Discovering the American Past

Discovering the American Past

A LOOK AT THE EVIDENCE

Volume II: Since 1865

William Bruce Wheeler
University of Tennessee

Susan D. Becker
University of Tennessee

HOUGHTON MIFFLIN COMPANY   Boston
Dallas   Geneva, Illinois   Lawrenceville, New Jersey   Palo Alto

ACKNOWLEDGMENTS

Pages 171–172: "Over There" by George M. Cohan © 1917, renewed 1945 Leo Feist, Inc. Rights assigned to CBS Catalogue Partnership. All rights controlled & administered by CBS Feist Catalog Inc. All rights reserved. International copyright secured. Used by permission.

Page 173: "Hello Central! Give Me No Man's Land" by Sam M. Lewis, Joe Young, and Jean Schwartz copyright © 1918 by Mills Music, Inc. Copyright renewed. Used with permission. All rights reserved.

Pages 202–203: Excerpt from Madison Grant, *The Passing of the Great Race* (Scribner's, 1916), used by permission of D. G. Brinton-Thompson.

Pages 209–210: Excerpt from Julian Warne, *The Immigrant Invasion*, reprinted with the permission of Dodd, Mead & Company.

Pages 212–213: Extract from John R. Commons, *Races and Immigrants in America*, 2nd ed. (Macmillan, 1911), reprinted by permission of Anne Commons Polisar.

Page 227: "Oral History Deed of Gift" from Betty McKeever Key, *Exploring Oral History*, reprinted by permission of the Maryland Historical Society.

Pages 230–236: Excerpts from *Hard Times: An Oral History of the Great Depression*, by Studs Terkel. Copyright © 1970 by Studs Terkel. Reprinted by permission of Pantheon Books, a Division of Random House, Inc.

Pages 254–275: Excerpts from Michael Wilson, "Salt of the Earth," reprinted by permission of Berthold Fles.

Pages 277–278: Excerpts from Bosley Crowther, "*Salt of the Earth* Opens at the Grande— Filming Marked by Violence," copyright © 1954 by The New York Times Company. Reprinted by permission.

Pages 278–281: Excerpt from *Variety* reprinted by permission.

Pages 282–283: Excerpts from "Salt and Pepper," copyright 1954 Time Inc. All rights reserved. Reprinted by permission from *Time*.

Pages 299–300: "For What It's Worth," Words and Music by Stephen Stills © 1966 by Cotillion Music, Inc., Ten East Music & Springfield Toones. Used by permission. All rights reserved.

Cover photograph courtesy of Keystone Aerial Surveys, Philadelphia, Pennsylvania, © 1984

Printed in the U.S.A.
Library of Congress Catalog Card Number: 85–80136
ISBN: 0–395–36094–3

DEFGHIJ-H-898

Contents

Preface

Those of us who are historians find ourselves surrounded by a wealth of primary evidence that can be used to reconstruct American history. This evidence ranges from the more traditional sources such as letters, newspapers, public documents, speeches, and oral reminiscences to the less traditional sources such as photographs, buildings, statistics, film scripts, and cartoons. Moreover, as historians we know how exciting it can be to sort and analyze this evidence, arrange it in various ways, formulate a hypothesis, and arrive at a probable explanation for at least a part of our collective past.

In addition, the study of American history can contribute to an understanding of the contemporary world. It does this in two important ways: (1) it can put the present in perspective by giving us an appreciation of the trends, forces, and people who served to shape contemporary American life, and (2) it can teach us the skills we need in order to examine and analyze our present environment and culture. To be sure, other disciplines (sociology, psychology, political science, anthropology, computer science, to name but a few) can be of enormous help in understanding our contemporary world. It is our belief, however, that because of its dual function of teaching both perspective and skills, the study of American history can make a significant contribution to becoming a truly educated person. Our goals, then, are to interest students in historical issues and to help them develop and sharpen the crucial skills that people need to live in today's society.

Too often, however, students in the United States history survey course perceive American history as the story of *someone else's* distant past, not their own history, or they see history as only dry facts, names and dates. Yet we believe that the majority of college students really are interested in the past, their own history as well as those of other peoples. The immense popularity of historical fiction, films, and television miniseries is but one indication of that underlying but often untapped interest. Another indication is the number of unsolicited questions we receive from students, alumni, and other teachers concerning the historical background of some present issue or crisis. In sum, then, we firmly believe that the interest in history is strong, but that students curiously leave that interest outside when they enter an American history survey classroom.

We began this book with an urgent desire to tap the already existing interest students have in the past. In addition, we wanted our students to be more than just passive observers of the historical process, allowing others to do their thinking for them. We wanted our students to go beyond just reading about the past, that is, beyond merely watching historians' minds at work. To a certain degree, we wanted our students actually to *do* history, to reach *their own* conclusions based upon a guided examination of historical evidence.

In *Discovering the American Past: A Look at the Evidence*, we have tried to present a series of historical issues and events in a lively way so as to engage students' interest. We have also tried to provide a good mixture of types of historical situations and a balance among political, social, diplomatic, intellectual, and cultural history. In addition, each type of historical evidence is combined with an introduction to the appropriate methodology in an effort to teach students a variety of historical skills. As much as possible, we have tried "to let the evidence speak for itself" and have avoided leading students to one particular interpretation or another. In this book, then, we have created a kind of historical sampler that we believe will help students learn the methods and skills historians use, as well as help them learn historical content. This approach is effective in many different classroom situations: seminars, small classes, large lecture classes with discussion sections.

Each chapter is divided into five parts: The Problem, The Method, The Evidence, Questions to Consider, and Epilogue. The section entitled "The Problem" gives the historical background and context for the evidence to be presented later in the chapter. The section called "The Method" gives students suggestions for studying and analyzing the evidence. "The Evidence" section is the heart of the chapter, providing a variety of primary source material on a particular historical event or issue. The section called "Questions to Consider" focuses students' attention on specific evidence and on linkages among different evidence material. The "Epilogue" section gives the aftermath or the historical outcome of the evidence — what happened to the people involved, who won the election, the results of a debate, and so on.

Discovering the American Past is not intended to replace a textbook or other reading material used in class. "The Problem" section in each chapter provides only a minimal factual context, and students are encouraged to return to their texts, readings, or lectures for information that will help them analyze the evidence presented in the chapter. An Instructor's Manual suggests ways that might be useful in guiding students through the evidence, questions students often ask, and a variety of ways in which the students' learning may be evaluated. By the time students complete this book, we believe they will know how to work with a great variety of historical evidence and how to use that evidence to answer historical questions about what happened and why.

We would like to thank the following people who read and critiqued the manuscript throughout its development. Their advice has been invaluable in helping to shape the book in its final form.

Frank Abbott, University of Houston
William Barney, University of North Carolina, Chapel Hill
John Cary, Cleveland State University
Howard Chudacoff, Brown University

Nancy Dye, University of Kentucky
Jack Elenbaas, California State University, Fullerton
Marcia Haubold, Triton College
Donald Jacobs, Northeastern University
James Lorence, University of Wisconsin
Robert McCaughey, Barnard College, Columbia University
Thomas G. Paterson, University of Connecticut
John Trickel, Richland College
William Walker, III, Ohio Wesleyan University
Darold Wax, Oregon State University

Our colleagues in the History Department at the University of Tennessee have been generous with both their ideas and their time, particularly Professors John R. Finger, Charles Johnson, Cathy Matson, and Jonathan Utley. The willing cooperation of our graduate teaching assistants enabled us not only to try out our ideas but also to evaluate their effectiveness in a variety of classroom situations. Finally, the staff of Houghton Mifflin Company have supported, encouraged, and helped us at every stage of this project.

Chapter 1

Reconstructing Reconstruction: The Political Cartoonist and the National Mood

The Problem

By early 1865 it was evident to most northerners and southerners that the Civil War was nearly over. While Grant was hammering at Lee's depleted forces in Virginia, Union general William Tecumseh Sherman broke the back of the Confederacy with his devastating march through Georgia and then northward into the Carolinas. Atlanta fell to Sherman's troops in September 1864, Savannah in December, and Charleston and Columbia, South Carolina, in February 1865. Two-thirds of Columbia lay in ashes. Meanwhile General Philip Sheridan had driven the Confederates out of the Shenandoah Valley of Virginia, thus blocking any escape attempts by Lee and further cutting southern supply routes. The Union naval blockade of the South was taking its fearful toll, as parts of the dying Confederacy were facing real privation. Hence, although northern armies had suffered terrible losses, by 1865 they stood poised on the brink of victory.

In the South all but the extreme die-hards recognized that defeat was inevitable. The Confederacy was suffering in more ways than militarily. The Confederate economy had almost completely collapsed and Confederate paper money was nearly worthless. Slaves were abandoning their masters and mistresses in record numbers, running away to Union armies or roaming through the South in search

Chapter 1
Reconstructing
Reconstruction:
The Political
Cartoonist and the
National Mood

of better opportunities. In many areas civilian morale had almost totally deteriorated, and one Georgian wrote, "The people are soul-sick and heartily tired of the hateful, hopeless strife. . . . We have had enough of want and woe, of cruelty and carnage, enough of cripples and corpses."[1] As the Confederate government made secret plans to evacuate Richmond, most southerners knew that the end was very near.

Yet, even with victory almost in hand, many northerners had given little thought to what should happen after the war was over. Would southerners accept the life-style changes that defeat would almost inevitably force on them (most especially the end of slavery)? What demands should the victors make upon the vanquished? Should the North assist the South in rebuilding after the devastation of war? If so, should the North dictate how that rebuilding, or reconstruction, should take place? What efforts should the North make to insure that the former slaves were receiving the rights of free men and women? During the war few northerners had seriously considered these questions. Now that victory was within their grasp, they could not avoid them.

One person who had been wrestling with these questions was Abraham Lincoln. In December 1863 the president announced his own plan for reconstructing the South, a plan in keeping with his later hope, as expressed in his second inaugural address, for "malice toward none; with charity for all; . . . Let us . . . bind up the nation's wounds."[2] In Lincoln's plan a southern state could resume its normal activities in the Union as soon as 10 percent of the voters of 1860 had taken an oath of loyalty to the United States. High-ranking Confederate leaders would be excluded, and some blacks might gain the right to vote. No mention was made of protecting the civil rights of former slaves, and it was presumed that this would be left to their former masters and mistresses.

To many northerners, later known as Radical Republicans, Lincoln's plan was much too lenient. In the opinion of these people, a number of whom had been abolitionists, the South, when conquered, should not be allowed to return to its former ways and life-style. Not only should slavery be eradicated, they claimed, but freed blacks should be assisted in their efforts to attain economic, social, and political equity. Most of the Radical Republicans favored education for blacks, and some advocated carving

1. The letter probably was written by Georgian Herschel V. Walker. See Allan Nevins, *The Organized War to Victory, 1864–1865*, Vol. IV of *The War for the Union* (New York: Charles Scribner's Sons, 1971), p. 221.

2. The full text of Lincoln's second inaugural address, delivered on March 4, 1865, can be found in Roy P. Basler, ed., *The Collected Works of Abraham Lincoln*, Vol. VIII (New Brunswick, N.J.: Rutgers University Press, 1953), pp. 332–333.

the South's plantations into small parcels to be given to the freedmen. To implement these reforms, Radical Republicans wanted detachments of the United States Army to remain in the South and favored the appointment of provisional governors to oversee the transitional governments in the southern states. Lincoln approved plans for the Army to stay and supported the idea of provisional governors. But he opposed the more far-reaching reform notions of the Radical Republicans, and as president was able to block them.

In addition to having diametrically opposed views of Reconstruction, Lincoln and the Radical Republicans differed over the constitutional question of which branch of the federal government would be responsible for the reconstruction of the South. The Constitution made no mention of secession, reunion, or reconstruction. But Radical Republicans, citing passages in the Constitution giving Congress the power to guarantee each state a republican government, insisted that the reconstruction of the South should be carried out by Congress.[3] For his part, however, Lincoln maintained that as chief enforcer of the law and as commander in chief, the president was the appropriate person to be in charge of Reconstruction. Clearly a stalemate was in the making, with Radical Republicans calling for a more reform-minded Reconstruction policy and Lincoln continuing to block them.

President Lincoln's death on April 15, 1865 (one week after Lee's surrender at Appomattox Court House),[4] brought Vice-President Andrew Johnson to the nation's highest office. At first, Radical Republicans had reason to hope that the new president would follow policies more to their liking. A Tennessean, Johnson had risen to political prominence from humble circumstances, had become a spokesperson for the common white men and women of the South, and had opposed the planter aristocracy. Upon becoming president, he excluded from amnesty all former Confederate political and military leaders as well as all southerners who owned taxable property worth more than $20,000 (an obvious slap at his old planter-aristocrat foes). Moreover, Johnson issued a proclamation setting up provisional military governments in the conquered South and told his cabinet he favored black suffrage, although as a states' rightist, he insisted that states adopt the measure voluntarily. At the outset, then, Johnson, appeared to be all the Radical Republicans had hoped

3. See Article IV, Section 4, of the Constitution. Later Radical Republicans also justified their position using the Thirteenth Amendment, adopted in 1865, which gave Congress the power to enforce the amendment ending slavery in the South.

4. The last Confederate army to give up, commanded by General Joseph Johnston, surrendered to Sherman at Durham Station, North Carolina, on April 18, 1865.

Chapter 1
Reconstructing
Reconstruction:
The Political
Cartoonist and the
National Mood

for, far preferable to the more moderate Lincoln.

Yet it did not take Radical Republicans long to realize that President Johnson was not one of them. Although he spoke harshly, he pardoned hundreds of former Confederates who quickly captured control of southern state governments and congressional delegations. Many northerners were shocked to see former Confederate generals, officials, and even former Confederate vice-president Alexander Stephens returned to Washington. The new southern state legislatures passed a series of laws, known collectively as black codes, that so severely restricted the rights of former slaves that they were all but slaves again. Moreover, Johnson privately told southerners that he opposed the Fourteenth Amendment to the Constitution, which was intended to confer full civil rights on the newly freed slaves. He also used his veto power to block Radical Republican Reconstruction measures in Congress and seemed to do little to combat the general defiance of the former Confederacy (exhibited in many forms, including insults thrown at Union occupation soldiers, the desecration of the United States flag, and the formation of organized resistance groups such as the Ku Klux Klan).

To an increasing number of northerners, the unrepentant spirit of the South and Johnson's acquiescence to it were nothing short of appalling. Had the Civil War been fought for nothing? Had over 364,000 federal soldiers died in vain? White southerners were openly defiant, blacks were being subjugated by white southerners and virtually ignored by President Johnson, and former Confederates were returning to positions of power and prominence. Radical Republicans had sufficient power in Congress to pass harsher measures, but Johnson kept vetoing them and the Radicals lacked the votes to override his vetoes. Indeed, the impasse that had existed before Lincoln's death continued.

In such an atmosphere the congressional elections of 1866 were bitterly fought campaigns, especially in the northern states. President Johnson traveled throughout the North, defending his moderate plan of Reconstruction and viciously attacking his political enemies. However, the Radical Republicans were even more effective. Stirring up the hostilities of wartime, they "waved the bloody shirt" and excited northern voters by charging that the South had never accepted its defeat and that the 364,000 Union dead and 275,000 wounded would be for nothing if the South was permitted to continue its arrogant and stubborn behavior. Increasingly, Johnson was greeted by hostile audiences as the North underwent a major shift in public opinion.

The Radical Republicans won a stunning victory in the congressional elections and thus broke the stalemate between Congress and the president.

[4]

Armed with enough votes to override Johnson's vetoes, the new Congress proceeded rapidly to implement the Radical Republican vision of Reconstruction. The South was divided into five military districts to be ruled by martial law. Southern states had to ratify the Fourteenth Amendment and institute black suffrage before being allowed to take their formal places in the Union. The Freedmen's Bureau, founded earlier, was given additional federal support to set up schools for blacks, negotiate labor contracts, and, with the military, help monitor elections. Only the proposal to give land to blacks was not adopted, being seen as too extreme by even some Radical Republicans. Congressional Reconstruction had begun.

President Johnson, however, had not been left completely powerless. Determined to undercut the Radical Republicans' Reconstruction policies, he issued orders increasing the powers of civil governments in the South and removed military officers who were enforcing Congress's will, replacing them with commanders less determined to protect black voting rights and more willing to turn the other way when disqualified white southerners voted. Opposed most vigorously by his own secretary of war, Edwin Stanton, Johnson tried to discharge Stanton. To an increasing number of Radicals, the president would have to be removed from office.

In 1868 the House of Representatives voted to impeach Andrew John-son. The president was tried in the Senate, where two-thirds of the senators would have to vote against Johnson for him to be removed.[5] The vast majority of senators disagreed with the president's Reconstruction policies. Yet they feared that impeachment had become a political tool that, if successful, threatened to destroy the balance of power between the branches of the federal government. The vote on removal fell one short of the necessary two-thirds, and Johnson was spared the indignity of removal. Nevertheless, the Republican nomination of General Ulysses Grant and his subsequent landslide victory (running as a military hero, Grant carried twenty-six out of thirty-four states) gave Radical Republicans a malleable president, one who, although not a Radical himself, could assure the continuation of their vision of Reconstruction.

By 1872 a renewed Democratic party believed it had a chance to oust Grant and the Republicans. For one thing, the Grant administration had been rocked by a series of scandals, some of them involving men quite close to the president. Although honest himself, Grant lost a good deal of popularity by defending the culprits and naively aiding in a cover-up of the corruption. These actions, along with some of his other policies, triggered a revolt within the Republican party, in

5. See Article I, Sections 2 and 3, of the Constitution.

Chapter 1
Reconstructing
Reconstruction:
The Political
Cartoonist and the
National Mood

which a group calling themselves Liberal Republicans bolted the party ranks and nominated well-known editor and reformer Horace Greeley to oppose Grant for the presidency.[6] Hoping for a coalition to defeat Grant, the Democrats also nominated the controversial Greeley.

Greeley's platform was designed to attract as many disparate groups of voters as possible to the Liberal Republican–Democratic political fold. Greeley favored civil service reform, the return to a "hard money" fiscal policy, and the reservation of western lands for settlers rather than for large land companies. He vowed an end to corruption in government. But the most dramatic part of Greeley's message was his call for an end to the bitterness of the Civil War, a thinly veiled promise to bring an end to Radical Reconstruction in the South. For their part, Radical Republicans attacked Greeley as the tool of die-hard southerners and labeled him as the candidate of white southern bigots and northern urban Irish immigrants manipulated by political machines. They took one of Greeley's phrases, "Let us shake hands over the bloody chasm" (a phrase with which Greeley intended to state his hope for an end to sectional hostilities), and warped that utterance almost beyond recognition. By contrast, Grant was labeled as a great war hero and a friend of

blacks and whites alike. The incumbent Grant won easily, capturing 55 percent of the popular vote and 286 electoral votes. Greeley died soon after the exhausting campaign.

Gradually, however, the zeal of Radical Republicanism began to fade. An increasing number of northerners grew tired of the issue. With their commitment to full civil rights for blacks never strong, they had voted into office Radical Republicans more out of anger at southern intransigence than out of any lofty notions of black equality. Hence northerners said little when, one by one, southern Democrats returned to power in the states of the former Confederacy.[7] As a mark of how little their own attitudes had changed in the years since the Civil War, white southerners labeled these native Democrats "Redeemers." Yet, as long as southern Democrats made no overt moves to subvert the rights of blacks, most northerners were willing to put the whole agony of Reconstruction behind them. Hence, while much that was fruitful and beneficial was accomplished in the South during the Reconstruction period (most notably black suffrage and public education), some of this was to be temporary, and many opportunities

6. See Volume 1, Chapter 9, for a discussion of Greeley's position on the emancipation of slaves in 1862.

7. Southerners regained control of the state governments in Tennessee and Virginia in 1869, North Carolina in 1870, Georgia in 1871, Arkansas and Alabama in 1874, and Mississippi in early 1876. By the presidential election of 1876, only South Carolina, Louisiana, and Florida were still controlled by Reconstruction governments.

for progress were lost. By the presidential election of 1876, both candidates (Rutherford B. Hayes and Samuel Tilden) promised an end to Reconstruction, and the Radical Republican experiment to all intents and purposes was over.

Many Americans formed their opinions about the events surrounding Reconstruction from newspapers. Especially influential were editorial cartoons, which captured the issues visually, often simplifying them so that virtually everyone could understand them. Perhaps the master of this style was Thomas Nast, a political cartoonist whose career, principally with *Harper's Weekly,* spanned the tumultuous years of the Civil War and Reconstruction. Congratulating themselves for having hired Nast, the editors of *Harper's Weekly* once exclaimed that each of Nast's drawings was at once "a poem and a speech."

Apparently Thomas Nast developed his talents early in life. Born in the German Palatinate (one of the German states) in 1840, Nast was the son of a musician in the Ninth Regiment Bavarian Band. The family moved to New York City in 1846, at which time young Thomas was enrolled in school. It seems that art was his only interest — one teacher admonished him, "Go finish your picture. You will never learn to read or figure." After unsuccessfully trying to interest their son in music, his parents eventually encouraged the development of his artistic talent. By the age

of fifteen, Thomas Nast was drawing illustrations for *Frank Leslie's Illustrated Newspaper.* He joined *Harper's Weekly* in 1862 (at the age of twenty-two), where he developed the cartoon style that was to win him a national reputation, as well as enemies. One of Nast's favorite targets, political boss William Marcy Tweed of New York's Tammany Hall, once shouted, "Let's stop these damn pictures. I don't care so much what the papers say about me — my constituents can't read; but damn it, they can see pictures!"

It is obvious from his work that Thomas Nast was a man of strong feelings and emotions. In his eyes, those people whom he admired possessed no flaws. Conversely, those whom he opposed were, to him, capable of every conceivable villainy. As a result his characterizations were often terribly unfair, gross distortions of reality, and more than occasionally slanderous. In his view, however, his central purpose was not to entertain but to move his audiences, to make them scream out in outrage or anger, to prod them to action.

Your task in this chapter is twofold:

1. By examining selected political cartoons of Thomas Nast dealing with Reconstruction, determine how Nast attempted to influence public opinion on Reconstruction's major issues.

2. By contrasting each cartoon with the treatment of Reconstruction in the introduction to this chapter and in supplementary readings, determine

[7]

Chapter 1
Reconstructing
Reconstruction:
The Political
Cartoonist and the
National Mood

the extent to which Nast's illustrations did or did not reflect northern public opinion at different times on the issues of Reconstruction.

Note carefully that the task is a dual one. All political cartoonists attempt to influence public opinion. Sometimes they are successful, sometimes not. To complete both parts of the assignment, you will have to do the following:

1. Read the introduction to this chapter and supplementary texts carefully to identify the principal issues of Reconstruction. You will want to make a list of those issues.

2. Examine closely the cartoons presented to determine where Nast stood on those issues.

3. Return to your readings to determine how the general public responded to those issues *at different times* during the Reconstruction period.

4. Finally, assess the extent to which Nast's illustrations did or did not reflect northern public opinion at different times on the issues of Reconstruction. Remember that public opinion shifts and changes. The public's stand on an issue at one point in time may not be its position at another point in time.

Public opinion is not always easy to measure. But we do have certain clues. Election results, for example, are a good gauge of public opinion. So

are audience responses to speakers (recall the audiences that President Johnson faced in 1866). As you read, looking for public opinion, be sensitive to these clues.

The Method

Although Thomas Nast developed the political cartoon into a true art form, cartoons and caricatures had a long tradition both in Europe and America before Nast. English artists helped to bring forth the cartoon style that eventually made *Punch* (founded in 1841) one of the liveliest-illustrated periodicals on both sides of the Atlantic. In America, Benjamin Franklin is traditionally credited with publishing the first newspaper cartoon in 1754, the multidivided snake (each part of the snake representing one colony) with the ominous warning "Join or Die." By the time Andrew Jackson sought the presidency, the political cartoon had become a regular and popular feature of American political life. Crude by modern standards, these cartoons influenced some people far more than did the printed word.

As noted above, the political cartoon, like the newspaper editorial, is intended to do more than objectively report events. It is meant to express an opinion, a point of view. Cartoons often praise or ridicule. Those who create them want to move people, anger them, make them laugh, or spur them to action. In short, political cartoons are poor devices for learning what was happening, but they are excellent devices for portraying popular reaction to what was happening.

How, then, can we analyze political cartoons? To begin with, cartoons almost always portray events. As you examine the cartoons in this chapter, try to determine what event is being portrayed. Often a cartoon's caption, dialogue, or other clues will help you to discover the event in question. By careful scrutiny, can you discern what the cartoonist's opinion of the event is? Is he or she approving or disapproving? How did you reach that conclusion?

Examine the people in each cartoon. Is the cartoonist aiming for a true likeness? Is he or she portraying the people sympathetically or unsympathetically? Nast often placed his characters out of their historical context (in Roman circuses, for example). Why did he do this? What did he intend to show? Sometimes cartoonists accentuate their subjects' physical features. Why do they do this?

After you examine a cartoon in detail, try to determine the message the cartoonist is trying to convey. What reactions does he or she hope those who see the cartoon will have? What do you think people's reactions might have been at the time the cartoon was published?

Before you begin the exercises in this chapter, it might be well to familiarize yourself both with the method

discussed above and with Nast by making a "trial run" on one of Nast's cartoons on another subject, that of public subsidy of private schools.

In 1868 the New York state legislature ruled that public funds could be made available to private schools. Most of the schools that benefited from this law were parochial schools of the Roman Catholic Church. Shortly thereafter, Roman Catholics complained about the compulsory use of the King James Version of the Bible in public schools.

The cartoon shown in Figure 1 appeared in *Harper's Weekly* on September 30, 1871. It graphically shows Nast's opinion on the issue. Examine the cartoon carefully. How are Roman Catholic clergymen portrayed? In the upper right, who is the woman being led to the gallows, and who is leading her? To the left of that, who are the adults at the top of the cliff and what are they doing? In what condition are the public schools? What is Tammany Hall (upper left), and what is the building intended to look like? In the foreground, what is stuck in the largest child's coat? What are the reactions of the children? Finally, what was Thomas Nast's opinion of Tammany Hall? The Irish Americans? The New York state legislature? The Roman Catholic Church? What feelings was Nast trying to elicit from those who saw this cartoon?

As you can see, a political cartoon must be analyzed to the most minute detail in order to get the full meaning

FIGURE 1 (*From Morton Keller, The Art and Politics of Thomas Nast (New York: Oxford University Press 1968), Plate 108 © Courtesy of the publisher.*)

THE AMERICAN RIVER GANGES.

The Priests and the Children.

September 30, 1871

the cartoonist is trying to convey. From that analysis, one can discover the creator's full meaning or message and can imagine the emotions the cartoon was likely to evoke.

Now you are ready to begin your analysis of the Reconstruction period through the cartoons of Thomas Nast. As you analyze each cartoon, be aware of the collective message of *all* of the cartoons. Most subscribers to *Harper's Weekly* saw all of the cartoons. What was their general reaction likely to be?

The Evidence

Figures 2 through 9 from Morton Keller, The Art and Politics of Thomas Nast *(New York: Oxford University Press, © 1968), Plates 14 (Figure 2), 55 and 56 (Figure 3), 22 (Figure 4), 27 (Figure 5), 32 (Figure 6), 47 (Figure 7), 48 (Figure 8), and 50 (Figure 9). Courtesy of the publisher. Figure 10 from J. Chal Vinson,* Thomas Nast, Political Cartoonist *(Athens: University of Georgia Press, © 1967), Plate 103. Courtesy of the publisher.*

FIGURE 2

[12]

FIGURE 3 *The Evidence*

PARDON.

Columbia.—"Shall I Trust These Men,

Chapter 1
Reconstructing
Reconstruction:
The Political
Cartoonist and the
National Mood

FIGURE 3, *Continued*

FRANCHISE.

And Not This Man?"

August 5, 1865

FIGURE 4 *The Evidence*

THE CONTRAST OF SUFFERING. ANDERSONVILLE & FORTRESS MONROE.

TREASON MUST BE MADE ODIOUS.

June 30, 1866

Chapter 1
Reconstructing
Reconstruction:
The Political
Cartoonist and the
National Mood

FIGURE 5

September 5, 1868

"This Is a White Man's Government."

"We regard the Reconstruction Acts (so called) of Congress as usurpations, and unconstitutional, revolutionary, and void."—*Democratic Platform.*

FIGURE 6

The Modern Samson.

[17]

Chapter 1
Reconstructing
Reconstruction:
The Political
Cartoonist and the
National Mood

FIGURE 7

August 3, 1872

Baltimore 1861–1872.

"Let Us Clasp Hands over the Bloody Chasm."

FIGURE 8

"Let Us Clasp Hands over the Bloody Chasm."—Horace Greeley.

[19]

Chapter 1
Reconstructing
Reconstruction:
The Political
Cartoonist and the
National Mood

FIGURE 9

The Whited Sepulchre.

Covering the monument of infamy with his white hat and coat.

FIGURE 10

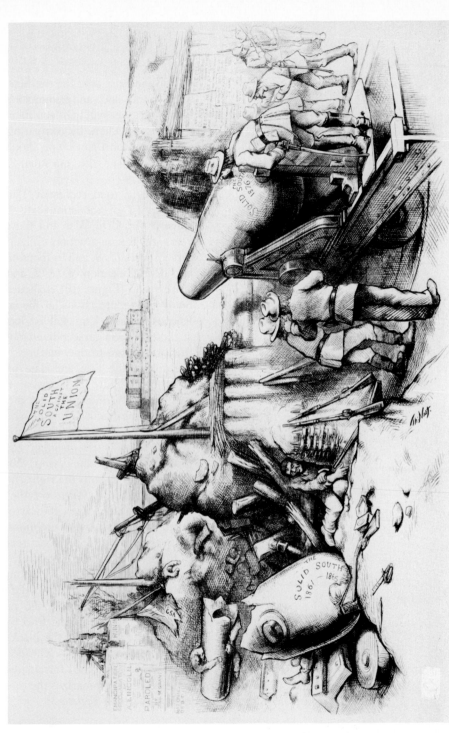

Chapter 1
Reconstructing
Reconstruction:
The Political
Cartoonist and the
National Mood

Questions to Consider

A review of the process you must use to complete this exercise should prove helpful. First, you are to identify the principal issues of the Reconstruction period. Second, determine where Nast stood on each of those issues. Third, describe how the general northern public stood on these issues at different times during the period (using clues such as election results). And, fourth, determine the extent to which Nast's illustrations did or did not reflect northern public opinion at different times on each of these issues. The process readily lends itself to a chart:

_____

Issues:

_____

Nast's Position:

_____

Public Opinion:

_____

Did Nast Reflect?

_____

A close reading of the introduction to this chapter and supplementary texts will provide the data for the first and third rows, and an examination of Nast's cartoons will help you fill in the second row. Then, by comparing the second and third rows, you should be able to answer the question, "Did Nast reflect?"

Figures 2 to 6 represent Thomas Nast's view of the immediate aftermath of the Civil War and the early years of Reconstruction. The next three figures (7, 8, and 9) focus on the presidential election of 1872, and the last cartoon (Figure 10) evaluates the South of the late 1870s, at the end of Reconstruction. You will be looking at these cartoons first individually and then in relation to one another.

Look at the title and date of the cartoon in Figure 2. To what event was Nast referring? Who are the two men shaking hands? How do you explain the contrast in their appearances? Who is the woman by the grave, and why is she crying? What is being shown in both the right and the left background? What do the two flags symbolize? When the cartoon is taken as a whole, what emotions was Nast trying to arouse in his readers?

Figure 3 must first be examined for its symbolism. Who is Columbia? What emotions do her two different poses suggest? Who are the people asking for pardon in the first frame? Now look carefully at the black man in the second frame — who does he represent? Can you formulate one sentence that summarizes the message of both parts of Figure 3?

Figure 4 is more complex: two drawings within two other drawings. If you do not already know, consult a text on this time period, an encyclopedia, or a good Civil War history book to discover what purpose Andersonville and Fortress Monroe served. Then look at the upper left and right outside drawings. Contrast the appearance of the man entering with the man leaving. Now examine the lower left and right outside drawings the same way. What was Nast trying to tell you? The explanation of the contrast is found in the larger inside drawings. What were the conditions like at Andersonville? At Fortress Monroe? What did the cartoonist think were the physical and psychological results?

Each of the three people standing in Figure 5 represents part of the Democratic Party coalition, and each has something to contribute to the party. Can you identify the groups that are being represented by the man on the right and the man in the center? What do they offer the party? Notice the facial features of the man on the left as well as his dress, particularly the hatband from Five Points (a notorious slum section of New York City). Who is this man supposed to represent, and what does he give the party? Notice what the black man lying on the ground has dropped. Who does he represent? What is he reaching for? What is happening in the background of the cartoon?

Figure 6 also explores the question

of rights for freed blacks, this time within the setting of the well-known story of Samson and Delilah. Who is Nast's Delilah, and what has she done? Who are her supporters at the left? What other things do they advocate? Now look carefully at the figure in the upper right-hand corner. Who is he? What has he promised blacks? What has he done?

Figures 7, 8, and 9 were all published just before the election of 1872. Who is the plump little man with the white beard and glasses who appears in all three cartoons? What part of this character's campaign did Nast find especially objectionable? Why? What is wrong with what the character is trying to do? (Since these cartoons show many reasons for Nast's disgust, you might find it helpful to keep a list as you study each separately.)

The last cartoon (Figure 10) shows Nast's opinion of the South in 1876, near the end of Reconstruction. What scene was Nast re-creating? Of what significance is this? How is the black man depicted? What was Nast trying to show?

You should now return to the questions asked in the Problem section of this chapter (and perhaps to supplementary readings). What were the major issues and events of the Reconstruction period? Who were the principal personalities? Think about all of Nast's cartoons collectively. In what ways did Nast try to influence public opinion about these events, issues, and people? How did he want his readers

Chapter 1
Reconstructing
Reconstruction:
The Political
Cartoonist and the
National Mood

to feel about them? In Nast's view, what were the worst failures of Reconstruction? Historians have sometimes characterized this era's Republican politics as "waving the bloody shirt." Can you explain why?

Epilogue

Undoubtedly Nast's work had an important impact on northern opinion of Reconstruction, the Democratic Party, Horace Greeley, the Irish Americans, and other issues as well. Yet gradually northern ardor began to decline as other issues and concerns eased Reconstruction out of the limelight and as it appeared that the crusade to reconstruct the South would be an endless one. Radical Republicans, who insisted on equality for the freed slaves, received less and less attention, and southern Democrats, who regained control of southern state governments, were essentially allowed a free hand as long as they didn't obviously violate the Constitution and federal law. By 1877 the South was once again in the hands of white Democrats.

Yet as long as blacks did not insist on their rights, white southern leaders allowed them to retain, in principle, all that the Civil War and Reconstruction had won. In other words, as long as black voters didn't challenge the

Redeemers, they were allowed to retain their political rights. Economically, many blacks gradually slipped into the status of tenant farmer, sharecropper, or even peon. The political structure, local courts, and law-enforcement agencies tended to support this arrangement. For his part, black leader Booker T. Washington was praised by white southerners for urging that blacks seek education and economic opportunities but not "rock the boat" politically in the white-controlled South.

In the 1890s the farmers' revolts that swept through the South and Midwest threatened southern white Democratic control, for the revolts threatened to unite white and black farmers in a political coalition that could drive the Redeemers from power. In response, southern white Democrats moved to restrict formally the rights of blacks, taking away the right to vote as well as racially segregating educational facilities, public transportation, parks, restaurants and theaters, elevators and drinking fountains. Not until the 1950s did these chains begin to be broken.

As the reform spirit waned in the latter years of Reconstruction, Nast's popularity suffered. The public appeared to tire of his anger, his self-righteousness, his relentless crusades. The new publisher of *Harper's Weekly* sought to make the magazine less political, and in that atmosphere there was no place for Nast. He resigned in 1886.

Nast continued to do freelance work for a number of magazines and tried unsuccessfully to start his own periodical, *Nast's Weekly*. Financially struggling, he appealed to friends who influenced President Theodore Roosevelt to appoint Nast to a minor consular post in Ecuador. He died there of yellow fever in 1902.

Yet Thomas Nast was a pioneer of a tradition and of a political art form. His successors, people such as Herbert Block (Herblock), Bill Mauldin, Oliphant, and even Garry Trudeau ("Doonesbury"), have continued to prick the American conscience, fret and irritate newspaper readers, and assert through their art the proposition that no evildoer can escape the scrutiny and ultimate justice of the popular will. Sometimes they are effective, sometimes not.

Chapter 2

Washington and DuBois:
Black Alternatives in the New South

The Problem

Years after the Civil War, Atlanta editor and sectional booster Henry Grady celebrated what he chose to call the "New South," a South that had risen out of the ashes of defeat to embrace the modern industrial age with a fervor usually confined to religious crusades. Although Grady and his New South cohorts often confused what they hoped for with what was actually accomplished, it is clear that in the years immediately following the Civil War a new spirit was manifesting itself in most of the states of the former Confederacy, a spirit that discarded older notions of an agricultural South and turned instead to industrialization, urbanization, and economic diversification.

In many ways the New South movement[1] was an undisguised attempt to imitate the industrialization that was sweeping through the North just prior to, during, and after the Civil War. Indeed, the North's industrial prowess had been one reason for its ultimate victory. As Reconstruction gradually came to an end in the southern states, many southern bankers, business leaders, and editors became convinced that the South should not return to its previous, narrow economic base of plantations and one-crop agriculture but instead should

1. Some of the material on the New South is drawn from Michael J. McDonald and William Bruce Wheeler, *Knoxville, Tennessee: Continuity and Change in an Appalachian City* (Knoxville: University of Tennessee Press, 1983), used with permission.

follow the North's lead toward modernization through industry. Prior to the Civil War many of these people had been calling for economic diversification, but they had been overwhelmed by the plantation aristocracy who controlled southern state politics and who used that control to further their own interests. By the end of Reconstruction, however, the planter elite had lost a good deal of their power, thus creating a power vacuum into which advocates of a New South could move.

Nearly every city, town, and hamlet of the former Confederacy had its New South boosters. Getting together in industrial societies or in chambers of commerce, they called for the erection of mills and factories. Why, they asked, should southerners export their valuable raw materials elsewhere, only to see them return from northern and European factories as costly finished products? Why couldn't southerners set up their own manufacturing establishments and become prosperous within a self-contained economy? And if they were short of capital, why not encourage rich northern investors to put up money in return for promises of great profits? In fact, the South had all the ingredients required of an industrial system: raw materials, a rebuilt transportation system, labor, potential consumers, and the possibility of obtaining capital. As they fed each other's dreams, the New South advocates pictured a resurgent South, a prosperous South, a triumphant South, a South of steam and power rather than of plantations and magnolias.

In an effort to obtain northern investment capital, New South boosters traveled across the northern states, selling their concept of an industrial South to all who would listen. In this activity Atlanta's Henry Grady had no peer. Addressing a group of potential investors in New York in 1886, Grady delighted his audience by saying that he actually was glad the Confederacy had lost the Civil War, for that defeat had broken the power of the plantation aristocracy and had provided the opportunity for the South to move into the modern industrial age. Northerners, Grady continued, were no longer unwelcome: "We have sown towns and cities in the place of theories, and put business above politics . . . and have . . . wiped out the place where Mason and Dixon's line used to be."[2]

To those southerners who envisioned a New South, the central goal was a harmonious, interdependent society in which each person and thing had its clearly defined place. Industry and the growth of cities were stressed most by New South boosters, since

2. Grady's speech may be found in Richard N. Current and John A. Garraty, eds., *Words That Made American History*, Vol. II (Boston: Little, Brown and Company, 1962), pp. 23–31.

the South had few factories and mills and almost no cities of substantial size. But agriculture too would have its place, although it would not be the same as the cash-crop agriculture of the pre–Civil War years. Instead New South spokesmen advocated a diversified agriculture that would still produce cash crops for export but would also make the South more self-sufficient by producing food crops and raw materials for the anticipated factories. Small towns would be used for collection and distribution, a rebuilt railroad network would transport goods, and northern capital would finance the entire process. Hence each part of the economy and, indeed, each person would have a clearly defined place and role in the New South, a place and role that would ensure a piece of the New South's prosperity for everyone.

But even as Grady and his counterparts were fashioning their dreams of a New South and selling those dreams to both northerners and southerners, a less beneficial, less prosperous side of the New South was taking shape. For in spite of the New South advocates' successes in establishing factories and mills (for example, Knoxville, Tennessee, witnessed the founding of over ninety such enterprises in the 1880s alone), the post-Reconstruction South remained primarily agricultural. Further, most of the farms were worked by sharecroppers or tenant farmers who eked out a bare subsistence while the profits went to the landowners or to the banks. This situation was especially prevalent in the lower South, where by 1890 a great proportion of farms were worked by tenants: South Carolina (61.1%), Georgia (59.9%), Alabama (57.7%), Mississippi (62.4%), and Louisiana (58.0%). Hence, even as factory smokestacks were rising on portions of the southern horizon, a high percentage of southerners remained in agriculture and in poverty.

Undeniably, blacks suffered the most. Over four million black men, women, and children had been freed by the Civil War. During the period of Reconstruction some advances were made, especially in the areas of public education and voter registration. Yet even many Radical Republicans were reluctant when it came to the issue of giving land to the former slaves. Thus most Afro-Americans were forced either to take menial, low-paying jobs in southern cities or to work as farmers on land they did not own. As poor urban laborers or as tenant farmers, blacks were dependent on their employers, landowners, or bankers and prey to rigid vagrancy laws, the convict lease system, peonage, and outright racial discrimination. Moreover, soon after white southerners regained control of their state governments, they moved to reinstitute rigid segregation laws affecting nearly every aspect of southern life and to restrict black voting (at first informally or through intimida-

[28]

tion, and then through more formal means, such as poll taxes and literacy tests). Blacks who protested or who strayed from their "place" were dealt with harshly: between 1880 and 1918, more than 2,400 blacks were lynched by white southern mobs, each action being a grim reminder to blacks of what could happen to those who challenged the New South status quo. For their part, the few southern whites who spoke against such outrages were themselves subjects of intimidation and even of violence. Indeed, although most black men and women undoubtedly would have disagreed, the blacks' relative position had in some ways deteriorated since the end of the Civil War.

Many New South advocates openly worried about how potential northern investors would react to this state of affairs. While the dream of the New South rested on the concept of a harmonious, interdependent society in which each component (industry, agriculture, and so forth) and each person (white, black) had a clearly defined place, it appeared that the blacks were being kept in their "place" largely by intimidation and force. Who would want to invest in a region in which the status quo of mutual deference and "place" often was maintained by force? To calm northern fears, Grady and his cohorts assured northerners that the position of blacks was improving and that southern society was one of mutual respect be-

tween the races. "We have found," Grady stated, "that in the summing up the free negro counts more than he did as a slave. . . ." Most northerners believed Grady because they wanted to believe Grady, because they had no taste for another bitter Reconstruction, and in many cases because they shared the white southerners' prejudices toward blacks. Grady was able to reassure them because they wanted to be reassured.

For southern blacks the options were clear. Short of migrating to Africa (which a few advocated), they seemed to have but two choices: accommodate to the system, or protest against it. By the early twentieth century each choice had its champion. Former slave and founder of Tuskegee Institute (a vocational school for blacks), Booker T. Washington was the leading accommodationist. Harvard-educated sociologist W. E. B. DuBois (pronounced DuBoys') spoke for the protesters.

In this chapter you are presented with three types of evidence: statistics on the situation facing southern blacks in the post-Reconstruction period; a speech delivered by Washington in Atlanta in 1895; and a portion of DuBois's Niagara Address of 1906. Your task is to analyze the evidence, determine what the competing philosophies and goals were, and decide which option you think was the better one for blacks at the turn of the twentieth century.

The Method

This is not the first time you have examined statistics or speeches. Indeed, our society is inundated daily with statistics that we must absorb, analyze, and understand. At the same time we are bombarded by speeches delivered by politicians, business figures, educators, and others, most of whom are trying to convince us to adopt a set of ideas or actions. As we listen to such speeches we invariably weigh the options presented to us, often using other available evidence (like statistics) to help us make our decisions. One purpose of this exercise is to help you think more critically and use evidence more thoroughly when assessing different options.

It is logical to begin by carefully defining the alternatives open to southern blacks in the late nineteenth and early twentieth centuries. For that you must go to the speeches of Washington and DuBois. Both were black and both wanted a complete integration of their race into the political, social, and economic mainstream of American life. Yet each had a different idea of how that could be accomplished. Read each speech carefully, looking for the particular method espoused. A rough chart may prove helpful:

	What Blacks Should Do
Washington	
DuBois	

Once you have carefully defined the options Washington and DuBois presented, you will be ready to *evaluate* which was the better option. To do this you will need other evidence. The statistics can be extremely useful here, especially those concerning the way blacks were faring in the post-Reconstruction South. The introduction to this chapter and supplementary reading will provide helpful clues about blacks' political and social status, anti-black violence, and so forth. Combine these clues with the statistics provided in this chapter to help you assess which alternative, Washington's or DuBois's, was the better one.

The Evidence

Tables 1 through 12 from Roger L. Ransom and Richard Sutch, One Kind of Freedom: The Economic Consequences of Emancipation *(Cambridge, London, New York: Cambridge University Press, 1977), pages 5 (Table 1), 65 (Table 2), 85 (Tables 3 and 4), 183 (Table 5), 184 (Tables 6 and 7), 226 (Table 8), 227 (Table 9), 30 (Table 10), 29 (Table 11), and 28 (Table 12). Table 13 from Bureau of the Census,* Historical Statistics of the United States, Colonial Times to 1970 *(Washington, D.C.: Government Printing Office, 1975), Vol. I, p. 95.*

TABLE 1   Comparison of Per Capita Output and Material Income Measures, Slaves on Large Plantations in 1859 with Black Sharecroppers in 1879

	Plantations with 51 or More Slaves, 1859	Black-Operated Sharecropped Family Farms, 1879	Percent Change, 1859–1879
Expressed in 1859–1860 dollars per capita			
Total output	147.93	74.03	−50.0
Product of labor	78.78	41.39	−47.5
Material income	32.12	41.39	28.9
Expressed as percent of total output			
Product of labor	53.3	55.9	4.9
Material income	21.7	55.9	157.6

TABLE 2   Annual Wages Earned by Black Males, Five Cotton States: 1867, 1868

State	Annual Wage ($)		Percent Decline
	1867	*1868*	
South Carolina	100	93	7.0
Georgia	125	83	33.6
Alabama	117	87	25.6
Mississippi	149	90	39.6
Louisiana	150	104	30.7

TABLE 3   Landownership by Race in Georgia: 1874, 1876, 1880

Year	Acres of Land Owned by		Percent of Total Acreage Owned by Blacks
	Whites	*Blacks*	
1874	34,196,870	338,769	1.0
1876	35,313,351	457,635	1.3
1880	36,792,243	586,664	1.6

TABLE 4   Value of Assets Held in Rural Counties of Georgia, by Race: 1876

Asset Class	Whites		Blacks	
	Value (Thousands of Dollars)	*Percent of All Assets Held*	*Value (Thousands of Dollars)*	*Percent of All Assets Held*
Land	84,613	50.1	922	21.6
City and town property	15,906	9.4	441	10.4
Money and liquid assets	21,335	12.6	84	2.0
Kitchen and household furniture	8,279	4.9	450	10.6
Horses, mules, hogs, etc.	21,086	12.5	238	5.6
Plantation and mechanical tools	2,337	1.4	121	2.8
All other property	15,314	9.1	2,003	47.0
Aggregate taxable wealth	168,870	100.0	4,259	100.0

TABLE 5   Inputs of Capital on Farms, by Race and Tenure, Cotton South: 1880

Type of Farm	Average Value of Farm Implements per Acre Reported in Crops ($)		Number of Untilled Acres per Tilled Acre	
	White	*Black*	*White*	*Black*
Small family farms	1.80	0.79	2.72	0.63
Owned	2.25	1.28	4.01	2.02
Tenanted	0.90	0.66	0.88	0.37
Rented	0.80	0.64	1.65	0.42
Sharecropped	0.93	0.67	0.69	0.34
Other small farms	3.06	0.86	3.83	0.90
Owned	3.64		4.77	
Tenanted	1.39	0.82	1.14	0.90
Medium-scale farms	1.08	0.69	3.92	1.40
Owned	1.15	0.67	4.43	1.58
Tenanted	0.83	0.71	2.23	1.31
Large farms	1.04		2.23	

TABLE 6   Number of Acres of Cropland per Worker on Family Farms, by Race and Tenure, Cotton South: 1880

Form of Tenure	Acres of Crops per Worker	
	White	*Black*
Owner-operated farms	12.5	6.6
Rented farms	14.5	7.3
Sharecropped farms	11.7	8.0
All farms	12.4	7.5

TABLE 7 Value of Output per Worker and Value of Output per Family Member on Family Farms, by Type of Farm, Tenure, and Race of Farm Operator, Cotton South: 1880

Type of Farm	Value of Output Per Worker($)		Value of Output Per Family Member ($)	
	White	Black	White	Black
Small family farms	255.74	159.62	81.35	63.57
Owned	283.70	155.78	88.12	58.11
Tenanted	212.47	160.40	70.87	64.67
Rented	260.19	159.51	88.02	67.63
Sharecropped	200.69	160.81	66.64	63.30
Other small farms	262.78	153.79	143.73	127.94
Owned	262.29		149.18	
Tenanted	264.17	147.23	127.93	117.65

TABLE 8 Distribution of Male Workers, Ten Years Old and Older, by Occupation, Five Cotton States: 1890

Occupation	All Colored	Native Whites		Foreign-Born Whites	Total
		Native Parents	Foreign Parents		
Agriculture	73.6	70.3	14.5	14.3	69.1
Laborer	41.9	22.1	4.3	5.5	31.5
Farm operator	31.7	48.2	10.2	8.8	37.6
Nonagriculture	26.4	29.7	85.5	85.6	30.9
Low-skilled	19.2	8.4	23.0	25.0	14.8
High-skilled	7.3	21.3	62.5	60.6	16.1
Total	100.0	100.0	100.0	100.0	100.0
Lower class	61.0	30.5	27.3	30.5	46.3
Privileged classes	39.0	69.5	72.7	69.5	53.7
Number gainfully occupied	985,280	801,369	49,763	47,652	1,884,064

TABLE 9 Distribution of Female Workers, Ten Years Old and Older, by Occupation, Five Cotton States: 1890

| | | Percent of Each Race and Nativity Class | | | |
| | | Native Whites | | | |
Occupation	All Colored	Native Parents	Foreign Parents	Foreign-Born Whites	Total
Agriculture	62.2	51.4	6.1	6.2	58.8
Laborer	56.3	30.7	2.8	3.0	50.2
Farm operator	5.9	20.7	3.3	3.2	8.6
Nonagriculture	37.8	48.6	93.9	93.8	41.2
Low-skilled	34.8	23.0	30.7	42.0	32.6
High-skilled	3.0	25.6	63.3	51.9	8.5
Total	100.0	100.0	100.0	100.0	100.0
Lower class	91.1	53.7	33.5	45.0	82.9
Privileged classes	8.9	46.3	66.5	55.1	17.1
Number gainfully occupied	515,894	120,750	10,076	6,189	652,909

TABLE 10 Percent of Persons Unable to Write, by Race and Age Group, Five Cotton States: 1870, 1880, 1890

Age and Race	1870	1880	1890
10–14 years			
Colored	78.9	74.1	49.2
White	33.2	34.5	18.7
15–20 years			
Colored	85.3	73.0	54.1
White	24.2	21.0	14.3
Over 20 years			
Colored	90.4	82.3	75.5
White	19.8	17.9	17.1

TABLE 11 Public Schools by Race of Students and Number of Children Five to Seventeen Years Old in Alabama, Georgia, and Mississippi: 1871, 1873

State, Year	Whites			Blacks		
	Number of Public Schools	*Number of Children Aged 5–17*	*Number of Children per School*	*Number of Public Schools*	*Number of Children Aged 5–17*	*Number of Children per School*
Alabama, 1871	2,399	184,441	76.9	922	165,601	179.6
Mississippi, 1871	1,742	131,570	75.5	860	156,424	181.9
Georgia, 1873	1,392	228,866	164.4	360	207,167	575.5

TABLE 12 Public School Enrollment of Blacks in Four Cotton States: 1871–1880

State, Year	Number of Students	Enrollment as Percent of School-Age Population	Enrollment as Percent of Colored Population 5–17
South Carolina			
1871	33,834	27.0	23.2
1875	63,415	41.6	36.9
1880	72,853	43.4	34.5
Georgia			
1873	19,755	13.2	9.5
1874	42,374	24.2	19.8
1880	86,399	37.4	33.7
Alabama			
1871	54,336	33.7	32.8
1875	54,595	31.6	29.6
1880	72,007	42.3	34.1
Mississippi			
1871	45,429	n.a.	29.0
1875	89,813	50.8	48.2
1880	123,710	49.2	53.3

TABLE 13 Estimated Net Intercensal Migration* of Negro Population by States, 1870–1920 (by Thousands)

	1910–1920	1900–1910	1890–1900	1880–1890	1870–1880
New England					
Maine	.1	.2	.3	−.1	−.2
New Hampshire	(Z)†	(Z)	.1	(Z)	.1
Vermont	−.9	.8	−.1	(Z)	(Z)
Massachusetts	6.9	5.9	9.9	4.4	3.0
Rhode Island	.6	.6	1.5	1.2	.8
Connecticut	5.3	.5	2.5	1.1	.8
Middle Atlantic					
New York	63.1	35.8	33.8	9.9	7.6
New Jersey	24.5	18.5	17.7	8.4	2.9
Pennsylvania	82.5	32.9	39.2	20.8	8.7
East North Central					
Ohio	69.4	15.6	5.2	5.2	2.6
Indiana	20.3	4.1	8.1	3.9	6.6
Illinois	69.8	23.5	22.7	8.4	8.7
Michigan	38.7	1.9	.4	−1.2	1.6
Wisconsin	2.2	.5	3.0	.1	1.3
West North Central					
Minnesota	2.1	2.3	5.9	1.5	1.5
Iowa	3.9	2.1	1.6	.4	2.3
Missouri	27.2	1.0	(Z)	−4.0	−4.3
North Dakota	−.1	.3	4.9	} (Z)	.3
South Dakota	(Z)	.3	14.0		
Nebraska	5.2	1.6	−2.3	7.3	1.2
Kansas	5.4	2.6	−.6	2.7	14.7
South Atlantic					
Delaware	−.6	−.4	−.7	.3	−1.4
Maryland	7.0	−11.4	−6.5	−7.5	−7.5
District of Columbia	18.3	9.8	8.7	13.4	6.2
Virginia	−27.2	−49.3	−70.8	−53.4	−37.6
West Virginia	15.5	15.3	5.8	3.6	2.1
North Carolina	−28.9	−28.4	−48.7	−38.4	−7.9
South Carolina	−74.5	−72.0	−65.5	−18.6	15.7
Georgia	−74.7	−16.2	−27.3	12.3	−20.3
Florida	3.2	40.7	23.4	15.8	1.4
East South Central					
Kentucky	−16.6	−22.3	−12.2	−22.4	−13.1
Tennessee	−29.3	−34.3	−19.0	−18.7	−24.6
Alabama	−70.8	−22.1	−1.7	−5.8	−36.1
Mississippi	−129.6	−30.9	−10.4	−13.2	17.6
West South Central					
Arkansas	−1.0	22.5	−7.9	44.7	25.4
Louisiana	−51.2	−16.1	−21.6	3.3	−1.3
Oklahoma	.8	54.8	79.3	2.3	(NA)‡
Texas	5.2	−10.2	7.1	12.6	21.0

* A net intercensal migration represents the amount of migration that took place between United States censuses, which are taken every ten years. The net figure is computed by comparing in-migration with out-migration to a particular state. A minus figure means that out-migration from a state was greater than in-migration.
† Z = under 50 people
‡ NA = not available

From Louis R. Harlan, ed., The Booker T. Washington Papers *(Urbana: University of Illinois Press, 1974), Vol. 3, pp. 583–587.*

The Standard Printed Version
of Booker T. Washington's
Atlanta Exposition Address

[Atlanta, Ga., Sept. 18, 1895]

Mr. President and Gentlemen of the Board of Directors and Citizens:

One-third of the population of the South is of the Negro race. No enterprise seeking the material, civil, or moral welfare of this section can disregard this element of our population and reach the highest success. I but convey to you, Mr. President and Directors, the sentiment of the masses of my race when I say that in no way have the value and manhood of the American Negro been more fittingly and generously recognized than by the managers of this magnificent Exposition at every stage of its progress. It is a recognition that will do more to cement the friendship of the two races than any occurrence since the dawn of our freedom.

Not only this, but the opportunity here afforded will awaken among us a new era of industrial progress. Ignorant and inexperienced, it is not strange that in the first years of our new life we began at the top instead of at the bottom; that a seat in Congress or the state legislature was more sought than real estate or industrial skill; that the political convention or stump speaking had more attractions than starting a dairy farm or truck garden.

A ship lost at sea for many days suddenly sighted a friendly vessel. From the mast of the unfortunate vessel was seen a signal, "Water, water; we die of thirst!" The answer from the friendly vessel at once came back, "Cast down your bucket where you are." A second time the signal, "Water, water; send us water!" ran up from the distressed vessel, and was answered, "Cast down your bucket where you are." And a third and fourth signal for water was answered, "Cast down your bucket where you are." The captain of the distressed vessel, at last heeding the injunction, cast down his bucket, and it came up full of fresh, sparkling water from the mouth of the Amazon River. To those of my race who depend on bettering their condition in a foreign land or who underestimate the importance of cultivating friendly relations with the Southern white man, who is their next-door neighbour, I would say: "Cast down your bucket where you are" — cast it down in making friends in every manly way of the people of all races by whom we are surrounded.

Cast it down in agriculture, mechanics, in commerce, in domestic service, and in the professions. And in this connection it is well to bear in mind that whatever other sins the South may be called to bear, when it comes to business, pure and simple, it is in the South that the Negro is given a man's chance in the commercial world, and in nothing is this Exposition more eloquent than in emphasizing this chance. Our greatest danger is that in the great leap from slavery to freedom we may overlook the fact that the masses of us are to live by the productions of our hands, and fail to keep in mind that we shall prosper in proportion as we learn to dignify and glorify common labour, and put brains and skill into the common occupations of life; shall prosper in proportion as we learn to draw the line between the superficial and the substantial, the ornamental gewgaws of life and the useful. No race can prosper till it learns that there is as much dignity in tilling a field as in writing a poem. It is at the bottom of life we must begin, and not at the top. Nor should we permit our grievances to overshadow our opportunities.

To those of the white race who look to the incoming of those of foreign birth and strange tongue and habits for the prosperity of the South, were I permitted I would repeat what I say to my own race, "Cast down your bucket where you are." Cast it down among the eight millions of Negroes whose habits you know, whose fidelity and love you have tested in days when to have proved treacherous meant the ruin of your firesides. Cast down your bucket among these people who have, without strikes and labour wars, tilled your fields, cleared your forests, builded your railroads and cities, and brought forth treasures from the bowels of the earth, and helped make possible this magnificent representation of the progress of the South. Casting down your bucket among my people, helping and encouraging them as you are doing on these grounds, and to education of head, hand, and heart, you will find that they will buy your surplus land, make blossom the waste places in your fields, and run your factories. While doing this, you can be sure in the future, as in the past, that you and your families will be surrounded by the most patient, faithful, law-abiding, and unresentful people that the world has seen. As we have proved our loyalty to you in the past, in nursing your children, watching by the sick-bed of your mothers and fathers, and often following them with tear-dimmed eyes to their graves, so in the future, in our humble way, we shall stand by you with a devotion that no foreigner can approach, ready to lay down our lives, if need be, in defense of

yours, interlacing our industrial, commercial, civil, and religious life with yours
in a way that shall make the interests of both races one. In all things that are
purely social we can be as separate as the fingers, yet one as the hand in all
things essential to mutual progress.

There is no defense or security for any of us except in the highest intelligence and development of all. If anywhere there are efforts tending to curtail
the fullest growth of the Negro, let these efforts be turned into stimulating, encouraging, and making him the most useful and intelligent citizen. Effort or
means so invested will pay a thousand per cent interest. These efforts will be
twice blessed — "blessing him that gives and him that takes."

There is no escape through law of man or God from the inevitable: —

"The laws of changeless justice bind
   Oppressor with oppressed;
And close as sin and suffering joined
   We march to fate abreast."

Nearly sixteen millions of hands will aid you in pulling the load upward, or
they will pull against you the load downward. We shall constitute one-third and
more of the ignorance and crime of the South, or one-third [of] its intelligence
and progress; we shall contribute one-third to the business and industrial prosperity of the South, or we shall prove a veritable body of death, stagnating, depressing, retarding every effort to advance the body politic.

Gentlemen of the Exposition, as we present to you our humble effort at an
exhibition of our progress, you must not expect overmuch. Starting thirty years
ago with ownership here and there in a few quilts and pumpkins and chickens
(gathered from miscellaneous sources), remember the path that has led from
these to the inventions and production of agricultural implements, buggies,
steam-engines, newspapers, books, statuary, carving, paintings, the management of drug stores and banks, has not been trodden without contact with
thorns and thistles. While we take pride in what we exhibit as a result of our
independent efforts, we do not for a moment forget that our part in this exhibition would fall far short of your expectations but for the constant help that has
come to our educational life, not only from the Southern states, but especially
from Northern philanthropists, who have made their gifts a constant stream of
blessing and encouragement.

The wisest among my race understand that the agitation of questions of social equality is the extremest folly, and that progress in the enjoyment of all the privileges that will come to us must be the result of severe and constant struggle rather than of artificial forcing. No race that has anything to contribute to the markets of the world is long in any degree ostracized. It is important and right that all privileges of the law be ours, but it is vastly more important that we be prepared for the exercise of these privileges. The opportunity to earn a dollar in a factory just now is worth infinitely more than the opportunity to spend a dollar in an opera-house.

In conclusion, may I repeat that nothing in thirty years has given us more hope and encouragement, and drawn us so near to you of the white race, as this opportunity offered by the Exposition; and here bending, as it were, over the altar that represents the results of the struggles of your race and mine, both starting practically empty-handed three decades ago, I pledge that in your effort to work out the great and intricate problem which God has laid at the doors of the South, you shall have at all times the patient, sympathetic help of my race; only let this be constantly in mind, that, while from representations in these buildings of the product of field, of forest, of mine, of factory, letters, and art, much good will come, yet far above and beyond material benefits will be that higher good, that, let us pray God, will come, in a blotting out of sectional differences and racial animosities and suspicions, in a determination to administer absolute justice, in a willing obedience among all classes to the mandates of law. This, coupled with our material prosperity, will bring into our beloved South a new heaven and a new earth.

From Virginia Hamilton, ed., The Writings of W. E. B. DuBois *(New York: Thomas Y. Crowell Co., 1975), pp. 64–69.*

DuBois's Niagara Address, 1906

The men of the Niagara Movement coming from the toil of the year's hard work and pausing a moment from the earning of their daily bread turn toward the nation and again ask in the name of ten million the privilege of a hearing. In the past year the work of the Negro hater has flourished in the land. Step by step the defenders of the rights of American citizens have retreated. The work of stealing the black man's ballot has progressed and the fifty and more representatives of stolen votes still sit in the nation's capital. Discrimination in travel and public accommodation has so spread that some of our weaker brethren are actually afraid to thunder against color discrimination as such and are simply whispering for ordinary decencies.

Against this the Niagara Movement eternally protests. We will not be satisfied to take one jot or tittle less than our full manhood rights. We claim for ourselves every single right that belongs to a freeborn American, political, civil and social; and until we get these rights we will never cease to protest and assail the ears of America. The battle we wage is not for ourselves alone but for all true Americans. It is a fight for ideals, lest this, our common fatherland, false to its founding, become in truth the land of the thief and the home of the Slave — a by-word and a hissing among the nations for its sounding pretensions and pitiful accomplishment.

Never before in the modern age has a great and civilized folk threatened to adopt so cowardly a creed in the treatment of its fellow-citizens born and bred on its soil. Stripped of verbiage and subterfuge and in its naked nastiness the new American creed says: Fear to let black men even try to rise lest they become the equals of the white. And this is the land that professes to follow Jesus Christ. The blasphemy of such a course is only matched by its cowardice.

In detail our demands are clear and unequivocal. First, we would vote; with the right to vote goes everything: Freedom, manhood, the honor of your wives, the chastity of your daughters, the right to work, and the chance to rise, and let no man listen to those who deny this.

We want full manhood suffrage, and we want it now, henceforth and forever.

Second. We want discrimination in public accommodation to cease. Separation in railway and street cars, based simply on race and color, is un-American, undemocratic, and silly. We protest against all such discrimination.

Third. We claim the right of freemen to walk, talk, and be with them that wish to be with us. No man has a right to choose another man's friends, and to attempt to do so is an impudent interference with the most fundamental human privilege.

Fourth. We want the laws enforced against rich as well as poor; against Capitalist as well as Laborer; against white as well as black. We are not more lawless than the white race, we are more often arrested, convicted and mobbed. We want justice even for criminals and outlaws. We want the Constitution of the country enforced. We want Congress to take charge of Congressional elections. We want the Fourteenth amendment carried out to the letter and every State disfranchised in Congress which attempts to disfranchise its rightful voters. We want the Fifteenth amendment enforced and no State allowed to base its franchise simply on color.

The failure of the Republican Party in Congress at the session just closed to redeem its pledge of 1904 with reference to suffrage conditions [in] the South seems a plain, deliberate, and premeditated breach of promise, and stamps that party as guilty of obtaining votes under false pretense.

Fifth. We want our children educated. The school system in the country districts of the South is a disgrace and in few towns and cities are the Negro schools what they ought to be. We want the national government to step in and wipe out illiteracy in the South. Either the United States will destroy ignorance or ignorance will destroy the United States.

And when we call for education we mean real education. We believe in work. We ourselves are workers, but work is not necessarily education. Education is the development of power and ideal. We want our children trained as intelligent human beings should be, and we will fight for all time against any proposal to educate black boys and girls simply as servants and underlings, or simply for the use of other people. They have a right to know, to think, to aspire.

These are some of the chief things which we want. How shall we get them? By voting where we may vote, by persistent, unceasing agitation, by hammering at the truth, by sacrifice and work.

We do not believe in violence, neither in the despised violence of the raid nor the lauded violence of the soldier, nor the barbarous violence of the mob, but we do believe in John Brown, in that incarnate spirit of justice, that hatred of a lie, that willingness to sacrifice money, reputation, and life itself on the altar of right. And here on the scene of John Brown's martyrdom we reconsecrate ourselves, our honor, our property to the final emancipation of the race which John Brown died to make free.

Our enemies, triumphant for the present, are fighting the stars in their courses. Justice and humanity must prevail. We live to tell these dark brothers of ours — scattered in counsel, wavering and weak — that no bribe of money or notoriety, no promise of wealth or fame, is worth the surrender of a people's manhood or the loss of a man's self-respect. We refuse to surrender the leadership of this race to cowards and trucklers. We are men; we will be treated as men. On this rock we have planted our banners. We will never give up, though the trump of doom find us still fighting.

And we shall win. The past promised it, the present foretells it. Thank God for John Brown! Thank God for Garrison and Douglass! Sumner and Phillips, Nat Turner and Robert Gould Shaw,* and all the hallowed dead who died for freedom! Thank God for all those today, few though their voices be, who have not forgotten the divine brotherhood of all men, white and black, rich and poor, fortunate and unfortunate.

We appeal to the young men and women of this nation, to those whose nostrils are not yet befouled by greed and snobbery and racial narrowness: Stand up for the right, prove yourselves worthy of your heritage and whether born north or south dare to treat men as men. Cannot the nation that has absorbed ten million foreigners into its political life without catastrophe absorb ten million Negro Americans into that same political life at less cost than their unjust and illegal exclusion will involve?

Courage, brothers! The battle for humanity is not lost or losing. All across the skies sit signs of promise. The Slav is rising in his might, the yellow millions are tasting liberty, the black Africans are writhing toward the light, and everywhere the laborer, with ballot in his hand, is voting open the gates of Opportunity and Peace. The morning breaks over blood-stained hills. We must not falter, we may not shrink. Above are the everlasting stars.

Questions to Consider

The statistics are intended to provide you with some information about the economic and educational progress of southern blacks roughly from emancipation to the turn of the century. How did blacks fare with respect to

1. output and income on black-operated sharecropper farms?

2. annual wages?

3. land ownership?

4. value of assets owned?

5. value of farm implements and number of untilled acres, as compared to whites?

6. amount of crops per acre, as compared to whites?

7. value of output, as compared to whites?

8. distribution of male workers? female workers?

9. illiteracy?

*John Brown, William Lloyd Garrison, Frederick Douglass, Charles Sumner, and Wendell Phillips were all abolitionists. Nat Turner led a slave revolt, and Robert Gould Shaw was a Union colonel killed in the Civil War. Only Douglass and Turner were black. [*Hamilton's note*]

10. public school students and enroll-ment?

11. out-migration?

Now turn to other evidence, provided in the introduction to this chapter and in your supplementary reading. How much political power did southern blacks possess? How could they effect changes in local and state political structures? What social rights did they possess? What might have been whites' reactions if southern blacks had protested against political, eco-nomic, and social inequities? How would the majority of white north-erners have reacted?

The statistics and other evidence show portions of the *reality* that for-mer slaves faced; the two speeches represent the *reactions* to that reality. What was Washington's response to the reality confronting the former slaves? How did he propose to rectify the problems he saw? How did he support his argument? What did Washington conceive to be the role of southern whites in black progress?

Before you consider the next speech, think a moment. Be willing to use some inference. How would south-ern whites have greeted Washington's speech? Southern blacks? What about northern blacks? Northern whites? To whom was Washington speaking?

Now move on to DuBois's speech. How does DuBois differ from Wash-ington with respect to goals? Timing? Tactics? Tone? How does he support

his arguments? To whom was DuBois speaking? Engage in inference again. How would DuBois's address have been greeted by each group named above?

It is now time to assess the alterna-tives offered by Washington and DuBois. To determine which option was the better one, you will have to answer the following questions:

1. How do I define "better"? More realistic? More morally defensible? Better in the long range? Better in the short range?

2. What would happen if southern blacks adopted Washington's alterna-tive? How long would it take for blacks to realize Washington's goals?

3. What would happen if southern blacks adopted DuBois's alternative?

4. Would white assistance be neces-sary to Washington? To Dubois? How did each man perceive the roles of the federal government and the federal courts? How did the government and courts stand on this issue at the time? [Clue: What was the Supreme Court decision in *Plessy v. Ferguson* (1896)?]

Epilogue

For the advocates of a New South the realization of their dream seemed to be just over the next horizon, always just beyond their grasp. Many of the factories did make a good deal of money. But profits often flowed out of the South to northern investors. And factory owners often maintained profits by paying workers pitifully low wages, which led to the rise of a poor white urban class that lived in slums and faced enormous problems of malnutrition, poor health, family instability, and crime. To most of those who had left their meager farms to find opportunities in the burgeoning southern cities, life there appeared even worse than it had been in the rural areas. Many whites returned to their rural homesteads disappointed and dispirited by urban life.

For an increasing number of southern blacks the solution seemed to be to abandon the South entirely. Beginning around the time of World War I (1917–1918), a growing number of blacks migrated to the industrial cities of the Northeast, Midwest, and West Coast. But there too they met racial hostility and racially inspired riots.

But at least in the North blacks could vote and thereby influence public policy. By the late 1940s it became clear that northern urban black voters by their very number could force American politicians to deal with racial discrimination. By the 1950s it was evident that the South would have to change its racial policies, if not willingly then by force. It took federal courts, federal marshals, and occasionally federal troops, but the crust of discrimination in the South began

to be broken in the 1960s. Attitudes changed slowly, but the white southern politician who draped himself in the Confederate flag and called for resistance to change became a figure of the past. Although much work still needed to be done, changes in the South had been profound, laying the groundwork for more changes ahead. Indeed, by the 1960s the industrialization and prosperity (largely through in-migration) of the Sunbelt seemed to show that Grady's dream of a New South might become a reality.

By this time, of course, both Washington and DuBois were dead. Washington had stubbornly clung to his notion of self-help, although he realized privately that whites could use him as an apologist for the status quo and a supporter of racial segregation. He died in Tuskegee, Alabama, in 1915. For his part, DuBois had grown more and more embittered, turning toward Marxism and Pan-Africanism when he believed "the system" had failed him and his people. He died in Africa in 1963.

Yet in their time both men were giants, important and respected figures. Although publicly at odds, they both privately dreamed of an America in which blacks would enjoy the full rights of citizens. In an era in which few people would champion the causes of black people, Washington and DuBois stood as heroic figures that time has only partially tarnished.

Chapter 3

America in the Gilded Age: Architecture as Living History

The Problem

Writing in the early years of the twentieth century, historian and author Henry Adams reflected on the profound and rapid changes that had taken place in America since his birth in 1838.[1] In the opinion of Adams and many of his generation, "the old universe was thrown into the ash-heap and a new one created," a new universe in which changes in science and technology, in industrialization and urbanization, and in social and political structures were occurring more rapidly than perhaps during any previous age of human history. For Adams and others, it was both an exciting and frightening era.

At approximately the same time that Adams was writing *The Education,* sociologist Thorstein Veblen published his book *The Theory of the Leisure Class* (1899). To Veblen, one of the most important things about the age that Adams and others had analyzed was the creation of a new, fabulously wealthy industrial elite, the "captains of industry" and their families, who had by their very wealth displaced the old American elite and had become America's new heroes and heroines. Without naming them specifically, Veblen was writing about the Rockefellers, Carnegies, Vanderbilts, and others of the new American aristocracy.

In *The Theory of the Leisure Class,*

1. Adams completed, privately published, and circulated *The Education of Henry Adams* to friends in 1907. He ordered that the book not be made available to the general public until after his death, which was in 1918. *The Education of Henry Adams* has since become an American classic, as important and relevant now as when it was first published.

Veblen was somewhat less concerned with how this new class acquired its money than with how it spent that money. It was as if, he asserted, the new elite felt the need to demonstrate their status through ostentation, showing others how wealthy they were by purchasing things they obviously did not need. Veblen called this kind of purchasing "conspicuous consumption," the buying of unnecessary furnishings, clothes, and other items simply to display one's wealth. In a society in which real poverty and want were widespread (for example, among both the sharecroppers of the New South and the immigrants and industrial laborers of the industrial North), Veblen found conspicuous consumption a convincing piece of evidence that the priorities of the post–Civil War nation were badly skewed and shockingly wrong. Why, he argued, should some keep pampered house pets, which consume food and perform no useful service (thus showing the pet owners' status), while humans went hungry? Something was wrong with a society, Veblen asserted, in which some spent huge amounts of money for antique furniture so brittle as to be nonfunctional while others could not afford the barest necessities. That era, to follow Veblen's reasoning, was truly what authors Mark Twain and Charles Dudley Warner had called it: a "Gilded Age," resplendent and glittering on the outside but dirty and sordid at the core.

Taken together, Adams and Veblen were reacting to an age best characterized by enormous and profound changes in American life. Unquestionably the most important of those changes were the nation's rapid industrialization and urbanization. Aided and accelerated by the rapid growth of railroads, emerging industries could extend their tentacles throughout the nation, collecting raw materials and fuel for the factories and distributing finished products to the growing American population. By 1900 that industrial process had come to be dominated by a few energetic and shrewd men, "captains of industry" to their friends and "robber barons" to their enemies. Almost every conceivable industry, from steel and oil to sugar refining and meat packing, was controlled by one or two gigantic corporations that essentially had the power to set prices on the raw materials bought and the finished products sold. In turn, the successes of those corporations created a new class of fabulously rich industrialists, and names like Swift, Armour, Westinghouse, Pillsbury, Pullman, Rockefeller, Carnegie, and Duke literally became almost household words as much for the notoriety of the industrialists as for the industries and products they created.

As America became more industrialized, it also became more urban. In the past the sizes of cities had been limited by the availability of nearby food, fuel, and employment opportunities. But the network of railroads and the rise of large factories had removed those limitations, and American cities grew phenomenally. Between 1860 and 1910 urban population increased sevenfold, and by 1920 over half of all Americans lived in cities. These gigantic urban complexes not only dominated the regions in which they were located but eventually set much of the tone for the entire nation as well.

Both processes — industrialization and urbanization — profoundly altered nearly every facet of American life. Family size began to decrease: the woman who might have had five or six children in 1860 was replaced by the "new" woman of 1900 who had only three or four children. The fruits of industrialization, distributed by new marketing techniques such as mail-order catalogues, could be enjoyed by a large portion of the American population. Electric lights, telephones, and eventually appliances virtually revolutionized the lives of the middle and upper classes, as did Ford's later mass production of the Model T automobile.

The nature of work was also changed, for factories required a higher degree of regimentation than did farm work or the "putting out" system. Many industries found it more profitable to employ women and children than adult males, thus altering the home lives of many of the nation's lower-middle and lower class citizens. Moreover, the lure of employment brought millions of immigrants to the United States, most of whom huddled together in cities, found low-paying jobs, and dreamed of the future. And as the cities grew grimy with factory soot and became increasingly populated by laborers, immigrants, and what one observer referred to as the "dangerous classes," upper and middle class Americans began to abandon the urban cores and retreat to fashionable suburbs on the peripheries, to return to the cities either in their automobiles or on streetcars only for work or recreation.

Industrialization and urbanization not only changed how most Americans lived, but how they *thought* as well. Faith in progress and technology was almost boundless, and many felt that America was about to enter a golden age of universal prosperity in which all problems could be solved by science and technology. The poor, especially the immigrant poor, were seen as biologically inferior, and most people believed that the industrial barons had reached their exalted positions less through shrewdness and ruthlessness than by virtue of their biological preeminence. It followed, then, that efforts to help the less fortunate through charity or government intervention were somehow tampering with both God's will and Darwinian evolution. In such a climate of opinion the leaders of gigantic corporations became national heroes, superior in prestige to both preachers and presidents. Voices of dissent were often ignored or brushed aside, and evidence of the excesses of the industrial barons (as when steel magnate Henry Clay Frick imported a genuine throne from Europe so he could be comfortable while reading the *Saturday Evening Post*) were viewed as merely the just rewards for superiority and toil. Many young boys read the rags-to-riches tales of Horatio Alger while girls learned to be "proper ladies" so that they wouldn't embarrass their future husbands as they rose in society together. Indeed, by how detailed the reports of the balls and parties of the industrial barons were, it was almost as if Americans were living their lives vicariously through the excesses of the new rich.

The collective mentality and values of that rapidly changing society were reflected in nearly everything the society created. Economies of scale meant that a large factory could lower the price per unit of goods it manufactured by buying raw materials and producing finished products in large quantities. For example, economies of scale combined new systems of mass marketing and distribution, made fashionable store-bought clothing easier to obtain, caused a decline in homemade clothing, and brought about a standardization of dress among all but the richest and poorest Americans. At the same time the new industrial elite became even more ostentatious in their dress and personal adornments (beard and hair styles, lace and jewelry, and so forth), as if to show that they could

afford more than the new factory items (see Figures 1 and 2).

So too with architecture. As American architects designed public buildings, factories, banks, apartment houses, offices, and residential structures during the period from approximately 1865 to 1900, their work mirrored the ideas, values, mood, and collective mentality of their times. In this, as with other human accomplishments of the era, they were aided by technological advances that allowed them to do things that had been impossible in the past. For instance, as American cities grew in size and population density the value of real estate soared. Therefore, it made sense to design higher and higher buildings, taking advantage of every square foot of available land. The perfection of central heating systems; the inventions of the radiator (1874), the elevator (1850s), and the flush toilet; and the use of steel framing (1880s) allowed architects like William LeBaron Jenney, Louis Sullivan, and others of the Chicago school of architecture to erect the modern skyscraper, a combined triumph of architecture, engineering, ingenuity, and construction. At the same time the new industrial elite were hiring the same architects to design and build their new homes.

Unfortunately, most people, including professional historians, are not used to looking for values and ideas in architecture. Every day we pass by buildings that could tell us a good deal

Figures 1 and 2 from John Maass, The Gingerbread Age: A View of Victorian America (New York: Rinehart, © 1957), pp. 24, 27. Courtesy of the publisher.

FIGURE 1   Examples of Late Nineteenth Century Male and Female Hair Styles

FIGURE 2 Late Nineteenth Century Female Dress, Upper Class

about the life-styles and values of the past, if we would only stop and take the time to look at them. In this chapter we will do precisely that. We will concentrate on private residences designed and built for America's industrial elite between the Civil War and World War I. Your task is to identify the prevalent values of the time by closely examining the residential architecture of the era.

The Method

At one time or another you have probably looked at a certain building and thought, "That is truly an ugly, awful looking building! Whatever possessed the lunatic who built it?" Yet when that building was designed and built, it was likely to have been seen as a truly beautiful structure and may have been widely praised by its occupants as well as by those who merely passed by. Why is this so? Why did an earlier generation believe the building was beautiful?

All of us are aware that standards for what is good art, good music, good literature, and good architecture change over time. What may be pleasing to the people of one era might be considered repugnant or even obscene by those of another time. But is this solely the result of changing fads, like the sudden rises and declines in the popularities of movie and television stars, rock'n'roll groups, or fashionable places to vacation?

The answer, of course, is partly yes, but only partly. Tastes do change, and fads like the hula-hoop and the yo-yo come and inevitably go. However, we must still ask why a particular person or thing becomes popular or in vogue at a certain time. Do these changing tastes in art, music, literature, and architecture *mean* something? Can they tell us something about the people who embraced these various styles? More to the point, can they tell us something about the *values* of those who embraced them? Obviously they can.

Your task is to induce the important values and collective mentality of Americans from roughly the Civil War to World War I by examining and analyzing selected residential structures built during that period for the nation's industrial elite. Since these structures were praised and accepted by far more people than those who actually built or lived in them, we may assume that they mirror the values and collective mentality of a great proportion of the American population.

Architects ask their clients and professional colleagues to examine closely both the interior and exterior of a building to understand the main concepts the architect had in mind when he or she designed the structure. First, examine closely the exterior of each house, paying special attention to size, detail work, special features (such as porches), symmetry, style of windows, and so forth. What features are common to all the exteriors? What do those commonalities tell us? Finding those commonalities will take some time, effort, and imagination, but the results will be well worth it.

It may help you to make a chart listing the features and commonalities of the exteriors. It might begin something like this:

Common Features of Exteriors	Values They Communicate
Size all very large Ostentatious	

As you study your list, think about each feature. For example, why would someone want an ostentatious house, especially a member of the new industrial elite, most of whom had risen from the middle class or in some cases even below?

Next, look at the floor plans. What strikes you about them? What rooms in the plans are no longer in houses today? Why is that? Study the plans, again jotting down the features that you see. Then try to interpret what you have seen. Some social scientists call this "massaging" or "cooking" the data.

Now look at the photographs of the interiors of the houses. Repeat the process: what features stand out? What do they tell you about the era?

Finally look at the values you have identified from the exteriors, floor plans, and interiors. Summarize them to determine what they tell you about the Gilded Age. Can you see why Twain and Dana might have chosen that term?

By the end of this exercise you should have been able to make a series of houses tell you a great deal about the times in which they were built and admired. Other buildings from other times, including buildings being constructed today, can tell equally interesting stories.

As you analyze the evidence, keep in mind what Thorstein Veblen referred to in 1899 as "conspicuous consumption." Is there evidence of that here? If so, why do you believe there is? If not, why not?

Figure 3 from John Maass, The Gingerbread Age: A View of Victorian America *(New York: Rinehart, © 1957), p. 79. Courtesy of the publisher. Figures 4 through 10 from A. J. Bicknell and William T. Comstock,* Victorian Architecture: Two Pattern Books *(New York: American Life Foundation and Study Institute, © 1976), Plates 36 (Figure 4), 38 (Figure 5), 45 (Figure 6), 8 (Figure 7), 49 (Figure 8), 21 and 22 (Figure 9), and 18 (Figure 10). Courtesy of the publisher.*

FIGURE 4

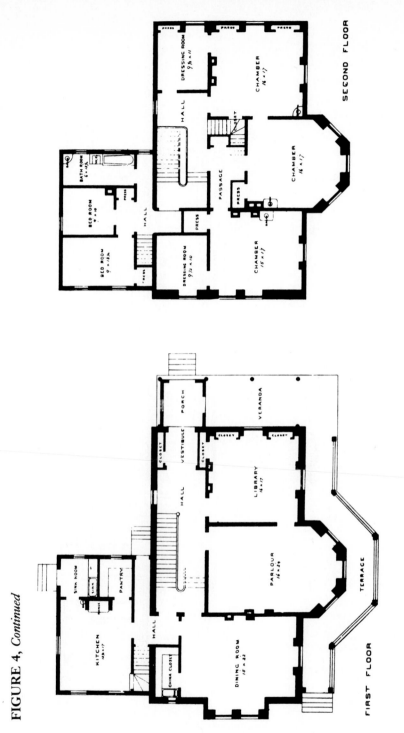

FIGURE 4, *Continued*

FIGURE 5

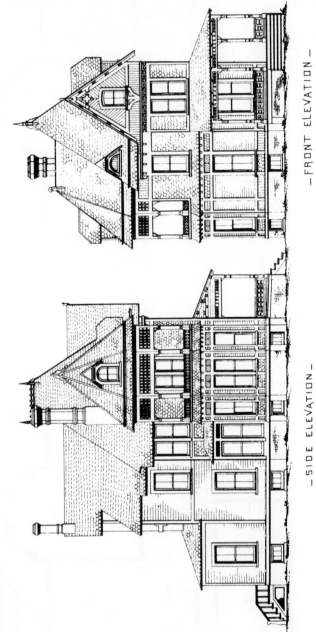

– FRONT ELEVATION –

– SIDE ELEVATION –

[58]

FIGURE 5, *Continued*

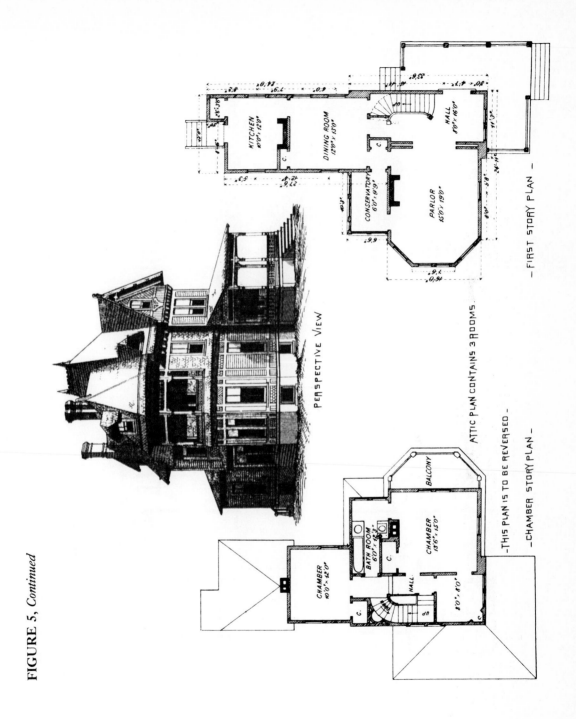

PERSPECTIVE VIEW

KITCHEN
10'0" x 12'0"

DINING ROOM
12'0" x 13'0"

CONSERVATORY
6'0" x 9'9"

HALL
8'0" x 16'0"

PARLOR
15'0" x 19'0"

– FIRST STORY PLAN –

ATTIC PLAN CONTAINS 3 ROOMS.

– THIS PLAN IS TO BE REVERSED –

– CHAMBER STORY PLAN –

CHAMBER
10'0" x 12'0"

BATH ROOM
6'0" x 9'3"

HALL

CHAMBER
13'6" x 15'0"

BALCONY

[59]

FIGURE 6

Perspective View.

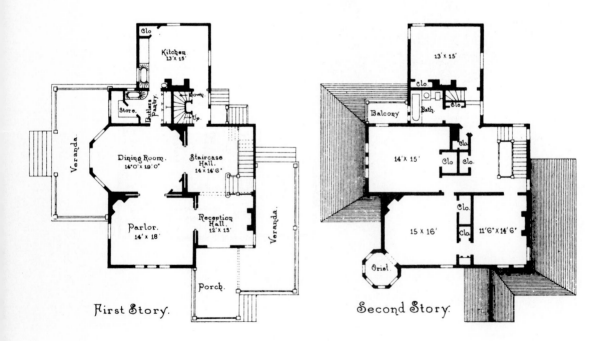

First Story.

Second Story.

FIGURE 7

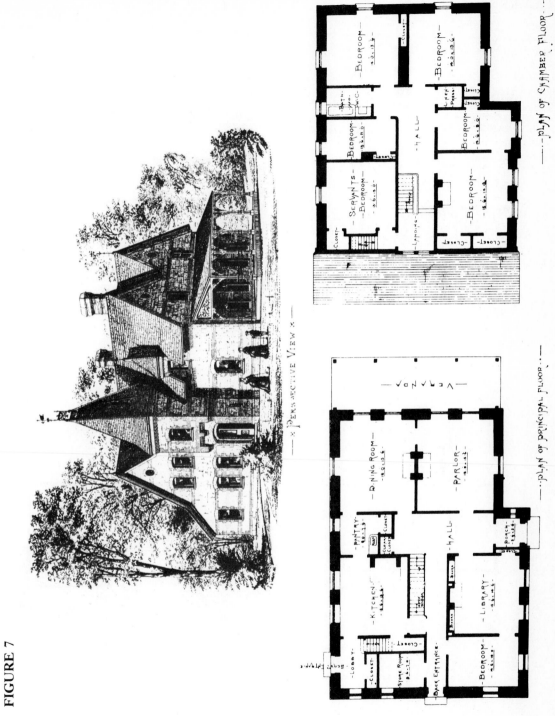

— Perspective View —

— Plan of Chamber Floor —

— Plan of Principal Floor —

[61]

FIGURE 8

Sea or Lake Shore Cottage,

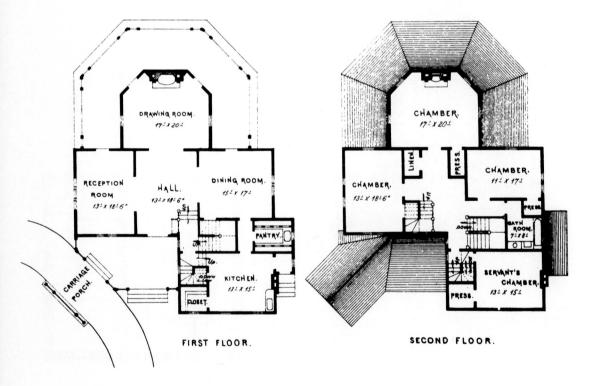

FIRST FLOOR.

SECOND FLOOR.

FIGURE 9

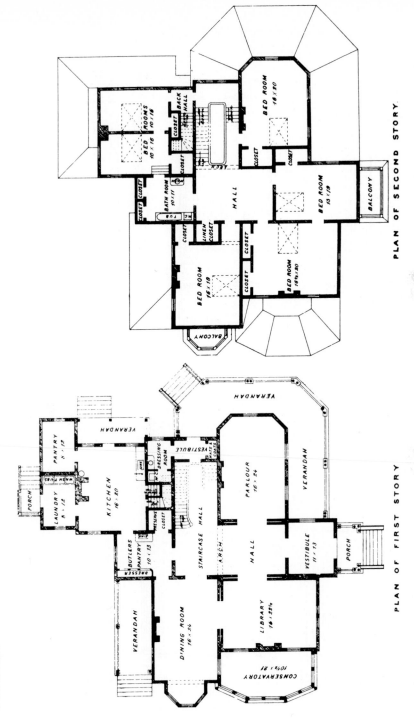

PLAN OF SECOND STORY.

PLAN OF FIRST STORY.

FIGURE 10

INTERIOR FINISH FOR DOORS AND WINDOWS.

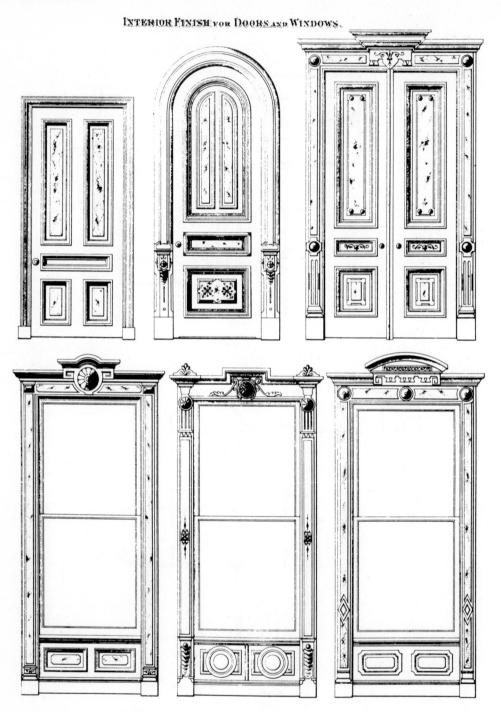

Figures 11 through 32 from Frederick Platt, America's Gilded Age: Its Architecture and Decoration *(South Brunswick: A. S. Barnes, © 1976), pp. 36 (Figures 11 and 25), 97 (Figure 12), 46 (Figures 13–16, 24, and 26), 83 (Figures 17 and 18), 87 (Figures 19–21, 30, and 31), 62 (Figures 22 and 23), 107 (Figure 27), 54 (Figure 28), 77 (Figure 29), and 80 (Figure 32). All figures courtesy of the publisher. Figure 12 courtesy of the Preservation Society of Newport County. Figures 22 and 23 courtesy of Biltmore House and Gardens. Figure 28 courtesy of Edison National Historic Site. Figure 30 courtesy of the Museum of the City of New York.*

FIGURE 11   Residence of Richard Townsend — Dining Room

FIGURE 12   Marble House: Summer Residence of William Kissam
Vanderbilt — Dining Room

FIGURE 13 Residence of Giraud Foster — Dining Room   *The Evidence*

FIGURE 14   Residence of Joseph Pulitzer — Breakfast Room

FIGURE 15   Residence of Giraud Foster — Living Room

FIGURE 16   Residence of Giraud Foster — Parlor

FIGURE 17   **Residence of A. Cass Canfield — Living Room**   *The Evidence*

FIGURE 18   **Residence of A. Cass Canfield — Library**

FIGURE 19 Residence of Richard Townsend — Library

FIGURE 20 Residence of Henry W. Poor — Library

FIGURE 21   Residence of Mrs. Phoebe A. Hearst — Library   *The Evidence*

FIGURE 22   Residence of George W. Vanderbilt — Mr. Vanderbilt's Bedroom

**FIGURE 23   Residence of George W. Vanderbilt — Mrs. Vanderbilt's
Bedroom**

FIGURE 24   Residence of Joseph Pulitzer — Second-Story Hall

FIGURE 26   Residence of Giraud Foster — Pergola and Fountain

FIGURE 27   Georgian Court: Summer Residence of George J. Gould —
Conservatory

FIGURE 28   Residence of Thomas Alva Edison — Conservatory   *The Evidence*

FIGURE 29   Residence of Henry W. Poor — Smoke Room

FIGURE 30   Elsie de Wolfe, in That Section of Her Irving Place, New York City, Home She Called Her "Cozy Corner"

FIGURE 31   Residence of Mrs. Phoebe A. Hearst — Music Room

FIGURE 32   Residence of P. A. B. Widener — Art Gallery

Questions to Consider

The first piece of evidence (Figure 3) is a photograph of the northern California mansion built in the 1880s by William Carson, a pioneer in the lumber business. The next several drawings (Figures 4 through 10) are taken from architects' "pattern books" published in the 1870s and 1880s. Figures 4, 5, and 6 are representative upper-class Victorian houses, while Figures 7 and 8 are cottages (we would call them vacation homes) intended for mountain or shore resort areas. Figure 9 illustrates an ambitious residence in the popular Italianate style, and Figure 10 illustrates detail work for doors and windows.

The remainder of the evidence consists of typical interiors of the houses of the newly rich, including residences of the Vanderbilts (shipping and railroads), of Pulitzer and Hearst (newspaper publishing), of Gould and Poor (financial speculation), of Widener (streetcars), and of Edison (inventions).

Begin by studying the exteriors of the houses. What are the outstanding features of the Carson mansion? Of the houses in Figures 4, 5, and 6? Look carefully at the floor plans. What kinds of rooms were included? How large were they? What were the purposes of the various rooms? Now look at the vacation cottages. To what degrees were they similar and in what

ways did they differ? Next, compare and contrast the elaborate Italian-style villa (Figure 9) with the earlier houses you have examined.

Figure 10 shows several ways in which interior doors and windows might have been decorated. How would you describe them to someone who had not seen these pictures? Figures 11, 12, 13, and 14 illustrate rooms designed for dining. What were their outstanding (and common) features? Can you imagine being a guest for lunch or dinner in one of these rooms? Use your imagination in the same way when looking at the living rooms and parlors (Figures 15–17), the home libraries (Figures 18–21), the bedrooms (Figures 22 and 23), the hallways (Figures 24 and 25), and the pergola[2] and conservatories (Figures 26–28). What impressions would you have if you were a visitor? Finally, think about the functions of the smoke room (Figure 29), cozy corner and music room (Figures 30 and 31), and art gallery (Figure 32).

Now try to put all the evidence together. What impressions did the newly rich of the Gilded Age want to convey through the exteriors, floor plans, and furnishings in their homes? What were the underlying values of the elite, portrayed by their life-styles and the homes they created?

2. A pergola is an arbor or passageway with a trellis for plants.

Epilogue

Of course, not all Americans lived like the elite. The poor and the immigrants of the cities were crowded into tenements (Figure 33). The early twentieth century saw the captains of industry come under attack for what many came to believe were their excesses. Evidence of their disdain for and defiance of the public good as well as of their treatment of workers, their political influence, and their ruthless business practices came more and more to light, due to the efforts of reformers and "muckraking" journalists. The society that once had venerated the industrial barons began to worry that they had too much power and came to believe that such power should be restricted.

FIGURE 33   A Dumbbell Apartment Plan. In such structures, there were four apartments per floor on each building lot. Except at the ends of blocks, ten of fourteen rooms looked out only on a light well. *(From David P. Handlin,* The American Home *(Boston: Little, Brown, © 1979), p. 202.)*

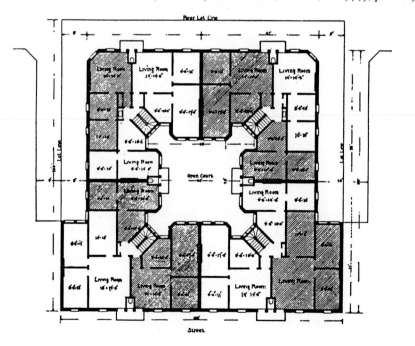

Reformers calling themselves Progressives (such as Robert LaFollette, Theodore Roosevelt, Jane Addams, and Woodrow Wilson) began to see government as a powerful referee, making decisions in the general public interest. In some cases that meant that the industrialists' activities had to be overseen, regulated, and occasionally prohibited. Antimonopoly legislation sought to restore competition by breaking up the huge corporations that industrial barons had patiently fashioned years before. Regulation of railroads, efforts to prohibit child labor and more closely oversee working conditions for workers (especially women and children), increased government efficiency with no favoritism to industrialists, and other reforms were part of the Progressives' program. Perhaps the high point of this movement was the passage of the Sixteenth Amendment to the Constitution (adopted in 1913), which gave Congress the power to institute a graduated income tax. Obviously, the Progressive era (roughly 1900–1915) marked a decided shift in values and ideas from those of the preceding decades.

Architecture was also undergoing a rapid transformation. Neoclassical and Georgian revivals occurred, and colonial and Dutch farmhouse styles signaled a shift toward less ostentation and increased moderation in private dwellings. But perhaps the most striking work was done by Chicago architect Frank Lloyd Wright, who sought to give functional and social meaning to his designs and to make each structure blend into its unique landscape. According to Wright's concepts there was no standard design for the "perfect house." Rather, a house was a "good house" if it conformed to the life-style of its owners and blended into the surrounding environment. Although Americans of the early twentieth century at first saw Wright's concepts and designs as extreme and "too modern," his work became the basis for a series of movements that ultimately changed the perspective and direction of American architecture.

In the 1970s and 1980s a rather curious phenomenon occurred. After over seven decades of architectural innovations based on the ideas of Frank Lloyd Wright and others, many Americans began to renew their love affairs with the architecture of the Gilded Age. Old Victorian homes were purchased and restored close to the centers of American cities. This was partly due to a movement called "gentrification," in which affluent young adults began returning from the suburbs to live in the cities. The energy shortage, clogged interstate highways, long and punishing daily commuter trips, and isolation of suburban living were all responsible. Still another reason was the sterility and conformity that had come to afflict modern suburban architecture. For whatever causes, the architecture of the Gilded Age, especially Queen Anne and High Victorian, again became the rage. Indeed, in 1983 the magazine *Victorian Homes,* a tasteful and lavishly illustrated quarterly that caters exclusively to this movement, had roughly forty thousand subscribers.

For those who could not own such homes another curious trend was taking place. Tens of thousands of adults began purchasing *miniature* houses (we would call them "dollhouses," although many would not like that term) that they patiently and expensively decorated with miniature furniture and accessories reflecting the tastes of the Gilded Age. In fact, the Miniature Industry Association of America (MIAA) claims that this hobby is one of the most popular of all American avocations in terms of numbers of enthusiasts and money spent.

What has caused this revival of interest in the architecture of the Gilded Age? If that architecture gave expression to the values and collective mentality of the late nineteenth century, why have Americans of the 1970s and 1980s found those styles so alluring? The answers to these questions will not tell us very much about architecture, but they may tell us a great deal about ourselves.

Chapter 4

The Consumer Society

The Problem

Every day Americans are surrounded, even bombarded, by advertising that tries to convince them to buy some product, use some service, or compare Brand X with Brand Y. Television, radio, billboards, magazines, and newspapers spread the message to potential consumers of a variety of necessary — and unnecessary — products. Underlying this barrage of advertisements is an appeal to a wide range of emotions — ambition, elitism, guilt, and anxiety, to name just a few — and a whole new "science" has arisen, called market research, that analyzes consumers' reactions and predicts future buying patterns.

Yet advertising is a relatively new phenomenon, one that began to develop after the Civil War and did not assume its modern form until the 1920s. P. T. Barnum, the promoter and impresario of mid-nineteenth-century entertainment, pointed the way with publicity gimmicks for his mu-

seum and circuses and, later, for the relatively unknown Swedish singer Jenny Lind (Barnum created such a demand for Lind's concert tickets that they sold for as much as $200 each). But at the time of the Civil War most merchants still announced special sales of their goods in simple newspaper notices, and brand names were virtually unknown.

In the late nineteenth and early twentieth centuries, America underwent a period of amazingly rapid growth. Cities expanded, taking in huge numbers of European immigrants as well as native born in-migrants from the surrounding countryside. In 1880 almost 75 percent of America's population lived in rural areas, but by 1920 approximately 46 percent lived in cities. American industry also expanded rapidly, mass producing a greater variety of products than ever before, instituting new managerial techniques, and forming new kinds of business combinations to reduce the fierce competition of an almost completely unregulated free-enterprise system. Gentlemen's agreements, pools, and trusts proliferated, and the Sherman Antitrust Act of 1890 was often used more effectively against workers who were trying to unionize than against industrial monopolies.

Taking advantage of the country's greatly improved transportation and communications systems, daring business leaders established innovative ways to distribute products, such as the mail-order firm and the department store. Sears and Roebuck was founded in 1893, and its "wish book," or catalogue, rapidly became popular reading for millions of people, especially those who lived in rural areas. Almost one thousand pages in length, these catalogues offered a dazzling variety of consumer goods and were filled with testimonial letters from satisfied customers. Lewis Thomas from Jefferson County, Alabama, wrote in 1897,

> I received my saddle and I must say that I am so pleased and satisfied with my saddle, words cannot express my thanks for the benefit that I received from the pleasure and satisfaction given me. I know that I have a saddle that will by ordinary care last a lifetime, and all of my neighbors are pleased as well, and I am satisfied so well that you shall have more of my orders in the near future.

And from Granite, Colorado, Mrs. Laura Garrison wrote, "Received my suit all right, was much pleased with it, will recommend your house to my friends. . . ."

For those who lived in cities, the department store was yet another way to distribute consumer goods. The massive, impressively decorated buildings erected by department store owners were often described as consumer "cathedrals" or "palaces." In fact, no less a personage that President William Howard Taft dedicated the new Wanamaker's department store in Philadelphia in 1911. "We are here," Taft told the crowd, "to celebrate the completion of one of the most important instrumentalities in modern life for the promotion of comfort among the people."

Many of the products being manufactured in factories in the late nineteenth and early twentieth centuries represented items previously made at home. Tinned meats and biscuits, "store bought" bread, ready-made clothing, and soap — all represented the impact of technology upon the functions of the homemaker. Other products were new versions of things already being used. For example, the bathtub was designed solely for washing one's body, as opposed to the large bucket or tub in which one collected rainwater, washed clothes, and, every so often, bathed. Still other products and gadgets (like the phonograph and the automobile) were completely new, the result of a fertile period of inventiveness (1860–1890) that saw over ten times more patents issued than were issued during the entire period up to 1860 (only 36,000 patents were issued prior to the Civil War, but 440,000 were granted during the next thirty years).

There was no question that American industry could produce new products and distribute them nationwide. But there *was* another problem: how could American industry overcome the traditional American ethic of thrift and create a demand for products that might not have even existed a few years earlier? It was this problem that the new field of advertising set out to solve.

America in 1865 was a country of widespread, if uneven, literacy and a vast variety of newspapers and magazines, all competing for readership. Businesses quickly learned that mass production demanded a national, even international, market, and money spent on national advertising in newspapers and magazines rose from $27 million in 1860 to more than $95 million in 1900. By 1929 the amount spent on advertising had climbed to more than one billion dollars. Brand names and catchy slogans vied with one another to capture the consumer's interest. Consumers could choose from among many biscuit manufacturers, as the president of National Biscuit Company reported to his stockholders in 1901: "We do not pretend to sell our standard goods cheaper than other manufacturers of biscuits

sell their goods. They always undersell us. Why do they not take away our business?" His answer was fourfold: efficiency, quality goods, innovative packaging, and advertising. "The trademarks we adopted," he concluded, "their value we created."

Advertising not only helped to differentiate one brand of a product from another, it also helped to break down regional differences as well as differences between rural and urban lifestyles. Women living on farms in Kansas could order the latest "New York–style frocks" from a mail-order catalogue, and people in small towns in the Midwest or rural areas in the South could find the newest furniture styles, appliances, and automobiles enticingly displayed in mass-circulation magazines. In this era, more and more people abandoned the old ways of doing things and embraced the new ways of life that resulted from the application of modern technology, mass production, and efficient distribution of products. Thus, some historians have argued that advertising accelerated the transition of American society from one that emphasized production to one that stressed consumption.

From the historian's viewpoint, advertising also created a wealth of evidence that can be used to reconstruct our collective past. By looking at and reading advertisements from the turn of the century, we can trace the changing habits, interests, and tastes of Americans. More than that, by analyzing the kinds of emotional appeals used in late nineteenth and early twentieth century advertisements, we can begin to understand the aspirations and goals as well as the fears and anxieties of the people who lived in such a rapidly changing society.

The Method

No historian would suggest that the advertisements of preceding decades (or today's advertisements, for that matter) speak for themselves — that they tell you how people actually lived. Rather, like almost all historical evidence, advertisements must be carefully analyzed for their message. Advertisements are intended to make people want to buy various products and services. They can be positive or negative. Positive advertisements show the benefits — direct or indirect, explicit or implicit — that would come from owning a product. Such advertisements, then, depict an ideal. Negative or "scare" advertisements demonstrate the disastrous consequences of not owning the product. Some of the most effective advertisements, of course, combine both negative and positive approaches ("I was a lonely 360-pound woman before I discovered Dr. Quack's Appetite Suppressors — now I weigh 120 pounds and am engaged to be married!"). Advertisements also attempt to evoke an emotional response from potential consumers that will encourage the purchase of a particular product or service.

Very early advertisements tended to be primarily descriptive, simply picturing the product. Later advertisements often told a story with pictures and words. In looking at the advertisements in this chapter, first determine whether the approach used is positive, negative, or a combination of both. What were the expected consequences of using (or not using) the product? How did the advertisement try to sell the product or service? What emotional response(s) were expected?

The preceding evaluation is not too difficult, but in this exercise you must go even further with your analysis. You are trying to determine what each advertisement can tell you about earlier generations of Americans and the times in which they lived. Look at (and read) each advertisement carefully. Does it reveal anything about the values of the time period in which the advertisement appeared? About the roles of men and women? About attitudes concerning necessities and luxuries? About people's aspirations or fears?

Historians are also concerned with continuity and change over time. In Part I of the evidence, you will notice that the Sears, Roebuck catalogue advertisements are dated 1897, 1902, and 1927. In Part II, the earliest advertisement is dated 1896, and the advertisements cover the period through the late 1920s. As you study this material, be alert to the aspects of the advertisements and the products portrayed in the advertisements that change during these decades, as well as those aspects that stay the same. These are only a few of the issues you might raise when analyzing advertisements as pieces of historial evidence.

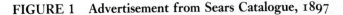

The Evidence

PART I: CHANGING LIFE-STYLES

Figures 1 through 16 from Sears, Roebuck and Company catalogues, 1897, 1902, and 1927. Courtesy of Sears, Roebuck and Company.

FIGURE 1   Advertisement from Sears Catalogue, 1897

[86]

FIGURE 2   Advertisement from Sears Catalogue, 1927   *The Evidence*

New Fall Colors and Fancy Weaves
High Quality Pure Wool Worsteds

It's pattern, men—new, colorful, rich looking—brand new, right from the style centers. And it's style, too. We've certainly gone one step ahead in these suits. Note the stylish lines of this fine "Clover Leaf" lapel coat and the three-button effect that college men and all well dressed men are demanding. The pattern is fancy weave with contrasting stripes—an altogether rich looking combination. Striped dark blue or the French (slate) gray, are the two new colors. The fabric is a weighty pure all wool worsted—strong, durable and slow to show signs of wear. Suit is well tailored and trim fitting. Coat full alpaca lined. Trousers have cuffs and are cut full. Regular vest. Yes, sir! We're proud of this suit and you will be, too. SIZES—34 to 42 inches chest, 29 to 40 inches waist and 29 to 34 inches inseam. State chest, waist and inseam measurements. Shipping weight, 5½ pounds.

45K8111—Striped Dark
Blue..................... **$16.75**
45K8112—Striped French (Slate)
Gray..................... **16.75**

"Warm as Toast"
Heavy Winter Overcoat

Nothing finer has ever happened before. We are featuring this coat because it is a representative value from our new "Great Store for Men." By representative value, we mean one of a great many bargains that you will find throughout this clothing section. The material in this particular coat is heavy-weight, a "Warm as Toast" fabric that will wear and give great service. In addition it is full twill lined. Snappy model with half belt in back. Tailored on stylish lines and strongly sewed. Two rich 1927 winter colors: Dark blue and dark brown. Length, about 44 inches. Big savings for you if you buy here. SIZES—34 to 44 inches chest. State chest measure taken over vest. Shipping weight, 7 pounds.

45K8367—Dark Blue............. **$12.75**
45K8368
Dark Brown..................... **12.75**

FIGURE 3   Advertisement from Sears Catalogue, 1927

FIGURE 4   Advertisement from Sears Catalogue, 1897   *The Evidence*

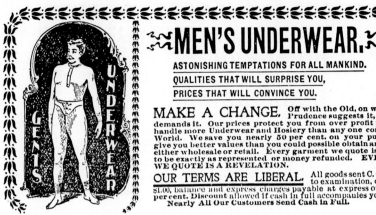

MEN'S UNDERWEAR.

ASTONISHING TEMPTATIONS FOR ALL MANKIND.
QUALITIES THAT WILL SURPRISE YOU,
PRICES THAT WILL CONVINCE YOU.

MAKE A CHANGE. Off with the Old, on with the New. Prudence suggests it, your health demands it. Our prices protect you from over profit paying. We handle more Underwear and Hosiery than any one concern in the World. We save you nearly 50 per cent. on your purchases and give you better values than you could possible obtain anywhere else either wholesale or retail. Every garment we quote is guaranteed to be exactly as represented or money refunded. EVERY PRICE WE QUOTE IS A REVELATION.

OUR TERMS ARE LIBERAL. All goods sent C. O. D., subject to examination, on receipt of $1.00, balance and express charges payable at express office. **Three per cent.** Discount allowed if cash in full accompanies your order. Nearly All Our Customers Send Cash in Full.

Ventilated Health Underwear.

Summer Weight Balbriggan.

No. 2830 Men's Ventilated Natural Gray Mixed Summer Undershirts. The most comfortable as well as the most healthful balbriggan underwear ever made; fine gauge and soft finish; fancy collarette neck, pearl buttons and ribbed cuffs; ventilated all over with small drop stitch openings. Highly recommended by the best physicians as conducive to good health. Sizes 34 to 42 only. Price each.. **$0.58**

MEN'S FANCY UNDERWEAR.
Men's Striped Balbriggan Underwear, 41 Cents.

No. 16R5078 Men's Fine Fancy Balbriggan Undershirts, knit from fine Egyptian cotton, made in a very narrow ¼-inch alternating white and blue stripe. A very pretty garment that never fails to give satisfaction. Fast color. Trimmed with collarette neck and pearl buttons. Perfect fitting ribbed cuffs. Never retails for less than 50 to 65 cents. Stitched throughout with never-rip seams. Sizes, 34 to 44 breast measure.
Price, each...................... **41c**

FIGURE 5   Advertisement from Sears Catalogue, 1897

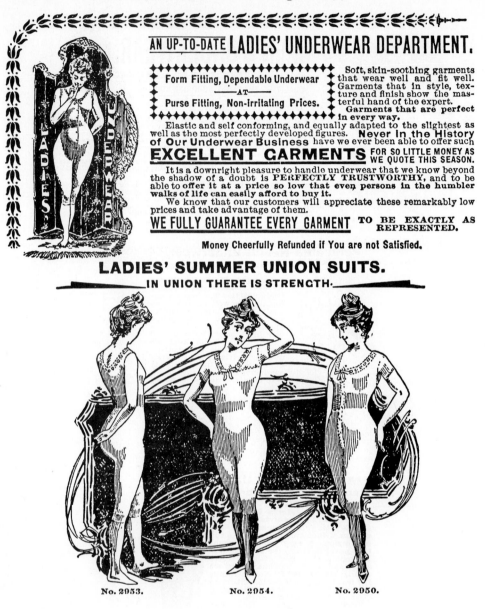

FIGURE 6   Advertisement from Sears Catalogue, 1902

Parisienne Hip Pad and Bustle.

No. 18R4880 The Parisienne Hip Pad and Bustle, made of best tempered, black enameled, woven wire with hip pads of padded cloth. Perfect in shape, and light in weight. Very durable.

Price, each...40c

If by mail, postage extra, each, 10 cents.

The Lenox Glove Fitting Hip Bustle.

No. 18R4886 It rounds out the figure and produces the effect desired in prevailing fashions, extending over the hips very lightly and gracefully. Made of blue black tempered steel and cannot get out of shape, neither can it be detected. Suitable for rainy day skirts.

Price, each 37c

If by mail, postage extra, 10 cents.

FIGURE 7   Advertisement from Sears Catalogue, 1927

38K534—Flesh.   55c.
Sizes to fit 30 to 44 inches bust measure. State bust measure. Shpg. wt., 3 oz.

The Boyshform Brassiere is very popular, as it gives your figure that smart boylike flat appearance that so many women desire. Made of fancy batiste of a firm durable quality with Rayon stripes. Cut in one piece; fitted under arms and has elastic waistline. Top neatly trimmed with lace. Hooks down back. No boning. Lingerie tape shoulder straps. If you have not tried this style, place an order for one or more now.

Our "Co-Ed"
New Soft Figure Former without Single Bone or Stay

$1.95

Its presence—so invisible under your frock. Soft corseting is preferred by many smartly dressed youthful figures and our "Co-Ed" fills the need. Made of Rayon striped pink material with elastic all the way down each side and across the thighs; no boning. The section across abdomen is lined and well stitched to impart just a little support. Hooks at left side and has four supporters. Lgt., center front, 19½ in.

18K125

Even sizes, 30, 32, 34, 36, 38, 40 and 42 inches bust measure. Measure bust over fullest part and state size; also give hip measure. Shpg. wt., 1¼ lbs. $1.95

FIGURE 8   Advertisement from Sears Catalogue, 1902

LADIES' LONG COATS
...OR AUTOMOBILES.

WHEN ORDERING, please state bust measure and length of sleeves, measured from under the arm to wrist, also the color you desire. Sizes are from 32 to 42 inches around bust. Shades or sizes different or larger than regular stock garment will be made to order at 20 per cent above the regular price quoted in catalogue and cash in full in advance. It takes about two weeks to make a special.

THESE GARMENTS ARE TOO HEAVY TO BE SENT BY MAIL.

No. 17R149 LADIES' AUTOMOBILE JACKET OR OVERCOAT. Made of all wool kersey, strictly tailor made; large collar and lapels made of South American beaver, otherwise called nutria; double breasted front trimmed with fancy buttons; side pockets stitched several times; bell sleeves; half tight fitting back; 36 inches long; facing in front made of same material; lined throughout with satin. Colors, black or castor. Price, each.............. **$13.50**

No. 17R151 LADIES' AUTOMOBILE OR OVERCOAT. Made 42 inches long, tailor made; large storm collar and lapels buttoning high at the neck; side pockets; several rows of stitching on collar, lapels, and cuffs; double breasted front; half tight fitting back; trimmed with kersey straps and fancy buttons; facing in front made of the same material; lined throughout with black mercerized sateen. Color, black only. Price, each...... .... **$7.95**

No. 17R152 LADIES' AUTOMOBILE OR OVERCOAT. Made of all wool kersey; storm collar, lapels buttoning at neck; silk stitching on collar, lapels and around the bottom as well as on the cuffs; double breasted front trimmed with fancy buttons; side pockets; half tight fitting back; facing in front made of same material; lined throughout with fine satin; watch pocket on inside. Made 42 inches long. Colors, black or tan. Price, each.... ... . **$9.50**

[92]

FIGURE 9   Advertisement from Sears Catalogue, 1927

A Fashion Review of Unusual Interest

On the Pages to Follow You'll Find the Latest and Smartest Spring and Summer Apparel Direct From New York

31H6000
All Silk Crepe Satin or All Silk Flat Crepe

$14⁷⁵

FIGURE 10 Advertisement from Sears Catalogue, 1897

Perfumes.

D 1027 Sears, Roebuck & Co.'s Perfume Extracts have given great satisfaction to everyone who has used them. They are sweet and lasting perfumes, put up in handsome packages. We import these perfume extracts in bulk from the flower gardens of France, and put them up ourselves in different sized bottles. By this method we can afford to give the choicest full strength perfume in a pretty bottle for a low price.

Lilac Blossoms.	Moss Rose.	Lily of the Valley.
Musk.	New Mown Hay.	Violet.
Indian Violet.	White Rose.	Wh'te Heliotrope.
Ylang Ylang.	English Violet.	Sweet Clover.
Jasamine.	Crab Apple.	Mignonette.
Sweet Pea.	Tea Rose.	Tuberose.
Wood Violet.	Shandon Bells.	Rose Geranium.
Carnation Pink.	Jockey Club.	Meadow Blossom.
Columbia Bouquet.		

Put up in glass stoppered bottles, 1 cz., each...25c
Put up in glass stoppered bottles, 2 oz., each...48c
Put up in glass stoppered bottles, 4 oz., each...89c
Put up in glass stoppered bottles, 8 oz., each.$1.60

TOILET ARTICLE COMBINATION.

10 Useful Articles at the Usual Price of Three.

EVERY LADY IN THE LAND Knows what a Luxury it is to have these Little Toilet Articles Around Handy.

$3.00 Worth of Useful Articles for the Toilet for 95c.

No. 26338 **THIS COMBINATION CONSISTS OF:**

95 c. for the entire outfit

1 bottle (8 oz.) Witch Hazel.
1 cake buttermilk soap.
1 bottle Petroleum Jelly (for burns, scalds, etc.)
1 box Swan Down Face Powder.
1 box Tooth Powder.
1 box Cold Cream (for freckles, sunburn, etc.)
1 box Toilet Powder.
1 Fancy Jug Shampoo (makes thirty shampoos.)
1 bottle Triple Extract Perfume (any odor.)
1 Face Chamois Skin.

The Entire Outfit for ....:...... 95c.

FIGURE 11 Advertisement from Sears Catalogue, 1902

FIGURE 12 Advertisements from Sears Catalogues, 1897 (Children's Reefer Jackets), and 1902 (Children's Toys)

SEARS ROEBUCK & CO. INC.

85¢

$1.50

24171

24172

REEFER JACKETS FOR CHILDREN FROM 1 TO 5 YEARS OLD.

Reefer Jackets for little toddlers, from one to four years, nobby, stylish little coats at little bits of prices. As usual S. R. & Co. will save you money on these goods.

Do not forget to mention age and color desired when ordering.

DRESSED SAILOR DOLLS.

Sailor Girl Dolls.

No. 29R735 Sailor Girl Doll, bisque head, flowing hair, solid eyes, dressed to represent a girl in sailor costume. A very pretty doll. Length, 13 inches.
Price, each................50c

Sailor Boy Dolls.

No. 29R739 Sailor Boy Doll, dressed to represent a boy in sailor costume, companion doll to sailor girl. Length, 13 inches.
Price, each......................50c

The Penny Saver.

No. 29R147 A perfect registering bank; no key, no combination. Each time a cent is dropped into the bank the bell rings and the register indicates. Opens automatically at each 50 cents. The total always in sight. **They are attractive and interesting to children.** The mechanism is made of steel, and will not break or get out of order. It is highly interesting to children, **and for this reason will encourage them to save. Shipping weight, 5 pounds.** Price, each........85c

[95]

FIGURE 13   Advertisement from Sears Catalogue, 1902

BOYS' WASH SUITS.

The extraordinary value we offer in Boys' Wash Suits can only be fully appreciated by those who order from this department.   A trial order will surely convince you that we are able to furnish new, fresh, up to date, stylish and well made wash suits at much lower prices than similar value can be had from any other house.

NOTE.—Boys' wash suits can be had only in the sizes as mentioned after each description.   Always state age of boy and if large or small of age.

Boy's Wash Crash Suit, 35 Cents.

Navy Blue and White Percale Wash Suit, 40 Cents.

38R2128 98c

38R2130 $1.39

38R2131 $1.48

GIRLS' WASH DRESSES.

AGES FROM 4 TO 14 YEARS.

WHEN ORDERING please state Age, Height, Weight and Number of Inches around Bust.

SCALE OF SIZES, SHOWING PROPORTION OF BUST AND LENGTH TO THE AGE OF CHILD

Age	4	6	8	10	12	14
Bust	24	27	28	29	80	81
Skirt length	18	20	22	24	26	28

FIGURE 14   Advertisement from Sears Catalogue, 1927

Bloomer Dresses
for Younger Girls
Ages 7-8-9 Years
To Fill a Long Felt Need

we have added this selection of younger girls' bloomer dresses to our catalog. Appropriately designed for the little girl who is not quite ready for the styles that "big sister" can wear. Mothers have long felt the need of just this particular class of dresses, for girls at this age.

Smart New Frocks
for Girls
Ages 7 - 8 - 10 - 12 - 14 Years

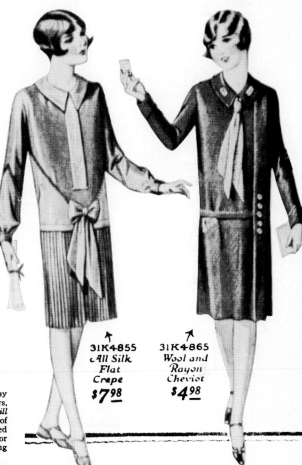

Smart and Dressy

Here is a charming frock of the dressy type, for the young girls of 7 to 9 years, adapted in rich looking good quality *Twill Back Velveteen.* It portrays a design of youthful chic and is attractively trimmed with ecru lace edged, contrasting color *Silk Broadcloth.* Comes with matching color lustrous sateen bloomers.

Ages—7, 8 and 9 years. State age size. See size scale. Shipping wt., 1½ lbs.

31K4965—Black.   **$4.79**

Ages, years	7	8	9
Fit chest measures, in	26	27	29
Come in lengths, in	26	28	30

31K4855
All Silk Flat Crepe
$7⁹⁸

31K4865
Wool and Rayon Cheviot
$4⁹⁸

FIGURE 15   Advertisement from Sears Catalogue, 1927

FIGURE 16   Advertisement from Sears Catalogue, 1927

Selected Toys for Girls

Our Great Special 4.95

It's Simply Marvelous Value!

Does your little girl, like most little girls the world over, want to play mother? This is the expression of a wish to be like her own mother and is a high ideal that should be encouraged. Why not give your daughter a really fine big doll now, like the one here pictured, with go-to-sleep eyes, hair eyelashes and fine Ma-Ma voice? The beautiful dress of colored, silky Rayon has a low neck, short sleeves and real wide lace edging with ribbon trim. Natural looking fine mohair wig with neat part and silk ribbon bow. New slender type composition legs and arms and fine body. Truly a wonderful purchase. 18K2952½ Shpg. wt., 5¼ lbs....**$4.95**

26 Inch Size

Combination Toy Gas Range and Stove
White With Blue Trimmings.

A new stove, just like Mother's. Top of stove measures 9x5⅝ inches; has four lids and four imitation gas burners. Total height, 10½ in. Complete with cast iron skillet, dinner kettle and lid lifter. Shpg. wt., 8 lbs. 69K7307 **$1.79**

Girls' Dresser Sets

Our Best Set
Beautifully hand decorated, pearl on amber filled pyralin. Just like mother's set. 8-inch beveled glass, mirror with brush and comb. In plain gift box. Shpg. wt., 2 pounds. 87K6133 **$2.98**

Chain Stitch **$3.98** *Some Beauty*

Little Girls Love to Sew

Everything for Dolly's Laundry

Here's a Complete Set at Low Price **$1.00**

DOLLY'S CLOTHES LINE

[99]

PART II: HOPES AND FEARS

Figures 17 through 24 and 26 through 31 from Edgar R. Jones, Those Were the Good Old Days: A Happy Look at American Advertising, 1880–1930 *(New York: Simon and Schuster,* © *1959), pp. 76 (Figure 17), 152 (Figure 18), 149 (Figure 19), 135 (Figure 20), 140 (Figure 21), 219 (Figure 22), 207 (Figure 23), 167 (Figure 24), 354 (Figure 26), 352 (Figure 27), 380 (Figure 28), 386 (Figure 29), 422 (Figure 30), and 448 (Figure 31). Courtesy of the publisher. Figure 25 from Frank Rowsome, Jr.,* They Laughed When I Sat Down *(New York: McGraw-Hill,* © *1959), p. 144.*

FIGURE 17   Advertisement, 1896

FIGURE 18   Advertisement, 1905   *The Evidence*

This illustration shows the Pierce Great
Arrow 28-32 Horse-Power Opera Coach,
body by Quinby & Co.   Price $5,000.

Great Arrow Enclosed Cars

THESE three types of enclosed cars have been built with a special thought for the user who expects the same perfection in the appointments of his automobile that he does in those of his carriages. These cars have the perfect mechanism of the Pierce cars together with the most attractive and tasteful bodies ever turned out by Quinby.   To appreciate their perfection they should be seen.   We have been working steadily toward a very high standard in car-building, and believe now that the Pierce cars are American cars built by Americans for American conditions, American roads and the American temperament.   Full descriptive booklet together with technical description of mechanisms will be mailed on request, or can be had of numerous Pierce agents all over the United States.

This illustration shows the Pierce Great Arrow
28-32 Horse-Power Suburban Car.   Price $5,000.

This illustration shows the Pierce Great Arrow
28-32 Horse-Power Landaulette Car.   Price $5,000.

THE GEORGE N. PIERCE COMPANY, Buffalo, N. Y.

Manufacturers of Pierce Cycles   MEMBERS OF ASSOCIATION OF LICENSED AUTOMOBILE MANUFACTURERS.

$1,000 IN PRIZES

EVERY artist and designer should write at once for full particulars of our offer of prizes as follows: First prize of $250 and a second prize of $100 for the best design of an open body for a motor car; first prize of $250 and a second prize of $100 for the best design of an enclosed or Limousine body for a motor car: first prize of $200 and a second prize of $100 for the best color scheme for motor car bodies.   Full description and outline drawings of Pierce cars will be supplied to artists for coloring.

[1905]

FIGURE 20 Advertisement, 1909

Why stir up the Dust Demon to Frenzy like this?

The Man
always wonders why some way of cleaning can't be found without tormenting him with choking clouds of dust.

The Woman
thinks she is performing praiseworthy and necessary work in an unavoidable manner.

You can Escape all this for $25

EVERY MAN AND WOMAN

should now realize that such laborious and tormenting "cleaning" methods, not only are absolutely unnecessary, but are **a relic of barbarism, a mockery and a farce.** "Cleaning" with broom and carpet-sweeper merely scatters more of the dirt over a wider area. Old dirt has to be *rehandled again and again.* The dust is never thoroughly clean. Disease germs are let to multiply, then are sent flying to infect all those whose powers of resistance may be lowered.

THE IDEAL VACUUM CLEANER

(Fully Protected by Patents)

Operated by Hand puts no tax on the strength.
Price $25

"IT EATS UP THE DIRT"

literally sucks out all the dust, grit, germs, moths and eggs of vermin that are *on* the object as well as *in* it—gobbles them down into its capacious maw, never to trouble you again.

Or by Electric Motor, at a cost of 2 cents per hour.
Price $55 or $60

This machine places in your hands a method of cleaning carpets, rugs, curtains, upholstery, wall decorations, etc., that hitherto has been limited to the very rich. It does exactly the same work as the Vacuum Cleaning systems that cost from $500 up—*and does it better and with more convenience.*
The Ideal Vacuum Cleaner is the perfection of the Vacuum Cleaning principle.

OPERATED BY HAND

Weighs only 20 pounds. Anybody can use it. Everybody can afford it. Compared with sweeping

It is ease itself.

It is absolutely dustless. Every machine guaranteed.

Our free illustrated Booklet tells an interesting story of a remarkable saving in money, time, labor, health, and strength. Send for it to-day.

The American Vacuum Cleaner Company
225 Fifth Avenue, New York City

[1909]

FIGURE 19 Advertisement, 1908

Don't Depend on Your Relatives When You Get Old

If you let things go kind o' slip-shod *now*, you may later have to get out of the 'bus and set your carpet-bag on the stoop of some house where your arrival will hardly be attended by an ovation.

If you secure a membership in the Century Club this sad possibility will be nipped in the bud. It is very, very comfortable to be able to sit under a vine and fig-tree of your own.

The Club has metropolitan headquarters and a national membership of self-respecting women and men who are building little fortunes on the monthly plan. Those who have joined thus far are a happy lot—it would do your heart good to read their letters.

We would just as soon send our particulars to you as to anybody else, and there is no reason in the world why you shouldn't know all about everything. You'll be glad if you do and sorry if you don't.

Be kind to those relatives—*and to yourself.*

Address, stating without fail your occupation and the exact date of your birth,

Century Life-Insurance Club
Section O

5, 7 and 9 East 42d Street, New York
RICHARD WIGHTMAN, Secretary

[1908]

[102]

FIGURE 21   Advertisement, 1908

The Electric Washer and Wringer

YOU can now have your washings done by electricity. The 1900 Electric Washer Outfit (Washer, Wringer and Motor complete) does all the heavy work of washing and wrings out the clothes.

Any electric light current furnishes the power needed. You connect up the washer the same way you put an electric light globe into its socket. Then all there is to do to start the washer is—turn on the electricity. The motion of the tub (driven by the electricity) and the water and soap in the tub wash the clothes clean. Washing is done quicker and easier, and more thoroughly and economically this way than ever before.

Washing

Wringing

30 Days' FREE Trial—Freight Prepaid

Servants will stay contented—laundry bills will be saved—clothes will last twice as long—where there is a 1900 Electric Washer to do the washing.

These washers save so much work and worry and trouble, that they *sell themselves.* This is the way of it—

We ship you an Electric Washer and *prepay the freight.*

Use the washer a month. Wash your linens and laces — wash your blankets and quilts—wash your rugs.

Then—when the month is up, if you are not convinced the washer is all we say— don't keep it. Tell us you don't want the washer and that will settle the matter. We won't charge anything for the use you have had of it.

This is the *only* washer outfit that does *all* the drudgery of the washing—*washes and wrings* clothes—saves them from wear and tear—and keeps your servants contented.

Our Washer Book tells how our washers are made and how they work. Send for this book today.

Don't mortgage your pleasure in life to dread of wash-day and wash-day troubles with servants. Let the 1900 Electric Washer and Wringer shoulder your wash-day burden—save your clothes and money, and keep your servants contented.

Write for our Washer Book at once. Address—

The 1900 Washer Co. 3133 Henry Street, Binghamton, N.Y. (If you live in Canada, write to the Canadian 1900 Washer Co., 355 Yonge Street, Toronto, Ont.)

[1908]

[103]

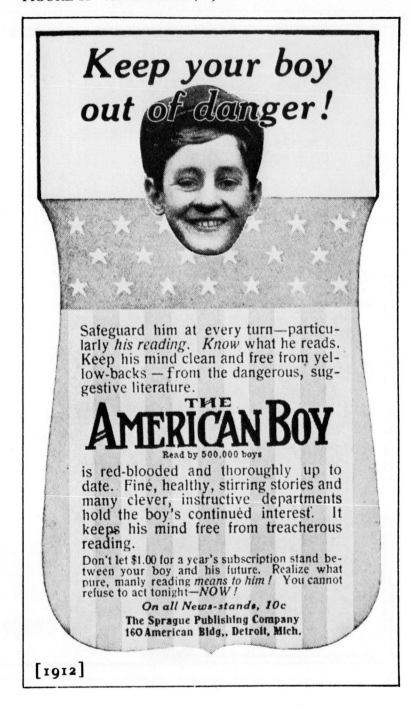

FIGURE 23   Advertisement, 1912   *The Evidence*

These are the watch chains now worn by men who set the styles

When a man buys a watch chain he chooses a *pattern* to suit his individual taste—but he wants a *style* which will always be in good taste.

A watch chain is the only piece of jewelry worn universally by men. It is the most prominent piece a man can wear. Every man with any regard for his personal appearance wants his watch chain right.

SIMMONS CHAINS
TRADE MARK

are always "correct" in style. That is one reason why first-class jewelers have handled them for forty years. A man in the smaller cities and towns can be just as sure as a New Yorker that he is getting the "proper thing" if he buys a *Simmons Chain*.

Waldemar and Dickens are the most popular styles this year. Lapels, vests and fobs are also in good taste. For women there are chatelaines, neck, eyeglass and guard chains and bracelets.

The beauty of design and finish and the satisfactory service of the *Simmons Chains*, have made them a standard among well-dressed men and women.

The surface of a *Simmons Chain* is not a wash or plate. It is a rolled tube of 12 or 14 karat *solid gold*, of sufficient thickness to withstand the wear of years.

If your jeweler hasn't *Simmons Chains* write us for Style Book—make your selection and we'll see that you are supplied.

R. F. Simmons Co.   (Established 1873)   177 N. Main St., Attleboro, Mass.
Look for SIMMONS stamped on each piece—your protection and guarantee for wear.

[1912]

FIGURE 24   Advertisement, 1914

Society's Town Car

The electric automobile has become a necessity to the woman with many social engagements. And the Detroit Electric has justly earned its title, "Society's Town Car." In the changeable spring weather—as at other times—this beautiful car carries you in elegant comfort and independent privacy to the reception, tea, theatre or dance. For shopping, also, it is the ideal of convenience

Remember, too, that the Detroit Electric is built and backed by the world's largest makers of electric pleasure vehicles. Your choice of many models.   Catalog on request

ANDERSON ELECTRIC CAR COMPANY
DETROIT, MICH.

Builders of the Detroit Electric

Largest manufacturers of electric pleasure vehicles in the world

[1914]

FIGURE 25   Advertisement, 1919

"Here's an Extra $50, Grace
—I'm making <u>real</u> money now!"

   "Yes, I've been keeping it a secret until pay day came. I've been pro-
moted with an increase of $50 a month. And the first extra money is yours.
Just a little reward for urging me to study at home. The boss says my
spare time training has made me a valuable man to the firm and there's
more money coming soon. We're starting up easy street, Grace, thanks to
you and the I. C. S.!"

FIGURE 26   Advertisement, 1921

Is Your Bathroom Ten Years Old?

If so, it is possible that the fixtures should be replaced.   They may not be up to date.   Like other home furnishings, plumbing fixtures should be replaced as new, more pleasing designs come into vogue. Let your Contracting Plumber be your adviser.   He is familiar with the modern developments in plumbing fixtures.   His knowledge of fixtures plus his knowledge of the technique of plumbing makes his advice authoritative.

Write for our catalog "Standard" Plumbing Fixtures for the Home."

Standard Sanitary Mfg. Co., Pittsburgh

In addition to the displays of "Standard" Plumbing Fixtures shown by Wholesale Dealers and Contracting Plumbers, there are permanent "Standard" exhibits in the following cities:

NEW YORK...................................35 W. 31ST	COLUMBUS...................................166 N. THIRD	DALLAS......................................1200 JACKSON
NEW YORK (EXPORT DEPARTMENT)..........50 BROAD	CANTON.................................1108 SECOND, N. E.	SAN ANTONIO................................212 LOBOYA
BOSTON................................186 DEVONSHIRE	YOUNGSTOWN.........................458 W. FEDERAL	FORT WORTH................................828 MONROE
PHILADELPHIA.............................1215 WALNUT	WHEELING............................48 EIGHTEENTH	KANSAS CITY......................301 RIDGE ARCADE
WASHINGTON...........................SOUTHERN BLDG.	HUNTINGTON..............SECOND AVE. AND TENTH	SAN FRANCISCO......................149-55 BLUXOME
PITTSBURGH.................................445 WATER	ERIE.....................................130 W. TWELFTH	LOS ANGELES....................216-224 S. CENTRAL
PITTSBURGH.................................106 SIXTH	ALTOONA................................918 ELEVENTH	SYRACUSE OFFICE....................303 HERALD BLDG
CHICAGO................................14 N. PEORIA	MILWAUKEE..............................428 BROADWAY	ATLANTA OFFICE.1217 CITIZENS & SOUTHERN BANK BLDG.
ST. LOUIS.....................4140 FOREST PARK BLVD.	MILWAUKEE................................311 FIFTH	DETROIT OFFICE....................414 HAMMOND BLDG.
EAST ST. LOUIS.............................18 N. MAIN	LOUISVILLE...............................323 W. MAIN	CHICAGO OFFICE..............1010 STANDARD OIL BLDG.
CLEVELAND................................4409 EUCLID	NASHVILLE.........................315 TENTH AVE., S.	SEATTLE OFFICE...............1326 L. C. SMITH BLDG.
CINCINNATI.................................633 WALNUT	NEW ORLEANS..........................846 BARONNE	TORONTO, CAN.......................59 E. RICHMOND
TOLEDO......................................311 ERIE	HOUSTON...............COR. PRESTON AVE. AND SMITH	HAMILTON, CAN..........................20 W. JACKSON

FACTORIES: Pittsburgh, Pa.; Louisville, Ky.; New Brighton, Pa.; Toronto, Can.   POTTERIES: Kokomo, Ind.; Tiffin, O.

[1921]

FIGURE 27 Advertisement, 1924   *The Evidence*

Often a bridesmaid but never a bride

EDNA'S case was really a pathetic one. Like every woman, her primary ambition was to marry. Most of the girls of her set were married—or about to be. Yet not one possessed more grace or charm or loveliness than she.

And as her birthdays crept gradually toward that tragic thirty-mark, marriage seemed farther from her life than ever.

She was often a bridesmaid but never a bride.

That's the insidious thing about halitosis (unpleasant breath). You, yourself, rarely know when you have it. And even your closest friends won't tell you.

Sometimes, of course, halitosis comes from some deep-seated organic disorder that requires professional advice. But usually—and fortunately—halitosis is only a local condition that yields to the regular use of Listerine as a mouth wash and gargle. It is an interesting thing that this well-known antiseptic that has been in use for years for surgical dressings, possesses these unusual properties as a breath deodorant.

It halts food fermentation in the mouth and leaves the breath sweet, fresh and clean. Not by substituting some other odor but by really removing the old one. The Listerine odor itself quickly disappears. So the systematic use of Listerine puts you on the safe and polite side.

Your druggist will supply you with Listerine. He sells lots of it. It has dozens of different uses as a safe antiseptic and has been trusted as such for a half a century. Read the interesting little booklet that comes with every bottle.
—*Lambert Pharmacal Company, Saint Louis, U. S. A.*

HALITOSIS   LISTERINE

[1924]

FIGURE 28   Advertisement, 1925

WRITE FOR—
An interesting booklet on furniture construction. Sent for the asking together with the name of your nearest Berkey & Gay dealer.

The
PRESCOTT
Dining Room Suite

Do they know YOUR *son at* MALUCIO'S?

THERE'S a hole in the door at Malucio's. Ring the bell and a pair of eyes will look coldly out at you. If you are known you will get in. Malucio has to be careful.

There have been riotous nights at Malucio's. Tragic nights, too. But somehow the fat little man has managed to avoid the law.

Almost every town has its Malucio's. Some, brightly disguised as cabarets—others, mere back street filling stations for pocket flasks.

But every Malucio will tell you the same thing. His best customers are not the ne'er-do-wells of other years. They are the young people—frequently the best young people of the town.

Malucio has put one over on the American home. Ultimately he will be driven out. Until then THE HOME MUST BID MORE INTELLIGENTLY FOR MALUCIO'S BUSINESS.

There are many reasons why it is

profitable and wise to furnish the home attractively, but one of these, and not the least, is—Malucio's!

The younger generation is sensitive to beauty, princely proud, and will not entertain in homes of which it is secretly ashamed.

But make your rooms attractive, appeal to the vaulting *pride* of youth, and you may worry that much less about Malucio's—and the other modern frivolities that his name symbolizes.

A guest room smartly and tastefully furnished—a refined and attractive dining room—will more than hold their own against the tinsel cheapness of Malucio's.

Nor is good furniture any longer a luxury for the favored few. The PRESCOTT suite shown above, for instance, is a moderately priced pattern, conforming in every detail to the finest Berkey & Gay standards.

In style, in the selection of rare and beautiful woods, and in the rich texture of the finish and hand decorating, it reveals the skill of craftsmen long expert in the art of quality furniture making.

The PRESCOTT is typical of values now on display at the store of your local Berkey & Gay dealer. Depend upon his showing you furniture in which you may take deep pride—beautiful, well built, luxuriously finished, and moderately priced.

There is a Berkey & Gay pattern suited for every home—an infinite variety of styles at prices ranging all the way from $350 to $6000.

* * * * * *

Write to the Berkey & Gay Furniture Company, Grand Rapids, Michigan, for an interesting booklet, "Some of the Things That Make Furniture Values," which points out sixteen important features of construction that you should consider in selecting furniture for your home.

THIS SHOP MARK IS INSET IN EVERY BERKEY & GAY PRODUCTION   IT IS THE CUSTOMERS PROTECTION WHEN BUYING AND HIS PRIDE EVER AFTER

BERKEY & GAY FURNITURE CO.

Wholesale Showroom: 115 W. 40th St., New York City

Associated Companies
WALLACE FURNITURE CO. ~ GRAND RAPIDS UPHOLSTERING CO
GRAND RAPIDS   MICHIGAN

[1925]

FIGURE 29   Advertisement, 1927   *The Evidence*

The song that **S**TOPPED !

A CHILD of five skipped down the garden path and laughed because the sky was blue. "Jane," called her mother from the kitchen window, "come here and help me bake your birthday cake." Little feet sped. "Don't fall," her mother warned.

Jane stood in the kitchen door and wrinkled her nose in joy. Her gingham dress was luminous against the sun. What a child! Dr. and Mrs. Wentworth cherished Jane.

"Go down cellar and get mother some preserves . . . the kind you like."

"The preserves are in the cellar," she chanted, making a progress twice around the kitchen. "Heigh-ho a-derry-o, the preserves are . . ." her voice grew fainter as she danced off. ". . . in the . . ."

The thread of song snapped. A soft thud-thud. Fear fluttered Mrs. Wentworth's heart. She rushed to the cellar door.

"Mother!" . . . a child screaming in pain. Mrs. Wentworth saw a little morsel of girl-hood lying in a heap of gingham and yellow hair at the bottom of the dark stairs.

The sky is still blue. But there will be no birthday party tomorrow. An ambulance clanged up to Dr. Wentworth's house today. Jane's leg is broken.

If a flashlight had been hanging on a hook at the head of the cellar stairs, this little tragedy would have been averted. If Jane had been taught to use a flashlight as carefully as her father, Dr. Wentworth, had taught her to use a tooth-brush, a life need not have been endangered.

An Eveready Flashlight is always a convenience and often a life-saver. Keep one about the house, in the car; and take one with you wherever you go. Keep it supplied with fresh Eveready Batteries — the longest-lasting flashlight batteries made. Eveready Flashlights, $1.00 up.

NATIONAL CARBON CO., INC.
New York   **UCC**   San Francisco
Unit of Union Carbide and Carbon Corporation

[1927]

EVEREADY FLASHLIGHTS & BATTERIES
—they last longer

A THOUSAND THINGS MAY HAPPEN IN THE DARK

FIGURE 30   Advertisement, 1926

FIGURE 31   Advertisement, 1926   *The Evidence*

"Why Was I Fired?"

"I've worked my head off for them people!" exclaimed Jones to his wife. "Yet the very minute business gets slack, out I go!"

"AND THIS IS THE SECOND JOB YOU'VE LOST, DEAR," answered his wife sorrowfully. "We're surely up against hard luck."

A few hours before this conversation, Jones was himself the subject of a conversation between the business manager and his assistant.

"I don't like to let Jones go," the manager said. "Married man with a wife to support. But I simply must. He's willing enough and faithful, too. *But his English! You know how he talks, Bill.* Maybe he didn't go to school long enough—but if that's the case why doesn't he try to improve himself. After hearing him talk to customers and hearing him dictate letters I can understand why his sales record stands still. He's not a very big asset to the house and it would never do to advance him."

Don't Be a Job Hunter

And so, Jones, because he was careless in his use of English, like many another man and woman before him, not only fails to advance, but is ACTUALLY REDUCED TO A JOB-HUNTING STATE—a condition he would never have reached if he had spent a few minutes of his spare time every day in improving his speech by a little study.

Be a Master of Words

To-day you have your destiny in your own hands, because—whoever you are, and whatever your walk in life, the little book which we are offering you will OPEN YOUR EYES TO A NEW WORLD OF UNTOLD POWER AND ACHIEVEMENT—to use good English and to build a personality that charms.

Stepping Stone to Success

Here is the stepping stone by which thousands have climbed to success. *Salesmen—doctors— lawyers— merchants — clergymen — teachers — clerks—* business men and women everywhere attribute their success to the advantage they derived from the study and application of Grenville Kleiser's unique course in English, endorsed by such distinguished people as Booth Tarkington, Mary Roberts Rinehart, Irvin S. Cobb, and thousands of others.

Use Your Spare Moments

This line of easy study places in your hands the systematized knowledge that others go to college for years to get—and sometimes leave without.

Grenville Kleiser can teach you by mail, in your home, at your own convenience, the power and use of words. This is no ordinary, lengthy course to be studied laboriously. On the contrary, you will find it marvelously simple, clear and concise. A few minutes a day spent in studying this course will soon make your speech, your conversation, your writing, vastly more interesting and profitable.

It is possible for people in all stations of life to enjoy the great benefits of Grenville Kleiser's wonderful course in English. For not only are we offering this course for an astonishingly small investment, but you may pay for it on easy monthly terms. So that you may know what Grenville Kleiser's English course contains, we will send you by mail the book

Get the Free Booklet

"HOW TO BECOME A MASTER OF ENGLISH"

This instructive little book which we will give you FREE will show you how the Kleiser Personal Mail Course in Practical English and Mental Efficiency will enable you to win promotion and higher pay—use correct and forceful words—write convincing letters, sermons, advertisements, stories, articles—become an interesting talker, win power, success, and popularity.

Remember—it costs you nothing to investigate. Your signature on the coupon puts you under no obligation whatever. But a single day's delay may mean that you will forget, or the coupon be lost, and so deprive you of your opportunity. MAIL THE COUPON TO-DAY!

The Coupon to Bigger Success

FUNK & WAGNALLS COMPANY
354 Fourth Avenue, New York

Gentlemen: Send me by mail, free of charge or obligation, the booklet, "How to Become a Master of English," together with full particulars of the Grenville Kleiser Course in Practical English and Mental Efficiency.   Dept. 966

Name.....................................

Local Address.............................

Post Office...............................

Date...................State..............

[1926]

[113]

Questions to Consider

In this chapter you are asked first to analyze each advertisement individually and then to analyze the advertisements collectively. You will find it helpful to jot down notes as you go through the advertisements, listing new products and changing styles. These notes will help in your collective analysis.

The evidence has been divided into two sections. Part I focuses on changing life-styles of men, women, and children as portrayed through clothing, cosmetics, and toy advertisements. The advertisements are from the Sears, Roebuck catalogues of 1897, 1902, and 1927, which were aimed at American consumers who lived outside the major cities. First look at the advertisements for men's clothing and underwear (Figures 1–4). Did the styles change very much during these thirty years? How did the advertisements attempt to persuade men to buy the clothes they offered? Now consider the women's underwear, clothing, and cosmetics advertisements (Figures 5–11). What changes do you see? How did the advertisements try to persuade women to buy the items? How would you compare the changes in women's styles with those in men's styles? Lastly, look at the styles for children's clothing in Figures 12, 13, and 14. Is there anything unusual about this clothing for young children? Compare

the advertisements for children's clothing in 1897, 1902 and 1927. What are the differences? Now look at the advertisements for toys (Figures 12, 15, and 16). What do they tell you about how parents were raising their children?

The second part of the evidence is drawn from various advertisements in magazines read by the middle class during the period from the 1880s to the 1920s. While these advertisements also tell us something about changing life-styles (notice all the new products), they may be used to understand the hopes and fears of people living in such a rapidly changing world. Both the gramophone and the later Berke & Gay furniture advertisements (Figures 17 and 28) were aimed at parents of young people. What was the message of these advertisements? What underlying fears might parents have had? How did the advertisements for the Pierce Arrow and Detroit Electric automobiles (Figures 18 and 24) try to persuade potential buyers? At whom were they directed? Now look at the insurance advertisement (Figure 19). What fears did it play on? Why? The next two advertisements (Figures 20 and 21) reflect the impact of the new technology upon housework. How did they try to persuade women to purchase the new products? Are these advertisements positive or negative in tone? How would you describe the message contained in the advertisements for the boy's magazine (Figure

22)? What kind of appeal did the watch chain advertisement (Figure 23) make to men? Now examine the 1921 bathroom advertisement (Figure 26). What are its tone and message? What do the I.C.S. (International Correspondence School), Prudential Insurance, and Funk and Wagnalls advertisements (Figures 25, 30, and 31) tell us about men's roles during this period? What do the advertisements for I.C.S., Listerine (Figure 27), Eveready Batteries (Figure 29), and Funk and Wagnalls tell us about women's roles? Finally, what does the furniture advertisement (Figure 28) tell us about parents' concern for their children during the 1920s?

Once you have gone through the evidence piece by piece, go back to the notes you have taken. Make a list of all the new products you saw. What were the most significant changes you noticed in the products and advertisements directed at men? At women? At parents who bought clothing and other items for their children? Are there any consistent themes that might tell us something about people's hopes or fears? If so, what are these themes, and what do they tell us about Americans and their reactions to a rapidly changing society?

Epilogue

While the muckrakers of the Progressive period criticized advertising, particularly the claims of patent medicine advertisements, such salesmanship was described as "the brightest hope of America" by the 1920s. Bruce Barton, a talented salesman and founder of a huge advertising agency, even discovered "advertisements" in the Bible, which he described as the first "best seller." Although its image was slightly tarnished by the disillusionment accompanying the Great Depression, advertising helped to "sell" World War II to the American public by encouraging conservation of scarce resources, and it emerged stronger and more persuasive than ever in the 1950s. Americans were starved for consumer goods after war-time rationing, and their rapid acceptance of a new form of media — television — greatly expanded advertising opportunities.

But advertising still had (and has) its critics. Writing in 1954, historian David Potter characterized advertising as the basic "institution of abundance." Advertising, he maintained, had become as powerful as religion or education had been in earlier eras — advertising, he said, now actually *created* the standards and values of our society. Because advertising lacked social goals or social responsibility, however, he believed that its power was dangerous. We must not forget, Potter warned, "that it ultimately regards man as a consumer and defines its own mission as one of stimulating him to consume."

Chapter 5

America's Rise to World Power: The Senate Debate over the Philippines, 1899

The Problem

Until the late nineteenth century the United States' transoceanic foreign policy clearly had been of minor concern to the nation's citizens. Westward expansion and settlement, the slavery controversy and the Civil War, postwar reconstruction of the Republic, and industrialization and urbanization had alternately captured the attention of Americans and pushed foreign affairs into the background. But beginning in the latter part of the nineteenth century, several factors prompted Americans to look beyond their own shores, and by the end of the century the United States had become a world power complete with a modest empire.

Initially the American business community opposed this drift toward expansion and colonialism, believing that American industry would do well just meeting the needs of the rapidly growing population, and fearing that a colonial empire would mean large armies and navies, increased government expenses, and the possibility of the nation's involvement in war. However, by the mid-1890s American business leaders were beginning to have second thoughts. The current national depression was creating large surpluses of goods, which many business leaders reasoned could be disposed of in foreign markets. Too, business leaders were constantly looking for areas in which to invest their surplus capital. Investments beyond the borders of the United States, they believed, would be more secure if the American government would act to stabilize the areas in which they invested. In 1895 the newly organized National Association of Manufacturers sounded both of those chords at its convention where the keynote speaker was soon-to-be-president William McKinley, an Ohio senator with decided expansionist leanings.

Yet it would be wrong to see American expansion and colonialism strictly as a scheme to better the nation's industrial and commercial interests. A number of other intellectual currents dovetailed with American commercial interests to create a powerful and popular urge toward imperialism. For example, those who advocated military growth (especially of a large, steam-powered navy) saw in American expansion a perfect justification for their position. Their interests were represented by increasingly influential lobbies in Washington. Especially important was Captain Alfred Thayer Mahan whose book *The Influence of Sea Power Upon History* (published in 1890) argued persuasively that national self-preservation depended upon international trade protected by a large and powerful navy with worldwide bases and refueling stations. Two of Mahan's disciples, Theodore Roosevelt and Henry Cabot Lodge, eventually achieved positions whereby they could put Mahan's philosophy to work.

Another current influencing American expansion was the dramatic increase in religious missionary zeal seen in the late nineteenth century. Working through both individual denominations and powerful congressional lobbies, missionaries argued that it was their duty to Christianize the world. In the United States, Methodists, Baptists, Presbyterians, and Congregationalists were especially active, giving money and attention to their denominational missionary boards as well as to those who went out to convert the "heathen." In large part these missionaries were selfless, committed men and women. Some of them, however, attempted to westernize as well as Christianize their flocks, often denigrating or destroying indigenous cultures and traditions even as they brought modern health and educational institutions with them. All argued for a more active role on the part of the United States government, both to protect the missionaries and to open up other areas around the world to missionary work.

Accompanying this religious zeal was latent racism, a racism that in some ways differed little from white Americans' long-held attitudes about American Indians. Since the popularization of the work of Charles Darwin (*The Origin of Species*, 1859), a number of people had taken Darwin's

Chapter 5
America's Rise to
World Power:
The Senate
Debate over the
Philippines, 1899

ideas of "survival of the fittest" and "struggle for existence" and had applied them to humans. Often the result was a notion of competition among races for world dominance. As Josiah Strong wrote in *Our Country: Its Possible Future and Its Present Crisis* (1885),

> this race of unequaled energy . . . will spread itself over the earth. If I read not amiss, this powerful race will move down upon Mexico, down upon Central and South America, out upon the islands of the sea, over upon Africa and beyond. And can anyone doubt that the result of this competition of races will be the "survival of the fittest"?

Clearly this idea of the racial superiority of Caucasians, together with other impulses, formed a powerful impetus to American expansion and colonization.

All of the above ideological impulses (economic, military, religious, racist) rested upon one common assumption: that the world was a great competitive battlefield and that those nations that did not grow and expand would wither and die. Indeed, this "growth mania," or fascination with growth and the measurement of growth, was perhaps the most powerful intellectual strain in all of American society. For those who accepted such an assumption the world was a dangerous, competitive jungle in which individuals, races, religions, na-

tions, corporations, and cities struggled for domination. Those that grew would continue to exist; those that did not grow would die.

The convergence of these intellectual strains in the late nineteenth century caused Americans to view the outside world as an area into which United States' influence should expand. Although the expansionist strain had appeared irregularly since the end of the Civil War in 1865, it was not until the Spanish-American War of 1898 that the various impulses for expansion and colonization began to converge. When Cubans began a revolt to secure their independence from Spain in 1895, most Americans were genuinely sympathetic toward the Cuban underdogs. Those genuine feelings were heightened by American newspaper reporters and editors, some of whom wrote lurid (and knowingly inaccurate) accounts of the Spanish "monsters" and the poor, downtrodden Cubans. President William McKinley tried to pressure Spain into making concessions and sent the American battleship *Maine* to Havana on a "courtesy call," an obvious move to underscore the United States' position toward Spain. But on February 15, 1898, the *Maine* blew up in the Havana harbor. Although we now know (as a result of a 1976 study) that the explosion on the *Maine* was an internal one almost surely the result of an accident at the time, many Americans, fired up by the press, were convinced that the

Spanish had been responsible. Yet war with Spain did not come immediately and, in the opinion of some, was not inevitable even after the *Maine* incident. However, on April 11, 1898, after two months of demands, negotiations, and arguments in which it sometimes appeared that war might be avoided, McKinley asked Congress for authorization to intervene in Cuba "in the name of humanity and civilization." On April 20 Congress granted authorization, and the Spanish-American War had begun. Genuine sympathy for Cuba coupled with expansionist impulses overcame the desires of some Americans to avoid war with Spain.

The first action of the Spanish-American War took place not in Cuba but in the Philippines, also a colony of Spain. Since the summer of 1897, the United States Navy Department had been collecting information on the Spanish squadron and defenses in the Philippines. In February 1898 (approximately two weeks after the sinking of the *Maine* but a month and a half before McKinley's war message) Commodore George Dewey of the United States Pacific fleet was ordered to prepare to attack the Spanish in the Philippines as soon as war was declared. On May 1, 1898, Dewey attacked the decrepit Spanish fleet in Manila Bay, destroying ten Spanish warships and killing over 350 men. Only one United States soldier died (of heat prostration) and only eight others were wounded in the attack.

Indeed, the Spanish fleet was so impotent that many of the ships had not been out of the harbor in fifty years and had to be towed into place for battle. Nevertheless, the Battle of Manila Bay was applauded by Americans as a great accomplishment, and Dewey became a military hero. In July, American soldiers arrived in the Philippines to secure Dewey's victory. In doing so, the American troops cooperated with Filipinos under General Emilio Aguinaldo, who had been fighting to oust the Spanish from the Philippines. In mid-August the Spanish in the Philippines surrendered to the United States.

The ten-week war against Spain was a comparatively bloodless one for the United States, which suffered only 5,462 fatalities (all but 362 died of diseases or food poisoning), and the immediate cost of the war was an inexpensive $250 million. However, the sudden Spanish surrender on July 16, 1898, thrust upon the United States momentous decisions that would alter American history and life for the next century. For some American political figures, editors, and business leaders, victory in the Spanish-American War presented the opportunity to acquire a colonial empire and thus make the United States a true world power. It was an opportunity they would not miss.

If the Spanish-American War had not begun as an imperialistic venture, the convergence of the economic, military, religious, and racist impulses

Chapter 5
America's Rise to
World Power:
The Senate
Debate over the
Philippines, 1899

mentioned previously and the prostrate condition of Spain gave American leaders the opportunity to use the war and victory for expansionist purposes. Keeping a close watch on American public opinion through newspaper polls and personal tours through the Midwest, West, and South, President McKinley concluded that the majority of Americans favored using the war to acquire a colonial empire. Therefore, he pressured the Spanish to include in the peace treaty the surrender of its colonial empire to the United States. The treaty was signed by the peace commissioners in Paris on December 10, 1898, and submitted to the United States Senate on January 4, 1899.

Debate both inside and outside the Senate tended to focus on whether or not the United States should acquire the Philippine Islands (McKinley himself admitted that he had to consult a globe to find out where these islands were). Outside the Senate, anticolonialists like Carl Schurz, William James, Mark Twain, Andrew Carnegie, Charles Francis Adams, Jane Addams, William Jennings Bryan, and the Anti-Imperialist League spoke articulately against the acquisition of an empire. Humorous editorialist Finley Peter Dunne (who spoke through the fictitious character Mr. Dooley) lampooned the expansionists:

An' now, ye mis'rable, childish-minded apes, we propose f'r to larn ye th' uses iv liberty . . . an' we'll larn ye our language, because 'tis aisier to larn ye ours than to larn oursilves yours. An' we'll give ye clothes, if ye pay f'r them; an', if ye don't, ye can go without. . . . We can't give ye anny votes, because we haven't more thin enough to go round now; but we'll threat ye th' way a father shud threat his childhen if we have to break ivry bone in ye'er bodies. So come to our ar-rms, says we.[1]

A month before President McKinley submitted the peace treaty to the Senate for ratification, the Senate had already taken up the question of American acquisition of the Philippines. The Senate's action was prompted by a resolution introduced by Senator George Vest (D, Missouri), which stated that empire "was alien to the American tradition." The debate on that resolution and on the treaty itself took approximately two months; the vote on the treaty came on February 6, 1899.

Your task in this chapter is to analyze the debates in the United States Senate over the peace treaty and the acquisition of the Philippines. What were the principal arguments for and against acquiring the Philippines? Which of the arguments do you believe were the most influential?

1. [Finley Peter Dunne], "Expansion," in *Mr. Dooley in the Hearts of His Countrymen* (Boston: Small, Maynard and Company, 1899), pp. 3–4.

TABLE 1 Debate over the Philippines

Senator's Name	Political Party	State	For or Against Treaty	Type of Argument	Additional Observations
Caffery	D	La.	A	Legal and racial	Said people in subtropics can't govern themselves, are unfit.

Just by reading the debates you should be able to see at a glance where each speaker stood on the issue and which arguments each speaker considered to have been most important. However, as with other types of evidence, with speeches you must be able to read between the lines. How does the careful use of words or phrases express some "hidden arguments" the speaker wants to make? How does word or phrase selection create images in the minds of the listeners? For example, how does each speaker depict the people of the Philippines? Be careful, then, to look for nuances, shadings, and arguments (hidden and open) that reflect the ideas and emotions of the times.

To assist you in reading between the lines, we have included biographical sketches of the senators whose speeches you will analyze. Sometimes these sketches can be extremely helpful to you. For example, Delaware senator George Gray is the only Democrat in the evidence provided who spoke in favor of the treaty — and one of only eleven Democrats who voted for the treaty. What in his bio-graphical sketch helps to explain his actions?

The Method

This is the first exercise in which you will be working almost exclusively with formal speeches. People who make speeches often try to include as many points as possible in support of their arguments, while at the same time refuting those points made by their forensic opponents. Thus it is not enough to simply summarize all the points made; you must also weigh the points for their comparative importance.

The Senate debate took place over a number of days, and the speeches in the evidence are selections taken from the *Congressional Record.* Read carefully through the speeches, making brief notes as you go along of the major *type* of argument (for example, legal, economic, moral, cultural) that each senator used. A chart such as that shown in Table 1 might prove helpful.

Chapter 5
America's Rise to
World Power:
The Senate
Debate over the
Philippines, 1899

| The Evidence |

SELECTIONS FROM THE
SENATE DEBATE

From the Congressional Record, *55th Cong., 3rd Sess., January through early February 1899, Vol. 32, pts. 1 and 2, pp. 436–1481* passim.

SEN. CAFFERY *(D, Louisiana)*

[Caffery began by arguing that no territory may be acquired without the consent of the people of that territory, that any territory that is acquired must ultimately become a state and not remain indefinitely as a colony, that all citizens of an acquired territory would automatically become United States citizens, and that it would be "impolitic, unwise," and dangerous if the land to be acquired was far away and was populated with a "dissimilar race, with different laws, religions, customs, matters, traditions and habits."]

In the first place, any people that we take jurisdiction over, by taking the territory in which they live, ought not to be, and, in my opinion, can not be, incorporated into our midst, to be bone of our bone and flesh of our flesh, without their free consent.

In the second place, if such a people are unfit and in all human probability never will be fit for the glorious privileges, franchises, and functions of an American citizen, we ought not in that case to even think of incorporating them into the United States, for we can not establish the principle of despotic sway in America. The first gun that was fired at Lexington sounded the knell of despotism in America; yea, sir, the civil strife sounded the knell of State citizenship as paramount to that of the United States. Every single step in our progress heretofore has been founded upon the glorious principle, the immutable principle, of the power of man to govern himself and the application of that principle to the great Territories we have acquired heretofore. . . .

Mr. President, even if we had the right — which I contend most earnestly we have not — to incorporate these distant islands, inhabited by these singular and strange people, then I say it is impolitic and unwise.

Sir, cast your eye over the map of the globe and find where freedom exists. Does it exist in the subtropics? Has it ever existed in the subtropics? Can it exist in the subtropics?

. . . The history of the world now, the history of the world in all times, shows us that God himself has set bounds to the habitations of the different peoples of the earth.

Sir, when I look at the condition of the world to-day, when I review the history of the past, I am unalterably convinced that no permanent sway can ever be held by the white man over the colored races of the Tropics; and if sway is held, it is held under the power of unlimited, cruel despotism. That is the only way the white man can rule in the Tropics. It is the only way he has ever ruled. Whether it is providential or whether it is not, it is a fact.

Is that the sort of "expansion" we want? Is that the sort of empire we are derided as old fogies and little Americans for not desiring to establish? Mr. President, we are told that duty and destiny and some undefinable power are pushing us on to a splendid and magnificent future that the fathers never dreamt of. This evil thing we are called on to do can not be painted in such bright, dazzling colors as to deceive the American eye. It is nothing but a wanton stretch of power. It is lust for power and greed for land, veneered with the tawdriness of false humanity. You can not hide its hideousness with the clothing of high-sounding phrases. You can not prostitute the flag made to float over freemen by driving under its fold millions of slaves. . . .

SEN. HOAR *(R, Massachusetts)*

Mr. President, the persons who favor the ratification of this treaty without conditions and without amendment differ among themselves certainly in their views, purposes, and opinions, and as they are so many of them honest and well-meaning persons, we have the right to say in their actual and real opinions. In general, the state of mind and the utterance of the lips are in accord. If you ask them what they want, you are answered with a shout: "Three cheers for the Flag! Who will dare to haul it down? Hold on to everything you can get. The United States is strong enough to do what it likes. The Declaration of Independence and the counsel of Washington and the Constitution of the United States have grown rusty and musty. They are for little countries and not for great ones. There is no moral law for strong nations. America has outgrown Americanism."

Mr. President, when I hear from some of our friends this new doctrine of constitutional interpretation, when I hear attributed to men in high places, counselors of the President himself, that we have outgrown the principles and the interpretation which were sufficient for our 13 States and our 3 million of people in the time of their weakness, and by which they have grown to 75 mil-

Chapter 5
America's Rise to
World Power:
The Senate
Debate over the
Philippines, 1899

lion and 45 States, in this hour of our strength, it seems to me these counselors would have this nation of ours like some prosperous thriving youth who reverses suddenly all the maxims and rules of living in which he has been educated and says to himself, "I am too big for the Golden Rule. I have outgrown the Ten Commandments."

[*Hoar then attacked those who argued that the American flag "must never be taken down where it has once floated."*]

If you can not take down a national flag where it has once floated in time of war, we were disgraced when we took our flag down in Mexico and in Vera Cruz, or after the invasion of Canada; England was dishonored when she took her flag down after she captured this capital; and every nation is henceforth pledged to the doctrine that wherever it puts its military foot or its naval power with the flag over it, that must be a war to the death and to extermination or the honor of the state is disgraced by the flag of that nation being withdrawn. . . .

This power to dispose of the territory or other property belonging to the United States, and to make all needful rules and regulations respecting it, and the power implied from that provision, to acquire and hold territory or other property, like other constitutional powers, is a power to be exercised only for constitutional purposes. . . . We have no more right to acquire land or hold it, or to dispose of it for an unconstitutional purpose than we have a right to fit out a fleet or to buy a park of artillery for an unconstitutional purpose. . . .

The Monroe doctrine is gone. Every European nation, every European alliance, has the right to acquire dominion in this hemisphere when we acquire it in the other. The Senator's doctrine put anywhere in practice will make of our beloved country a cheap-jack country, raking after the cart for the leavings of European tyranny. . . .

SEN. PLATT *(R, Connecticut)*

Mr. President, what did we do with the Indians of this country? I said that that doctrine would have turned back the *Mayflower* from Plymouth Rock. We found here a continent in the hands of the Indians, aborigines, who did not want us to come here, who did not want to be governed by us without their consent, and with them incapable of consenting, we have, nevertheless, gone on and legislated for them and governed them, and now, at last, have brought many of them to a state where they have become citizens and incorporated with us. If you attempt to make a literal application of this doctrine, what answer have you to make when the Indian raises his voice and says: "I did not want to be legislated for, I did not consent to be governed by the United States; you violated your Declaration of Independence when you attempted to legislate for and to govern me without my consent"?

. . . I am one who believes that we shall not have done a great wrong to humanity, that we shall not have imperiled our institutions, that we shall not have rung the doom knell of republican institutions if we extend over the people who reside in the territory which we may acquire those principles which protect them in their lives, which protect them in their property, which protect them in their efforts to secure happiness, and the American Senate and the American House of Representatives are not going to legislate in any other spirit, Mr. President. . . .

I believe in Providence. I believe the hand of Providence brought about the conditions which we must either accept or be recreant to duty. I believe that those conditions were a part of the great development of the great force of Christian civilization on earth. I believe the same force was behind our army at Santiago and our ships in Manila Bay that was behind the landing of the Pilgrims on Plymouth Rock. I believe that we have been chosen to carry on and to carry forward this great work of uplifting humanity on earth. From the time of the landing on Plymouth Rock in the spirit of the Declaration of Independence, in the spirit of the Constitution, believing that all men are equal and endowed by their Creator with inalienable rights, believing that governments derive their just powers from the consent of the governed, we have spread that civilization across the continent until it stood at the Pacific Ocean looking ever westward.

Westward the course of empire takes its way.

The English-speaking people, the agents of this civilization, the agency through which humanity is to be uplifted, through which despotism is to go down, through which the rights of man are to prevail, is charged with this great mission. Providence has put it upon us. We propose to execute it. We propose to proclaim liberty in the Philippines Islands, if they are ours. We propose to proclaim liberty and justice and the protection of life and human rights wherever the flag of the United States is planted. Who denies that? Who will haul down those principles?

SEN. MASON *(R, Illinois)*

I appreciate and agree with President Lincoln, who said, "In the long run you can trust the people;" but I want the people to hear both sides of this question before the verdict is rendered.

[125]

Chapter 5
America's Rise to
World Power:
The Senate
Debate over the
Philippines, 1899

Distinguished editors, writers, and statesmen tell us, and tell me almost constantly, that this doctrine of governing those people without their consent is a part of the platform of the Republican party, and they would discipline me because of my opposition.

That party sprang from the womb of conscience; its great fight was for human liberty; and if I may prophesy, as other gentlemen are indulged in prophecy, I prophesy that when the Republican party meets again in convention, if the delegates represent the conscience of its constituents, the old plank for human liberty will go in again, and the rafters of our convention hall will ring again and again, and yet again, when we declare, as we will, for independence in the Philippine Islands, as we did two years ago for independence for the people of Cuba.

Mr. President, I may be charged with speaking for rebels. When did they take the oath of allegiance to our flag? Name the hour when they have not claimed the right of independence. I am speaking one word for the Philippine Islands, but I am speaking two words for my own country. A boy treading upon an ant, his father said: "Don't, my boy; that is cruel." A learned man said, "The ant has no nerve centers and can not suffer." "Ah," said the father, "I am speaking one word for the ant and two words for my boy." A black man thanked a Senator here the other day. He said: "I thank you, Mr. Senator, for what you have said for my race." The Senator said: "I was speaking one word for your race and two for mine." The one thing that has dwarfed the white race more than any other is the stooping of a hundred years of the white man to hold the black man down. If I am to be branded as speaking for rebels, let me say at the outset I am speaking more for my country than for them. . . .

No, no; they [the Filipinos] can not govern themselves. I was told so the other day by one of my beloved constituents, who never governs himself fifteen minutes at a time; but he was willing to take an assignment under the present Administration to govern all the Philippines at a fair salary. [Laughter.]

Can not govern themselves! Every man who ever owned a slave always said: "Why, you poor, downtrodden slave, I own you for your own good, just to help you; I eat my bread in the sweat of your face just to keep you safe and sound from the ways of danger; and in order that I may continue to exercise this Christian duty do not let me catch you with a spelling book in your hand." [Laughter.]

Can not govern themselves! And we are to say that to-day to the poor, God-forsaken, downtrodden people of the Philippine Islands; and while we whisper the words of consolation into their ears that we are to give them liberty and life, we wink the other eye to the merchants of the country, and say: "We will extend commerce and sell more calico." [Laughter.] My distinguished friend suggested this morning that we ought to rake those islands with our guns and compel their people to wear shirts — not that they need the shirts, but to increase the demand for calico. [Laughter.]

Why, Mr. President, can not we now make those people our friends, as Fox pled to make America England's friend a hundred years ago? Why not give them what they ask? Why should we stingily withhold the jewel of independence? Why should we not finish this war as we began it — for humanity's sake? Why not with a free and open hand give them what we have promised to give to Cuba, and say, "Go and obey the Divine injunction, work out your own salvation with fear and trembling; go and learn by experience, as we did. Profit by your mistakes, as we have done. Yes, we have saved your life, Filipino, and in the future we will protect it against all comers from within or without while our flag floats." Then we shall have kept our promise, and only then. . . .

That we have assisted the Filipinos is undoubtedly true. That they assisted us is also true. We are told that Aguinaldo could not have got back there but for Dewey. Then Dewey put him back. Then under all the laws of common honesty he is an ally. Under all the laws of nations he is our ally. Caesar, with all his cruelty, aye, Nero, never accepted the assistance of an ally and whipped his enemy and then turned his guns upon the men who helped him. . . .

Spain is an expansionist and has been for centuries. And say, my friends, have you forgotten the first rule proved by all history, without exception, that every square inch of territory taken by force has to be held by force? . . . Are we to continue to imitate Spain? She has believed in the expansion of territory, expansion of commerce by force, without the consent of the governed, and her ships are lying at the bottom of the sea. Her men are rotting in the ocean and upon the land all over the world. Her flag has been dishonored, disgraced, defeated, and sent back to her peninsula, and the golden crown of imperialism that she has sought against the will of the people has turned to ashes in her palsied hands. . . .

Mr. President, we have had a very serious war, glorious in its inception, for liberty. We have set the high-water mark in patriotism.

I have seen men dying in hospitals without a murmur. They said to me, "I am going to die; it is all right, old man." I have stood by the open graves. I have

Chapter 5
America's Rise to
World Power:
The Senate
Debate over the
Philippines, 1899

seen the mother's tears dry and her face light up with hope — aye, with pride — when it was said to her that he died in a noble cause; that he died like the Master, for others. I have seen the tears dry and the face light with pride because her son was there, having died in the cause as sacred as the Nazarene's.

But, Mr. President, when your ships come home laden from Manila with the putrid remains of our boys, and you take the coffin to the mother's door, you never will dry her tears, you never will soothe her heart by telling her that you have extended your commerce at the cost of her dead boy. . . .

SEN. ALLEN *(Populist, Nebraska)*

I am led to introduce this resolution, because the press dispatches bring to us information that our Army and Navy are moving upon the Filipinos, with a view of attacking them and engaging them in war, unless they surrender the possession of the city of Iloilo. I introduce the resolution for the purpose of protesting against the use of the Army or Navy for that purpose without a declaration of war having first been made by Congress.

I think it is indisputable that the war-making power is exclusively in Congress; that the President of the United States is impotent and powerless to initiate or conduct war without a declaration of Congress first having been made that a state of war exists with a given people.

The Filipinos can not be said to be the enemies of the United States. Our possession of the archipelago was a possession obtained as a result of war with Spain.

MR. HOAR: We are solemnly bound not to use any military forces against Spain in the Philippine Islands while this truce lasts, and where is the constitutional power to use military force against anybody else?

MR. ALLEN: We have no power.

MR. HOAR: That is the question I desire to put to the Senate and to the Senator from Delaware, not as implying that he dissents from me at all, but only as having special knowledge of this subject.

MR. GRAY: Mr. President, I would not have presumed to say a word had not the Senator from Massachusetts referred to me in the question he has put to the Senator from Nebraska. But I wish to remark that the question of the Senator from Massachusetts seems to answer in part at least the technical position taken by the Senator from Nebraska. I was called out for a moment during the Senator's remarks, but as I understood the Senator from Nebraska he made the point that this Government was attempting or threatening to make war against the Filipinos.

MR. ALLEN: Yes, sir.

MR. GRAY: Without the authority of Congress, where the war-making power alone rests under the Constitution. That point would be very well taken — and now I am considering it technically, as the Senator from Nebraska is considering it technically — that point would be very well taken, in my humble judgment, if it were true that this country was threatening war against a people other than the Spaniards. But we must recollect, if we are to pursue a technical argument in this respect, that what the Senator from Massachusetts suggests is true. We are at war with Spain under the authority of a declaration of Congress, the war-making power.

MR. HOAR: It is a truce.

MR. GRAY: It is true that we are living now under a truce, which is a mere suspension of the hostilities incident to that war, and anything that is done now in the archipelago of the Philippines is done pursuant to the war power delegated or intrusted to the President by the resolution of Congress in the conduct of the war with Spain.

SEN. ALLEN

I want to enter my protest against the conclusion of the Senator from Delaware. I do not believe that Spain possesses or exercises sovereignty over the Philippines de facto or de jure. I think her jurisdiction is gone and has been gone for months. I do not think we are the residuary legatee of whatever Spanish authority may have existed there. I think when Spain withdrew her army from the archipelago the only de facto and de jure government in those islands was the government of the present chief, Aguinaldo, and his followers.

[*Allen then argued that when Spanish rule collapsed in the Philippines, the Filipinos established a lawful government "that was recognized by the great majority of the people."*]

MR. GRAY: Will the Senator pardon me for a moment while I seek to correct what I think is a misapprehension of my position?

MR. ALLEN: Certainly.

MR. GRAY: Mr. President, we must not forget that there is no treaty of peace existing between Spain and the United States at the present time. We are in a state of war with Spain technically, juridically. It is true that active military operations have been suspended by the agreement of August 12, 1898, and we are under the highest obligation of good faith to maintain to the letter the agreement in the protocol signed on that day. I will remind the Senator from Nebraska of the fact, of which, of course, he is aware, that our only right originally to have attacked any portion of the Philippine Islands was that they were part of the sovereignty of Spain, with whom we were and are at war.

MR. ALLEN: So I stated a moment ago.

MR. GRAY: Exactly. And that being so, and that war technically and in the light of international law still existing, though military operations are suspended for the time being by the truce of August 12, 1898, it is a question of good faith between the military authority of the United States and Spain whether we observe that protocol or no. I agree with the Senator from Massachusetts, as I said a while ago, that we can not violate it without flagrant violation of the good faith that rests upon us as a nation unless we have in some form the consent of Spain, either expressed or, I might say, implied.

MR. ALLEN: Mr. President, I agree perfectly with the Senator from Massachusetts and the Senator from Delaware that we may possess constitutional power to do many things that it would be dishonorable to do under the circumstances. I think myself it would be dishonorable to wage war upon those people.

SEN. FORAKER *(R, Ohio)*

I come now, Mr. President, to the speech of the Senator from Massachusetts [Mr. Hoar]. . . . It was a speech of great ability, a speech such as only few men could make. But, Mr. President, when it is all reduced to practical propositions, it amounted, as I understood it, simply to this, that the Government of the United States has no constitutional power to acquire territory except only for constitutional purposes, of which purposes the Senator from Massachusetts seems to constitute himself the sole and exclusive judge.

In other words, Mr. President, it must be a constitutional purpose according to the definition given by the Senator from Massachusetts of the purposes of the Constitution. He specifies that it is constitutional under the Constitution for the Government, in the exercise of its constitutional power with respect to the acquisition of territory, to secure a coaling station, a naval station, a place for a post-office or a custom-house, and remembering our experience last summer at the last session, he thought it was constitutional to acquire Hawaii; that that was a constitutional purpose because necessary to the national defense. I did not understand the Senator to say, but I understood him to admit, that when this Government acquires territory for one of these constitutional purposes it is not necessary to secure the consent of the people who may occupy that territory and who must by the acquisition pass under our jurisdiction and be governed by us.

MR. HOAR: I did not make any such admission.

MR. FORAKER: The Senator says he did not make any such admission. I say I did not understand him to say anything on the subject. I rather thought he had in mind the fact that when we were debating the Hawaiian resolution there was a protest filed here in this Chamber by the Senator from Massachusetts, signed by more than 14,000 of the Kanakas, or natives of that island, protesting against the acquisition by the United States Government of the Hawaiian Islands and the extension of our jurisdiction over them.

MR. HOAR: The Senator, I am sure, will pardon me?

MR. FORAKER: Certainly.

MR. HOAR: The people of Hawaii voted upon a constitution, and in that constitution they expressly authorized their legislative body to make provision for their annexation to the United States. Thereupon, in pursuance of the constitution, which had been in force for six or seven years, they proceeded to do it. Now, it is true that I presented a paper purporting to be signed (I do not know whether the signatures were or were not in every case verified) by a pretty large number of the Kanakas, but I believed then and stated then, and I believe now, that a majority of the citizens of Hawaii desired annexation to the United States; and that, in addition to that, everything in that island which could be called the germ of a national life was on that side; and so did the Senator from Ohio believe, I am sure.

MR. FORAKER: Surely; but I had no constitutional trouble about it. Now, all the Senator has said is quite true; but the fact remains, and that is what I am calling attention to, that he did not state in his speech — if he did it escaped me, and I allude to it now that he may correct me if I should be corrected — that when we acquire territory for a constitutional purpose the consent has anything to do with it. Suppose we acquire a coaling station that is situated upon an island in the sea. It is a constitutional purpose for which we have to acquire it. Suppose the inhabitants be of such a character that it is essential to the safety of our interests there that we acquire the whole island, though there be a thousand, or ten thousand, or one hundred thousand, as in the case of Hawaii, or a million people or more, as may be the case as to Luzon. Suppose we acquired it for a constitutional purpose, a purpose that is absolutely essential to the national welfare, for the purpose of national defense, must we stop in such a case and secure

[131]

Chapter 5
America's Rise to
World Power:
The Senate
Debate over the
Philippines, 1899

consent of the population? The Senator's statement was in regard to Hawaii. Would we stop and jeopardize the national interests, hesitating to acquire a place necessary to the national defense, because somebody there had not been consulted? And suppose we consult the population and they object, or some of them object. What then?

MR. HOAR: Will the Senator allow me to ask him if he claims that we have the right to do what nobody proposes to do?

MR. FORAKER: The right to do what?

MR. HOAR: To do what the Senator says nobody proposes to do.

MR. FORAKER: To allow them independence?

MR. HOAR: I ask if we have the right to hold them without giving them their independence if we want to?

MR. FORAKER: Unquestionably, if we take the Philippine Islands, so far as the question of power is concerned, I think there is no question whatever —

MR. HOAR: I used the word "right."

MR. FORAKER: I used the word "right" also. I am speaking, however, of the legal right; I am speaking of the power; I am speaking of the right; I am speaking of the authority of this Government. When it comes to the question of policy, I will tell you in a minute what I think about that. I am now telling you what we decided — and I think the Senator will agree with me — that those islands ought not to be given back to Spain or given to any other European power which would partition them out. Only two things were left — to leave them to themselves at once and retire immediately, taking no responsibility whatever for the condition there obtaining, or else take charge of them by cession from Spain, asking the world to have confidence in this great Government, which has ever sought to do right, that we will deal with them as they should be dealt with. . . .

I know whereof I speak when I say that of the four things we had the choice of doing — giving the islands back to Spain, giving them to other countries, leaving them to anarchy, or taking them ourselves — the President acted most wisely when he concluded that we should take them ourselves; and he comes now and says, when he submits this treaty, "You put me to war; here is the result; here are these people; do with them as you like." It is for the Congress of the United States to investigate and find out about the islands of the Philippines, what kind of inhabitants they may have, whether or not they are capable of government, and whether or not they want government, or whether or not only a few want government.

[*Hoar replied that, in his opinion, it would be wrong to annex a territory if the people of that territory objected, even if the United States had a legitimate motive for annexing. Better, he said, the United States should go "down beneath the Pacific in honor rather than disgrace itself by doing that thing."*]

SEN. McLAURIN *(D, South Carolina)*

I feel that a representative from South Carolina is peculiarly qualified to speak upon one phase of the question, and it is that pertaining to the incorporation of a mongrel and semibarbarous population into our body politic, a population that, so far as I can ascertain, is inferior to but akin to the negro in moral and intellectual qualities and incapacity for self-government. The experience of the South for the past thirty years with the negro race, is pregnant with lessons of wisdom for our guidance in the Philippines. It is passing strange that Senators who favored universal suffrage and the full enfranchisement of the negro should now advocate imperialism.

In other words, that territory can be acquired by conquest, held as a colony, and its inhabitants treated as vassals rather than citizens — governed by military rule or legislation not authorized by the Constitution. There is a glaring inconsistency in these positions. If they are sincere in their views as to the Philippines, they should propose an amendment to the Constitution which will put the inferior races in this country and the inhabitants of the Philippines upon an equality as to their civil and political rights, and thus forever settle the vexed race and suffrage questions in this country as well as the outlying territories.

How can they consistently, justly, and, I might add, constitutionally advocate a policy for outlying territories, embracing races so nearly akin to the negro, which differs so radically from the policy adopted as to that race in the South? There can be but one answer to that question, and that is that they substantially admit, in the light of a third of a century's experience, that universal suffrage is a monumental failure and that the time has come for the correction of this stupendous government error. . . .

Therefore, if the Philippine Islands were annexed and formed into States, this Chamber and the other House would contain about one-seventh Japanese, Malays, Chinese, or whatever mixture they have out there. We would have representatives with a voice in directing the affairs of this country from another continent, speaking another language, different in race, religion, and civilization — a people with whom we have nothing in common. For me, I can not tolerate the thought. The great strength of our country is not merely its isolated posi-

[133]

Chapter 5
America's Rise to
World Power:
The Senate
Debate over the
Philippines, 1899

tion, washed on each side by the waters of a great ocean, but in a homogeneous population, speaking a common language, and with similar aspirations and ideas of liberty and civilization.

In a commercial point of view, I believe the importance of the Philippines per se is greatly exaggerated. They are chiefly valuable as the key to the Orient, but we need not colonize to obtain that advantage. The exports of the Philippines, according to the Statistical Abstract, in 1896 amounted to $30,806,250. If this entire trade was monopolized by us it would be insignificant. We will have to teach them to wear shirts and breeches before we can trade with them much. But England and Germany have large trade interests in the Philippines, and under our agreement with Spain she must have equal trade privileges with the United States. As a matter of dollars and cents, I doubt its advantage. . . .

If we embark in a colonial system, it means the inauguration of a despotic power in Washington. It means a large standing army that will not only be used to rule outlying territories with an iron hand, but that sooner or later will be used at home to overawe and override the popular will. An imperialistic democracy, like an atheistic religion, is an impossible hybrid.

[*McLaurin then claimed that it was unconstitutional to acquire a territory if statehood for that territory was not the "ultimate object."*]

SEN. BACON *(D, Georgia)*

They were there engaged at that time in a rightful rebellion, or they were bandits; they were, in the latter case, outlaws, and the United States authorities had no right to accept of their cooperation and their alliance. There is no refinement of reasoning, there is no finesse of logic which can get away from the conclusion that when we sailed into Manila Bay and recognized those people as rightful belligerents, put arms and ammunition in their hands, and accepted of their cooperation and their alliance, we not only became, by every high and honorable obligation, bound to see to it that the power of Spain was broken in the Philippines, but we fell under an obligation, no less imperative, that when it was broken the Filipinos should get the benefit of it, and not the American people. My contention is that we certainly incurred that obligation, and that it is the only obligation. . . .

What is the effect of the acquisition of the Philippine Islands? It will be an entirely new departure. It will commit us to a colonial policy necessarily, because it is not possible, it is not within the contemplation of the American people, that the Philippine Islands should ever be converted into a State or into States and admitted into participation in the affairs of this Government.

That is out of the question. That is an absolute impossibility. Not only is there the consideration of great distance, but the people are absolutely foreign in every particular, foreign in religion, foreign in race, totally unassimilable to our people, and absolutely unqualified for the exercise of such duties as are devolved upon States and their representatives in the Government. So it comes down squarely to the proposition, Will you hold the Philippine Islands as a colony? . . .

If the Philippines are annexed this territory must either be in the end admitted as States in the Union with their people as citizens, entitled to equal rights and power with the citizens of other States, or the territory must be held as colonies with their people as subjects and vassals of the United States.

What is the result if these islands are acquired and held as colonies? The logic of the situation will be to acquire more Asiatic territory, and after that to reach out for still more. There is no reason for the acquisition of the Philippines which will not apply to the acquisition of other parts of Asia.

If we become involved in a war with a foreign power, the Philippine Islands would be our weak spot. It was the weak spot of Spain, and we struck it first because it was the weak spot, and if we succeeded to her dominion it would be our weak spot, and any foreign government with which we engaged in war would strike that first. Mr. President, if we were to maintain our authority, if we were to meet that stroke, at least 100,000 men must be transported across the Pacific Ocean, 7,000 miles. . . .

Now, Mr. President, as I was saying, if we are to maintain dominion over this foreign, alien people, these Mohammedans, these people accustomed to revolution, and to blood, and to disorder, if you please, we will be compelled to do it with an iron hand, regardless of the shedding of blood. And I repeat, I want no such transactions under the American flag. I do not want it to be that we will have to send governors and judges there to be brought back here to be tried for their oppressions of a people like them. I want no Warren Hastings arrayed before the bar of the Senate to be tried upon impeachment articles for oppressions of a people whom we are seeking to rule.

I want to hear nothing of another Black Hole or another Lucknow in the Philippine Islands. I want to hear nothing, Mr. President, about the blowing of people from cannon by Americans. I want to hear nothing of the shooting of

Chapter 5
America's Rise to
World Power:
The Senate
Debate over the
Philippines, 1899

hundreds of men of one regiment, all done in the name of the United States and under the American flag. . . .

MR. RAWLINS: Mr. President —

THE PRESIDING OFFICER: Does the Senator from Ohio yield to the Senator from Utah?

MR. FORAKER: Certainly.

MR. RAWLINS: Do I correctly understand the position of the Senator to be that in so far as political privileges like the right of voting and holding office in a Territory are concerned, because of the absence of an act of Congress the people in a Territory do not possess those privileges, and therefore the Senator holds that the Constitution does not apply to the Territories in and of itself?

MR. FORAKER: Mr. President, there is hardly an excuse for the interrogatory the Senator from Utah has propounded to me. I have not said anything even like that.

MR. RAWLINS: I wanted —

MR. FORAKER: What I said is that the Constitution of the United States does not operate in the Territories of the United States until legislative machinery has been supplied to set it in motion there.

MR. RAWLINS: Now, if the Senator —

MR. FORAKER: If the Senator from Utah will allow me, I think I can make it plain so that Senators will have no difficulty in comprehending what I have contended for. Nobody questions but that everywhere throughout the Territories of the United States citizens of the United States residing there are entitled to all the rights and privileges and immunities guaranteed by the Bill of Rights. . . .

. . . But how can he have the writ of habeas corpus; how can he have a trial by jury; how can he have an enforcement of any of these rights in the Territory before Congress has legislated and set these principles of the Constitution in motion in the Territory? That is the point I have made.

MR. RAWLINS: Now, may I interrupt the Senator?

MR. HOAR: May I ask the Senator from Ohio a practical question?

MR. FORAKER: The Senator from Utah wants to ask me a question.

MR. RAWLINS: I had not yet completed my question.

MR. FORAKER: Oh, I beg pardon; I thought the Senator had done so.

MR. RAWLINS: The point which I desired to make was, that no political privileges, such as the right of franchise, of voting, or holding office, are imparted to anyone by the Constitution.

MR. FORAKER: No.

SEN. NELSON *(R, Minnesota)*

[*Nelson reviewed the history of American territorial acquisition, from the Louisiana territory in 1803 to the Hawaiian Islands earlier in 1898.*]

Now, in none of these cases, with the exception of Texas and Hawaii, were the people of the annexed territory in any form or manner consulted.

This proposition has never been doubted until lately, but now we are confronted for the first time in the history of our country with a new gospel. It is contended that we have no right to govern a territory and hold it except for the purpose of statehood; that we have no right to acquire territory unless it is our immediate purpose to make it into a State. If you look into the decisions of our courts, if you look into the practice of our Government, you will find no warrant or basis for this contention.

We are met with the argument that under the Declaration of Independence all men are created equal, that there should be no taxation without representation, and that government derives its just powers from the consent of the governed.

Mr. President, all this is true only in a limited and qualified sense. It has never anywhere on the face of the earth been applied in its entirety. Neither women, minors, nor persons non compos mentis have a right to participate at the ballot box in our system of government. They are disfranchised, and yet we tax their property, and we make them in all respects, in their property and in their persons, liable to all the duties of citizenship. More than two-thirds of our population, if we count women, minors, and persons non compos mentis, are not consulted, and have no direct voice in our system of government. They are in this respect unequal to those who have the right of suffrage, and the Government does not derive its just powers from their consent. In their case taxation and representation do not go together, but they are nevertheless citizens of the United States, subject to its laws and entitled to its protection. To govern the people of the Philippine Islands without enfranchising them is no more unjust than to govern our own disfranchised people — by males over 21 years of age.

. . . I claim that we hold the Philippine Islands to-day practically as we held

Chapter 5
America's Rise to
World Power:
The Senate
Debate over the
Philippines, 1899

New Mexico and Upper California after the war with Mexico — we hold them by conquest; and the government there is lawfully in the hands of the executive department, under the President as the Commander in Chief; that our flag and our Government are as lawfully in the Philippine Islands to-day under the Constitution and laws of this country as they are in the State of Illinois, the Senator's own home.

What right have Senators to say that we are among the Philippine Islanders as a conquering and subjugating nation? They had been sold out by their leaders, bound hand and foot. They were still in the shackles of Spanish tyranny, and when our fleet entered Manila Bay on the 1st day of May we came there, not as conquerors to vanquish them, we came there by their invitation to help them, to relieve them from Spanish tyranny and Spanish oppression.

MR. TILLMAN: I am going to try to be as direct and straightforward as I know how to be, and I believe I understand that art a little, Mr. President.

I want to call the Senator's attention to the fact, however, that he and others who are now contending for a different policy in Hawaii and the Philippines gave the slaves of the South not only self-government, but they forced on the white men of the South, at the point of the bayonet, the rule and domination of those ex-slaves. Why the difference? Why the change? Do you acknowledge that you were wrong in 1868?

MR. NELSON: I do not think it is wholesome either for the Senator from South Carolina or for me to delve into the dreary past in these matters. So far as the negro question is concerned in this country, let the dead past bury its dead. Let us act in the living present.

. . . I fear that the Senator is so possessed with questions that grew out of slavery and that he is so possessed with all the conditions that grow out of that institution, that he can hardly see clear on this matter of the Philippine Islands or in the matter of territorial acquisitions.

. . . I have no desire to discuss those problems and questions of the South. I have no desire to antagonize anybody or to say anything harsh or unjust; and it is wholly unnecessary for the Senator from South Carolina to inject it into this inquiry. It is not germane.

SEN. WHITE *(D, California)*

Mr. President, ought we to grant the Filipino an opportunity? If we say that he is not fitted to govern himself, by what process of reasoning can we reach the conclusion that therefore, and on that account, we ought to absorb him, especially when we announce in advance that we are not acquiring possessions for the purpose of dominion or statehood? . . . When the Senator from New Hampshire absorbs, say, a broiled live lobster, he assimilates it, or at least he ought to. [Laughter.]

MR. CHANDLER: The trouble is that the Senator does not appreciate the different meanings that may be given to the same word. Undoubtedly the President thinks that we want to bring —
MR. WHITE: Will the Senator from New Hampshire allow me to ask whether he speaks by authority of the President?
MR. CHANDLER: Undoubtedly the President thinks as I do, if he is a wise man [laughter], and I think he is. Undoubtedly the President thinks that we ought to bring these people into a resemblance or a likeness to us, but not exactly to an identity; and I hope the Senator will not give too much stress, as the Senator from South Carolina did, to the use of the words "benevolent assimilation." They sound finely to me, and I am sorry the Senator from California does not like them. . . .

Permit me to say that I do not give undue weight to purely commercial considerations. . . . But I appreciate that in some quarters a different conception prevails. Boards of trade and chambers of commerce in various localities look forward to and with glowing words portray the riches which they seem to think will drop into our laps. Thus was the siren voice raised in the case of Hawaii, and yet it is demonstrable to-day, as some of us said it would be demonstrated, that the local sugar growers alone made fortunes from annexation. Then we were told that numerous laborers would go to Hawaii and find a long-sought opportunity for the development of their interests, and yet we have ascertained from experience that these anticipations were not realized and that there is no opening for such immigration. . . .

We hear much of our destiny, our *manifest* destiny. What "manifest destiny" can require any man or set of men or any nation to do that which should not be done? Are we destined for turpitude? What is that manifest destiny? Is it to conquer the world? Evidently many so think. Not long ago it was frequently said upon this floor, "wherever the flag is raised there let it float forever." This proposition was so absurd and the statement was so ridiculed here and elsewhere that a distinguished Senator of expansion tendencies informed me recently that the expression was only a figure of speech. . . .

Chapter 5
America's Rise to
World Power:
The Senate
Debate over the
Philippines, 1899

MR. MASON: Before the Senator leaves the point he is making, I want to ask him if he knows of any case in history where territory has been acquired by force that they did not require the same or a greater force to maintain it? Does it not mean a perpetual standing army?

MR. WHITE: Mr. President, especially in the Tropics, there is no occasion for civilization or capacity as we understand it, and there control is always by the sword.

MR. GEAR: Let me state to the Senator from Illinois that the acquisition of a part of California, Arizona, and New Mexico did not require any additional force.

MR. MASON: It was settled by a treaty, and it was settled finally by a treaty, by an agreement by a people who had a right to settle it by treaty. It was not questioned —

MR. TELLER: The people of New Mexico and California were not heard in the matter.

MR. MASON: They did not stand with guns as the Filipino does now, saying, "Keep off the grass!"

MR. TELLER: They did stand with guns when we went into California and Mexico. When the army went there, the Mexicans and Californians stood with guns.

MR. MASON: I know, but the whole thing was finally adjusted by treaty.

MR. TELLER: So is this being adjusted by treaty.

MR. MASON: By a treaty with a people who have no more title than the devil had when he offered to give the Saviour all the land in sight. He did not have a tax title to a square foot.

MR. WHITE: The Senator from Colorado [Mr. Teller] evidently has not exactly understood the line of argument I have been making. He was out of the Chamber during this explanation. I think he will concede perhaps that there is some difference in the character of population and the problems threatening us in the Philippine group and that which we encountered when we accepted California and annexed Arizona and the territory which he names under a treaty.

I have not made any statement with reference to my belief that the people of the island must necessarily be consulted. The region to which he refers was not densely populated. While there were Indians in considerable number, they were considered destined to removal or even obliteration. The Caucasian inhabitants were capable of "assimilation." They were contiguous. The tropical problem is altogether different. The inferior race in the Tropics does not diminish. The

Caucasian there never substantially increases. The number, the location, and the character of the inhabitants in the Philippines are conclusive to me from the standpoint of policy, and thus I am considering the matter.

SEN. LODGE *(R, Massachusetts)*

[*Lodge began with a ringing declaration that the United States has the "undoubted power" to acquire territory, hold it, and govern it. He then added that in his opinion it was for* Congress *to decide whether the purposes for acquiring a territory were constitutional, and that the United States' power in that territory was absolute (except for the limitations of the Thirteenth Amendment, which outlawed slavery).*]

Constitutions do not make people; people make constitutions. Our Constitution is great and admirable, because the men who made it were so and the people who ratified it and have lived under it were and are brave, intelligent, and lovers of liberty. There is a higher sanction and a surer protection to life and liberty, to the right of free speech and trial by jury, to justice and humanity, in the traditions, the beliefs, the habits of mind, and the character of the American people than any which can be afforded by any constitution, no matter how wisely drawn. If the American people were disposed to tyranny, injustice, and oppression, a constitution would offer but a temporary barrier to their ambitions, and the reverence for the Constitution and for law and justice grows out of the fact that the American people believe in freedom and humanity, in equal justice to all men, and in equal rights before the law, and while they so believe the great doctrines of the Declaration of Independence and of the Constitution will never be in peril.

[*Lodge then added that the United States could be expected to deal honorably with the Philippines even though its power in the islands would be absolute.*]

What our precise policy shall be I do not know, because I for one am not sufficiently informed as to the conditions there to be able to say what it will be best to do, nor, I may add, do I think anyone is. But I believe that we shall have the wisdom not to attempt to incorporate those islands with our body politic, or make their inhabitants part of our citizenship, or set their labor alongside of ours and within our tariff to compete in any industry with American workmen. I believe that we shall have the courage not to depart from those islands fearfully, timidly, and unworthily and leave them to anarchy among themselves, to the brief and bloody domination of some self-constituted dictator, and to the

Chapter 5
America's Rise to
World Power:
The Senate
Debate over the
Philippines, 1899

quick conquest of other powers, who will have no such hesitation as we should feel in crushing them into subjection by harsh and repressive methods. It is for us to decide the destiny of the Philippines, not for Europe, and we can do it alone and without assistance. I believe that we shall have the wisdom, the self-restraint, and the ability to restore peace and order in those islands and give to their people an opportunity for self-government and for freedom under the protecting shield of the United States until the time shall come when they are able to stand alone, if such a thing is possible, and if they do not themselves desire to remain under our protection. This is a great, a difficult, and a noble task. I believe that American civilization is entirely capable of fulfilling it, and I should not have that profound faith which I now cherish in American civilization and American manhood if I did not think so.

Take now the other alternative. Suppose we reject the treaty or strike out the clause relating to the Philippines. That will hand the islands back to Spain; and I can not conceive that any American should be willing to do that. Suppose we reject the treaty; what follows? Let us look at it practically. We continue the state of war, and every sensible man in the country, every business interest, desires the reestablishment of peace in law as well as in fact. At the same time we repudiate the President and his action before the whole world, and the repudiation of the President in such a matter as this is, to my mind, the humiliation of the United States in the eyes of civilized mankind and brands us as a people incapable of great affairs or of taking rank where we belong, as one of the greatest of the great world powers. . . .

There is much else involved here, vast commercial and trade interests, which I believe we have a right to guard and a duty to foster. But the opponents of the treaty have placed their opposition on such high and altruistic grounds that I have preferred to meet them there, and not to discuss the enormous material benefits to our trade, our industries, and our labor dependent upon a right settlement of this question, both directly and indirectly. For this reason I have not touched upon the commercial advantages to the country involved in the question of these islands, or the far greater question of the markets of China, of which we must have our share for the benefit of our workingmen. I have confined myself solely to the question which has been brought to the front here, and to the proposition that we could not be trusted to deal honestly with those islands of the East, for that is what the argument of the opposition, stripped of rhetoric and ornament, amounts to.

I want to get this country out of war and back to peace. I want to take the disposition and control of the Philippines out of the hands of the war power and place them where they belong, in the hands of the Congress and of the President. I want to enter upon a policy which shall enable us to give peace and self-government to the natives of those islands. The rejection of the treaty makes all these things impossible, and the delay in its ratification retards and endangers them. If I did not have faith in the American people and their Government, I would do my best to prevent the ratification of the treaty, and I can see no other ground of opposition. But as I have a profound faith in both, I want to take those islands from Spain in the only way in which it can be done, by the ratification of the treaty, and then leave it to the President — wise, humane, patriotic — to the American Congress, and to the American people, who have never failed in any great duty or feared to face any great responsibility, to deal with them in that spirit of justice, humanity, and liberty which has made us all that we are to-day or can ever hope to be.

SEN. CLAY *(D, Georgia)*

[Clay began by stating that while the United States had the constitutional right to acquire and govern the Philippines with the ultimate object of bringing them to statehood, it was most unwise to do so.]

We can not, in my judgment, have two forms of Territorial government — one for contiguous territory, which must be within the pale of the Constitution, and another for foreign territory, which must be subject to the arbitrary will of Congress without any constitutional check whatever. If Congress possessed such power, that is, to govern the people of those islands without any constitutional limitations, then Congress would have the right to establish a form of religious worship in the islands and to prohibit the free exercise of religion by the inhabitants. Such erroneous ideas of the powers of Congress to govern foreign territories would permit this Government to deny to the Filipinos the right to peaceably assemble and to petition the Government for a redress of grievances. Such erroneous construction would permit us to pass laws depriving the Filipinos of the right of trial by jury and place their lives and property at the disposal of Congress without any restraint except the conscience of our lawmakers.

Such a proposition, to my mind, is appalling.

The history of the past demonstrates that our race can not thrive and prosper in the Tropics. The area of these islands is about twice as large as my own State. This population is composed of Spaniards, half-castes, Chinese, Malays,

Chapter 5
*America's Rise to
World Power:
The Senate
Debate over the
Philippines, 1899*

and Japanese. Of the total population, Europeans and Americans compose less than 2 per cent. The English, Germans, French, and Americans, knowing the climatic conditions of the country, have never sought homes among the Filipinos. Now, why do we want such a population, situated at such great distance from us, and why do we want to become responsible for their future government, when such responsibility is almost sure to involve us in future wars with foreign governments? . . .

Since Spanish rule has ceased to exist in those islands we possess unmistakable evidence that the entire population, consisting of nearly 9,000,000 people, will be as hostile to any government that we may establish denying them the right of self-government as they were against the Government of Spain. We are not only liable to become involved in war by the permanent retention of this territory with foreign powers, but our troops are actually engaged in hostilities with the natives of their islands to maintain our supremacy. Mr. President, did you ever contemplate what a serious and difficult task it is to rule and govern eight or nine millions of people against their will, when this people were ready to sacrifice their fortunes and their lives for independence and self-government, especially when our ships and soldiers must travel from seven to fourteen thousand miles from eastern and western coast across the ocean to fight our battles on the native land of the insurgents?

[Concluding with a quotation from the Declaration of Independence, Clay argued that only a homogeneous people could "manage their own affairs under a popular constitution, and that the taste for imperialism ultimately would destroy free institutions among the conquerors as well as the conquered."]

SEN. MALLORY *(D, Florida)*

[Mallory began by reminding the Senate that the declaration of war against Spain said that the United States was fighting for noble and lofty purposes.]

Mr. President, our attitude at that time was one which gave to me an exalted sense of the honor of being one of the participants in the action that resulted in that declaration; but how is it to-day? What has become of that declaration? We are confronted with the fact that in face of that solemn proclamation of our disinterested and unselfish purpose we are about to take to ourselves not only the island of Porto Rico, but, under the pretense of having offered an equivalent in

[144]

the shape of a sum of money, we shall also take into our possession the Philippine Islands, heretofore belonging to Spain.

Mr. President, this Government can not afford to be inconsistent; the people of the United States can not afford to be inconsistent. It is true it has been said that we who are opposing the annexation of the Philippine Islands are to a certain extent inconsistent, inasmuch as we have offered no opposition to the annexation of Porto Rico; but the conditions are different. Porto Rico is close to our borders; she is in a similar position to Cuba. Her people are a civilized people, and, so far as we know, they themselves are perfectly willing to come in under the shelter of the American flag. They are a people who to a certain extent can be made homogeneous with the people of the United States, and with their consent there could be no objection to incorporating them into the body politic of this country. But in the case of the Philippine Islands we have, in the first place, an indefinite number of islands 10,000 miles distant from the capital of this country, seven thousand and odd miles distant from the nearest coast of the United States, inhabited by a very large population of mixed and different races, different in language, different in customs, different in religion, and to a large extent not only uncivilized, but even barbarous and savage. In addition to these objections, Mr. President, we have the fact, which I do not think can now be disputed, that the inhabitants of those islands are unwilling to become a part of the people of the United States. . . .

The wisdom and the necessities of the people of the United States urged Congress to pass a law prohibiting the immigration of people from the Chinese Empire into the United States. There were only a few thousand — one hundred and odd thousand, if I am not mistaken — that had gotten in; and here now we are seized with a spasm of apprehension lest 10,000 additional Japanese contract laborers get into Honolulu for the purpose of working on the sugar plantations in those islands. . . .

How is it with from seven to ten million of savages, barbarians, semicivilized, civilized, and partially enlightened people who constitute the population of the Philippine Islands? From seven to ten million are to be taken in in a day. They are not to be confined to the Philippine Islands, because it is out of the power of this Congress to deprive one of them of his liberty to pass from the confines of the Philippines and to go anywhere else on God's footstool he may choose to go. And here we are proclaiming to the laboring element of our population that we do not wish to see them distressed by the inroads of the pauper labor of Eu-

Chapter 5
America's Rise to
World Power:
The Senate
Debate over the
Philippines, 1899

rope, and are quaking with fear lest a few thousand Japanese get into Hawaii. At the same time, Mr. President, we propose to immediately incorporate into our body politic, and to permit to come here if it so suits them, from seven to ten million of the people of the Philippine Islands — an inferior but a strikingly imitative race.

MR. MASON: Or to send the product of their labor here.

MR. MALLORY: Or, as the Senator from Illinois suggests, to send the product of their labor here. That, Mr. President, is simply one possible ground of objection to the action which is proposed to be taken.

SEN. PLATT *(R, New York)*

All this talk about forcing our Government upon an unwilling people, all this eloquent invocation of the spirit of the Declaration of Independence, is far and away from any real point that concerns the Senate in this discussion. No Senator can suppose that there exists an American statesman who approaches the consideration of the Philippine problem with any other than the most benevolent intentions concerning the Filipinos and their future. There are reasons why the natives of these islands, after their experience with Spanish misrule, should misunderstand the presence at Manila of an American army, but there is no reason why an American Senator should misunderstand it, and no justification of his course in misrepresenting it. He knows that there is no American in all this broad land who wishes any other fate to any single native of the Philippine Islands than his free enjoyment of a prosperous life.

He knows that close in the wake of American rule there would come to the Filipinos a liberty that they have never known and a far greater liberty than they could ever have under the arrogant rule of a native dictator. He knows, moreover, that it would be self-rule, the rule of the islanders to the full extent of their capacity in that direction, and that each successive American President would welcome the time when he could recommend new leases of self-government to an advancing and improving people. The Filipinos may not know these things yet, but every American Senator knows them, and puts himself and his country in a false position when, by attributing the spirit of conquest and aggression to those whose policy has rescued the Filipinos from Spain and would now rescue them from native tyrants, he encourages them to doubt the generous sentiment of our people.

SEN. MASON

After having done that, and while your army is there subduing those people and teaching them the beauties of Christian civilization with guns and forts, the agricultural papers call attention to the fact that you do not even increase the demand for the produce of the farm, that the game is not worth the powder, and that you are spending money and spending men to carry out your desire of governing people without their consent, adding the tinsel and gewgaws of royalty to put upon the leaders of Tammany Hall or some other distinguished statesmen who may become the governors of those islands and govern them without their consent. It has been driven into the minds of the people of this country that we are about to do that. It is said we have had a great trust thrust upon us; that, like the good Samaritan, we have to give the man who has fallen by the wayside a dose of our medicine until he should draw on us a gun from his pocket and say, "Hands off!" telling us as good Samaritans we can increase our trade and commerce to furnish a market for our goods, and yet by the very statement of these people who represent the agriculturists of this country you show by your own conduct that you are feeding an American army with meat and vegetables from Australia. . . .

SEN. BERRY *(D, Arkansas)*

Mr. President, If in November, 1896, it had been known or generally believed throughout the United States that within less than two years from the date of his inauguration the President of the United States would be asking Congress to grant a standing army of 100,000 men for the purpose of being used to subjugate and subdue a people 7,000 miles away from our territory, who were seeking to form a government of their own, he would not have received the electoral vote of a single State in this Union. Prior to that time the Goverment of the United States had been the friend of all people in all places who were struggling for liberty and who sought to establish a government for themselves. To the people of France, the people of the South American Republics, the people of Poland, the people of Hungary, the people of Greece, the Government of the United States and all the people of the United States have extended their sympathy when they were fighting for liberty. The last year of the nineteenth century will hereafter mark the date that will show when the Government of the United States first aligned itself with those nations which seek to impose government upon other people contrary to their will. . . .

Chapter 5
America's Rise to
World Power:
The Senate
Debate over the
Philippines, 1899

Mr. President, it seems to me that the wholesale abuse, misrepresentation, and slander that daily come from the public press, and the intolerance shown by some Senators on this floor toward those who are unwilling to follow the President in his wild scheme of colonization and acquisition of territory is not the best and fairest way to determine and settle the great and important question which now confronts the American people. . . .

What has been the cause, Mr. President, of the remarkable change in the policy of our Government? What has been the mighty influence that has caused us to depart from the teachings of our fathers and to enter upon a course of action directly opposed to all that we have ever professed[?] Mr. President, men do not always agree as to causes and effects, but it seems to me that the all-powerful force that is pushing us on to destruction can be easily found. In 1896, for the first time since the organization of the Government, all of the great combinations of wealth, all of the great corporations, all of the trusts, all of the syndicates, boards of trade, merchants and manufacturers' associations and exchanges of the great cities, were united in the support of the same candidate for the Presidency. They were associated together as, and assumed for themselves, the name of the business men of the country. Many of them boldly claimed that the men who owned the wealth and property of the country had a right to dictate the policy of the Government and to name its Chief Magistrate. This powerful combination of wealth was able to control nearly all of the great daily newspapers, and they succeeded in electing William McKinley President of the United States.

Mr. President, it is largely the same element, the same mighty influence, which is to-day, under the plea that the United States must have a wider and broader field for trade and commerce, pushing us to a line of action that threatens the very foundations of the Republic. It is no doubt true that there are many earnest and honest people in all sections of the Union who believe that it is the duty of the government to sacrifice the lives of thousands and tens of thousands of our own people in order to force civilization and Christianity at the cannon's mouth upon the people of those distant islands; but the influence of this class is small compared with those I have first named. . . .

The pride and glory that the American people felt in the Army and Navy was greatly enhanced by the fact that all felt and knew that the war had been waged by us from unselfish and disinterested motives. We had fought to make others free as we ourselves were free; we had fought to enable the Cuban people to throw off their colonial dependence upon Spain and establish a free and independent government for themselves; we had disclaimed, in the act declaring war, any intention of acquiring territory in the island. The President himself had said that the forcible acquisition of territory would not be tolerated by the American people, and that such an attempt would be criminal aggression. The American people were proud because they had done a brave and generous and unselfish deed, which would be a gratification to them and to their children in all the years to come.

They had no thought then that the great combinations of wealth and greed would be able thereafter to unite and bring to bear such a mighty influence as would control the public press, to a large extent public sentiment, the President, and the Senate of the United Staes, and secure the adoption of a policy that would hereafter forever dim and obscure the glory that they had fairly won. We fought Spain in order to free the Cubans from her control. We can not, in my opinion, without placing a blot upon the fair name of the Republic, without dishonor to ourselves, fight the inhabitants of the Philippine Islands in order to subject them to our control. But such is the proposition made to us today. Under the terms of the protocol for peace signed by our Government and that of Spain, until the treaty of peace is ratified by the Senate the United States has no right in the Philippine Islands except to hold and defend the city of Manila, the harbor, and the bay.

It has been often said, Mr. President, that we hold those islands and that we can not turn them loose. That is not true. Except the city of Manila and the bay and harbor we do not hold those islands either in law or in fact, and, Mr. President, the city of Manila itself was never captured until after the protocol of peace was signed. This is admitted by those that supported the treaty; and it can not be denied that under the terms of the protocol of peace our rights were confined to the defenses of the city of Manila and its bay and its harbor.

Those who support the treaty urge this as a reason why there should be a speedy ratification of the treaty in order that General Otis may be at liberty to move forward his battalions to crush the Philippine government and slaughter those who resist. They insist that we must agree to a treaty by which we promise to pay Spain $20,000,000 in order to obtain her consent to make war upon those who were our allies in the recent contest; and we are told that any party or individual who refuses to give his consent to this proposition will meet with the indignation of the American people. Mr. President, it may be true; I do not

Chapter 5
America's Rise to
World Power:
The Senate
Debate over the
Philippines, 1899

know; but it seems to me that when the excitement of the hour has passed away and impartial history comes to be written the men who are urging the forcible acquisition of foreign territory will not be proud of the record they are making.

But I do know that any Senator upon this floor who earnestly and honestly believes that this policy endangers this country and who would be intimidated by any threat of indignation from any source or any power is unworthy of a seat upon the floor of the Senate. This matter is too great for any purpose, except that we stand by our convictions.

But it was said by the President of the United States, in his speech at Omaha, I think — at least in one of the speeches he made on his Western tour — that it is destiny, and we must meet it and accept it. Mr. President, the plea of destiny as an excuse for any course of action is an admission that no other reason can be given. If destiny is a sufficient excuse for wrong, then there is no crime however great and no infamy however degrading that a nation may not commit under that name. And we are told again that we must conquer these people in the interests of humanity and for their own good, that we must entail enormous expense upon our own people, that we must drag our youth to that far-off land, and kill and slaughter hundreds and, it may be, thousands of these people, in order that we may civilize and Christianize the remainder.

Mr. President, this is the same excuse, the same false pretense, that has been given by every nation of the world which sought to impose its government upon other people.

But I am asked if I think our people are as bad as theirs. I answer no, Mr. President, I do not think they are; but the reason why I do not think they are is because they have never indulged in these practices in the past. But the very moment we attempt to govern foreign territory against the will of the inhabitants, the chances are, if history can be relied upon, that we shall grow worse year by year. . . .

Mr. President, those of us who live in the States of the South have some knowledge of the wrongs and outrages that may be perpetrated even by Americans where they seek to govern by strangers and by military power an unwilling people. Fortunately for our Republic, the people of the North learned in time that such government could not be continued without danger to every part of the Union.

I say to-day that we are entering upon a dangerous field. We are doing it on the pretense, it may be, of humanity and Christianity, but behind it all, I repeat, is the desire for trade and commerce; and whenever and wherever considerations of money making are placed above the honor and fair fame of this Republic, the men who do it are undermining the very foundations of the Government under which we live.

SEN. PLATT *(R, Connecticut)*

But, Mr. President, while this treaty has been in process of negotiation an ambitious leader in the Philippine Islands has been raising revolt, and I say revolt against the United States and its Government and its Navy and its Army. He is to-day a Spanish citizen arraying Spanish subjects against the United States. He had a great opportunity to do so, because by the terms of the protocol, by the operation of international law, he had a free field for his operations. We had taken all effective Spanish soldiers in the island prisoners, so that Spain could not resist him. We had tied our hands by the protocol until a treaty of peace should be declared, so that the United States could not resist him.

By reason of the situation he was given free course in all his operations. He has gathered an insurgent band and to-day gives notice to the United States that unless he is recognized as the ruler of that territory he will contest his right by armed attack upon the armies of the United States. The situation is critical. He is in arms, using the arms which the United States furnished him, and in arms against the United States authority. That is the situation. Against whom else is Aguinaldo in arms? Against whom else are the threats of warfare? The ratification of a peace treaty will give the United States rights which it does not possess now. It will give the United States the right to say, "We are in control of these islands, attack us if you dare," and in a very short time, without warfare, this insurgent band will melt away, better counsels will prevail, and a government superior, immensely superior, to anything which Aguinaldo could establish there will bless the inhabitants of those islands.

MR. TILLMAN: I presume the Senator from Connecticut will not object to my calling his attention, or rather recalling his attention, to a statement in the papers of this city as to the speech that was made by General Shafter at a banquet two or three weeks ago in which he announced a willingness to disarm those people and, if necessary, to kill half of them to do it. I wish to know whether he sympathizes with that view.

MR. PLATT OF CONNECTICUT: Oh, well, Mr. President, I do not think it is required of me that I shall answer that question. It is entirely irrelevant. We are not discussing General Shafter.

Chapter 5
America's Rise to
World Power:
The Senate
Debate over the
Philippines, 1899

MR. TILLMAN: The Senator —

MR. PLATT OF CONNECTICUT: We are not discussing the newspapers; we are not discussing the peculiar ideas which the Senator from South Carolina seems by his interruptions to entertain.

SEN. RAWLINS *(D, Utah)*

Mr. President, the mere idea of expansion, of extending our borders, does not alarm me so much as some of the startling doctrines advanced in its justification. We are to-day confronted with the question as to whether we shall change the name of the Republic; and if so, what shall the new name be, and what shall it symbolize? Shall it be the United States of America and the Kingdom of the Philippines or shall it be the Empire of America and Asia? Already there are spectral visions of this in the political sky. . . .

Mr. President, what do we want the Philippines Islands for? Do we want them to furnish homes for our own people? No. Do we want them to furnish an outlet for our surplus labor? The sturdy American workingman could not live in that climate, competing with the meanest of the Tagalos. Do we want them to add a wholesome element to our population, that our sons may find wives and our daughters husbands? The blighting curse of the Almighty would rest upon such miscegenation. Do we want them in order to practice upon their inhabitants the same arts of philanthropy which, applied to the aboriginal inhabitants of this continent, have led to their extermination? Humanity says no. Do we want them for the sake of their trade and commerce? Already the spokesmen of the dominant Administration are seeking to devise unconstitutional methods for intercepting and preventing such traffic. Do we want them in order to send hither swarms of officeholders, carpetbaggers, to riot among them like slimy worms, eating out their substance? . . . No, there is no conceivable good which they can bring to us. Their retention bodes nothing but evil. They are made the pretext for emasculating our freedom, for overriding our Constitution and breaking down the safeguards of our liberty.

SEN. SPOONER *(R, Wisconsin)*

Senators do not like the word "colony." I do not like it. It is certainly not accurate as applied to the Philippines.

[*Spooner then contended that "territory" was the proper word, and said he knew of no constitutional prohibition to acquiring a territory that would "forever" be governed by Congress, that is, never become a State.*]

[152]

MR. TILLMAN: Will the Senator allow me to ask him a question?

MR. SPOONER: Yes.

MR. TILLMAN: Do those rights, which the Senator has just given us a list of, include the right to move from one part of this country to another?

MR. SPOONER: I think so.

MR. TILLMAN: From the Territories into the States?

MR. SPOONER: I think so.

MR. TILLMAN: In other words, the annexation of the Philippines would carry with it the right, under the law and the Constitution, for any one of those people to come here?

MR. SPOONER: I think so. I do not care to discuss that now, but for the purposes of what I have to say I am disposed to admit it.

MR. PLATT OF CONNECTICUT: They have that right now.

MR. SPOONER: We could exclude them now, and possibly we could then. Until they are excluded by law, every one has a right to come here. Whether we could prevent the people of a Territory from leaving the Territory, or prevent them from going into one of our States, I do not care to discuss. The Senator from Connecticut [Mr. Platt] thinks we could. I have grave doubts about it. . . .

. . . The Senator seemed to be very much aroused in behalf of the dignity of Aguinaldo, and I used the phrase which I ought not to have used and which I withdraw. . . .

We have had no participation in the struggles of the Old World nations over the balance of power. We have sympathized with them in their struggles; we have sympathized with their peoples in the terrible burdens put upon them to maintain great standing armies and great navies. But their quarrels have not been our quarrels; their policies have not been our policies. While they have fought we have fed them and manufactured products for their use.

It may not be sentimental or romantic, but it is true we have grown rich by staying at home and attending to our own business.

I have not been able to find persuasive the suggestion that we can benefit the United States by a policy which will make us in any larger sense than we are a political factor among the governments of the world — I mean in world matters — and I look with apprehension upon a policy which may place the United States in a position where by force of environment or neighborship we can be made a compulsory participant in the struggles of the Old World nations over the balance of power in the Orient. Nor can I contemplate with equanimity, Mr. President, the adoption of any policy which may bring into perpetual competition with our people, with the men who raise tobacco on our farms, with the

Chapter 5
America's Rise to
World Power:
The Senate
Debate over the
Philippines, 1899

men who labor in our factories, the products of a labor which in the very nature of things must be cheaper than ours, because of radical and unchangeable differences, for climatic and other reasons, in the standard of living, and in the wage of labor.

SEN. MONEY *(D, Mississippi)*

It is insisted that the commercial needs of the United States demand the possession of trading posts within the Orient, and I confess that the prospect of increasing trade has made a considerable impression upon my mind. There is in this proposition more of the accessory than of the necessary quality. I can say with the utmost frankness that this phase of the question is one of the most difficult that ever I have been called upon to decide. I have labored to a conclusion, endeavoring honestly to see whether it was better that the treaty should be ratified as it stands or that it should be amended. I felt that glow of enthusiasm which seemed to sweep like a wave over the country when the ensign of this Republic waved in supremacy in the Asiatic world. I felt the thrill of exultation that this Republic had at once become a potent factor in solving the world-wide questions. I felt in every ruddy drop that visited my heart a tingling of joyous pride when the great exploits of our sailors and soldiers astonished the world. The amazement of all Europe at the sudden, unexpected, and complete victory of our arms delighted me. In these things as an American citizen I have shared as fully as any man who advocates the treaty. . . .

[*Money conceded the economic advantages of taking the Philippines, especially that of helping United States trade with China. However, Money said that the Philippines were not indispensable to that commerce.*]

But are conquests and subjugation necessary to the spread of American products, either manufactured or raw? Have we depended heretofore upon those aids so much vaunted in this debate? . . .

It has been considered almost a crime here to oppose the Executive. That is another danger. The subserviency of the Senate to the Executive is one of the dangers of this situation. Let this coordinate branch of the Government maintain its dignity and power, such power as is granted to it by the Constitution.

SEN. DANIEL *(D, Virginia)*

Mr. President, peace! Peace! This treaty is not a treaty of peace except in formal ceremony with Spain. It is a declaration of war against the Philippine peo-

[154]

ple, not by Congress, but in necessary and logical effect. We know that the Filipinos are in arms. We know that they have an army of from 12,000 to
30,000. We know that they are seeking to work out their own destiny. The
moment that this treaty is adopted the Filipinos are made citizens, and the moment they are made citizens, if they do not instantly lay down their arms they
become rebels. The tie of allegiance is created with this Government, and when
the President or Commander in Chief says, "Our sovereignty is here; lay down
your arms," they bear them no longer, under the penalty of death.

SEN. CHILTON *(D, Texas)*

Now, I have great faith in the energy, in the ability, and in the strength of the
American people. I know our resources are tremendous. But we must never
lose sight of the important fact that one of the reasons why the other nations of
the earth have heretofore been unwilling and unable to measure arms with the
United States is because of the fact that we have stood here in a great continen-
tal area and serenity, and the countries of the Old World could not find a place
to strike us. They dared not seek to invade us, and hence they shrank from en-
countering the dangers of a war with this Republic.

But whenever we take the Philippine Islands we have furnished to the world
a place to strike us. It will be our one weak point. If we enter into an alliance
with England, as is proposed here by some, we will have to take part in the division of China or take side against the partition of China. In either case we will
be obliged to go across the sea and fight our future battles with the powers of
the Old World at a place which they and not we will select. . . .

Mr. President, we should take some observations from experience. I remember in reading history one very remarkable instance of the utter folly of ena-
bling your adversary to select the theater of war. After Napoleon Bonaparte
invaded Russia and left his army bleeding upon her plains of snow, no power in
Europe dared to undertake another Russian invasion. For a half century Russia
was deemed impregnable. But in an evil hour she set up certain rights upon the
Black Sea. Then England and France saw their opportunity. . . .

SEN. WOLCOTT *(R, Colorado)*

Bar England, there is not a country in Europe that is not hostile to us. During
all this war they stood in sullen hate, hoping for our defeat and that disaster
might come to us; and to-day they wait with eager and rapacious gaze, hoping
that some event may yet prevent our reaping the fruits of the treaty which has

Chapter 5
America's Rise to
World Power:
The Senate
Debate over the
Philippines, 1899

been agreed upon by the commissioners of the two countries. Yet, while this critical condition of affairs exists, it has become evident within the last few days that certain political leaders in this Chamber believe that a new issue should be brought before the American people to be determined at the next Presidential election. They intend that the American people shall be called to pass on the questions arising out of the war, and that this shall be the issue of the next campaign.

For one I believe that issue a fair one, and I am ready, as all good citizens ought to be, to meet the views of the whole American people upon the question of the conduct of the war, of its achievements, and of the policy this country should pursue at its close. But it is deplorable, Mr. President, that in formulating such an issue and in pursuit of such a policy those leaders should find it necessary to seek to dishonor this government and the Administration which has guided us so wisely through the troubled sea of international complications and brought us to the threshold of an honorable peace; that they should seek to degrade us in the face of the nations of the world. . . .

SEN. ALLEN

Now, Mr. President, because I shall vote for the treaty it does not follow that I am in favor of annexation. I do it for the simple reason that in my judgment the Government of the United States can not afford to open up negotiations with the Spanish dynasty again. We have the whole question within our jurisdiction and within our power, and here and by us alone it should be settled. If by amending the treaty we send it back for further consideration by the commissioners, or to new commissioners to be appointed; if we open up the subject-matter of the treaty, we will, in my judgment, especially in the light of very recent events, incur the danger of European interference and European complications.

BIOGRAPHICAL SKETCHES
OF SELECTED U.S.
SENATORS WHO DEBATED
THE PARIS PEACE TREATY

Donelson Caffery (1835–1906), D, La. Civil War veteran (CSA, lieutenant); admitted to the bar, 1867; sugar planter and lawyer; La. senate, 1892–1893; U.S. Senate, 1894–1901 (did not run for reelection, 1900); disagreed with his party's stand on free silver, 1896; opposed war with Spain, 1898.

George Frisbee Hoar (1826–1904), R, Mass. Son of Massachusetts congressman and abolitionist; Harvard Law School, graduated 1846; practiced law, 1846–1852; Mass. house, 1852; Mass. senate, 1857; U.S. House, 1869–1877; U.S. Senate, 1877–1904; opposed drift of Republican party to becoming the party of big business.

Orville Hitchcock Platt (1827–1905), R, Conn. Lawyer; clerk, Conn. senate, 1855–1856; secretary of state, Conn., 1857; Conn. senate, 1861–1862; Conn. house, 1864, 1869; U.S. Senate, 1879–1905; strong expansionist; author of Platt Amendment (1901), a chief feature of which was the authorization of the United States to intervene in Cuban affairs to preserve Cuba's independence.

William Ernest Mason (1850–1921), R, Ill. Born in Ohio; moved to Iowa, 1857; private in Union army; admitted to the bar, 1869; moved to Nebraska, 1885; judge, 1891–1893; filled U.S. Senate vacancy, 1899–1901.

William Vincent Allen (1847–1924), Populist, Neb. Born in Ohio; moved with parents to Iowa, 1857; served in Civil War as a private with the Iowa Volunteer Infantry; studied law at West Union, Iowa, and admitted to bar, 1869; moved to Nebraska, 1884; district judge, 1891–1893; permanent chairman of Populist state conventions in 1892, 1894, and 1896; U.S. Senate, 1893–1899; unsuccessful candidate for reelection, 1899; appointed to fill term of Nebraska's other U.S. senator, 1899–1901.

George Gray (1840–1925), D, Del. Graduated Princeton, 1859; Harvard Law School, 1863, attorney general of Delaware, 1879–1885; U.S. Senate, 1885–1899 (defeated 1899); one of the commissioners to the Paris Treaty negotiations with Spain, 1898; McKinley appointee as ambassador to The Hague, 1900.

Joseph Benson Foraker (1846–1917), R, Ohio. Lawyer; Union soldier in Civil War; graduated Cornell Law School, 1869; admitted to the bar, 1869; judge, 1879–1882; governor of Ohio, 1885–1889; defeated twice for governor, 1883, 1889; U.S. Senate, 1896–1909; strong political supporter of McKinley.

John Lowndes McLaurin (1860–1934), D, S.C. Graduated Carolina Military Institute and studied law at the University of Virginia; admitted to the bar, 1883; S.C. house, 1890; S.C. attorney general, 1891–1897; U.S. House, 1892–1897; U.S. Senate, 1897–1903.

Chapter 5
America's Rise to
World Power:
The Senate
Debate over the
Philippines, 1899

Augustus Octavius Bacon (1839–1914), D, Ga. Graduated University of Georgia Law School, 1860; Confederate veteran; Ga. house, 1871–1886; U.S. Senate, 1894–1914; introduced resolution urging the United States to grant independence to the Philippines.

Joseph Lafayette Rawlins (1850–1926), D, Utah. Professor of classics, University of Deseret, 1873–1875; admitted to the bar, 1875; U.S. House, 1893–1895 (defeated 1894); U.S. Senate, 1897–1903 (defeated 1902).

Knute Nelson (1843–1923), R, Minn. Immigrant from Norway, 1849; Union veteran (POW); graduated from Albion College; admitted to the bar, 1867; Wisc. house, 1868–1869; moved to Minnesota, 1870; Minn. senate, 1875–1878; U.S. House, 1883–1889; governor of Minnesota, 1892–1895; U.S. Senate, 1895–1923; noted as a conservative Republican, except for support of low tariff and federal income tax.

Benjamin Ryan Tillman (1847–1918), D, S.C. Confederate veteran; governor of South Carolina, 1890–1894; championed agricultural education and helped found Clemson University (1893) and Winthrop College (1895); organized and led uprising of farmers in South Carolina; supported disfranchisement of blacks in South Carolina, 1895; U.S. Senate, 1894–1918; advocated repeal of the Fifteenth Amendment; supported the use of force in disfranchising blacks.

Stephen Mallory White (1853–1901), D, Calif. Native of California; graduate of Santa Clara College, 1871; admitted to the bar, 1874; Calif. senate, 1886–1890; lieutenant governor of California, 1888; U.S. Senate, 1890, 1893–1899; opposed business monopolies and imperialism.

William Eaton Chandler (1835–1917), R, N.H. Graduate of Harvard Law School, 1854; admitted to the bar, 1855; N.H. house, 1862–1864, 1881; U.S. secretary of the navy, 1882–1885; established steel warship construction; U.S. Senate, 1887–1901.

John Henry Gear (1825–1900), R, Iowa. Born in New York; moved to Iowa; Iowa house, 1871–1873; governor, 1878–1881; U.S. House, 1887–1891, 1893–1895; U.S. Senate, 1895–1900.

Henry Moore Teller (1830–1914), R, Colo. Born in New York; admitted to the bar, 1858; moved to Illinois, 1858, and to Colorado, 1861; U.S. Senate,

1876–1882; Secretary of the Interior (Arthur appointee), 1882–1885; U.S. Senate, 1885–1909. Considered a reformer, he supported women's suffrage, federal income tax, government regulation of big business; author of Teller Resolution, pledging the United States to an independent Cuba; opposed U.S. policy in the Philippines, 1899–1902.

Henry Cabot Lodge (1850–1924), R, Mass. Graduate of Harvard, 1871, and Harvard Law School, 1875; admitted to the bar, 1876; Mass. house, 1880–1881; U.S. House, 1884; U.S. Senate, 1893–1924; helped draft Sherman Antitrust Act and Pure Food and Drug Act; strong protectionist; supported U.S. policy in the Philippines.

Alexander Stephens Clay (1853–1910), D, Ga. Admitted to the bar, 1877; Ga. house, 1884–1887, 1889–1890; Ga. senate, 1892–1894; U.S. Senate, 1896–1910.

Stephen Russell Mallory, Jr. (1848–1907), D, Fla. Son of a former U.S. senator; midshipman, Confederate navy; graduate of Georgetown College, 1869; admitted to the bar, 1872; Fla. house, 1876–1880; Fla. senate, 1880–1888; U.S. House, 1891–1895; U.S. Senate, 1897–1907.

Thomas Collier Platt (1833–1910), R, N.Y. Graduate of Yale, 1850; druggist, 1852–1872, also banker and lumber company executive; county clerk, 1859–1861; U.S. House, 1873–1877; U.S. Senate, 1881, 1896–1909; considered a "stalwart" (conservative) Republican; opposed "reform" Republicans; considered spokesman of big business.

James Henderson Berry (1841–1913), D, Ark. Born in Alabama, moved to Arkansas, 1848; Confederate soldier (lost leg at Battle of Corinth, 1862); Ark. house, 1866, 1872; judge, 1878–1882; governor, 1882–1885; U.S. Senate, 1885–1907 (defeated 1906).

John Colt Spooner (1843–1919), R, Wisc. Born in Indiana; moved to Wisconsin, 1859; graduate of University of Wisconsin, 1864; Union veteran; admitted to the bar, 1867; Wisc. house, 1872; U.S. Senate, 1885–1891; governor, 1892; U.S. Senate, 1897–1907; was an antireform "stalwart" Republican.

Hernando de Soto Money (1839–1912), D, Miss. Graduate of University of Mississippi Law School; Confederate veteran; planter-editor; U.S. House,

Chapter 5
America's Rise to
World Power:
The Senate
Debate over the
Philippines, 1899

1875–1885, 1893–1897; U.S. Senate, 1897–1911; noted as an "independent" in Congress.

John Warwick Daniel (1842–1910), D, Va. Confederate veteran (wounded at Wilderness, 1864); graduate of University of Virginia Law School; admitted to the bar, 1866; Va. house, 1869–1872; Va. senate, 1875–1881; U.S. House, 1885–1887; U.S. Senate, 1887–1910.

Horace Chilton (1853–1932), D, Tex. Printer-lawyer; U.S. Senate, 1891–1892, 1895–1901.

Edward Oliver Wolcott (1848–1905), R, Colo. Born in Massachusetts; served in Civil War as member of Ohio Volunteer Infantry; graduated from Harvard Law School, 1871; moved to Colorado where he was admitted to the bar; district attorney, 1876; Colo. senate, 1879–1882; U.S. Senate, 1889–1901; firm Republican.

SENATE VOTE,
FEBRUARY 6, 1899

In favor of treaty (and therefore annexation of the Philippines): 57
Opposed   27
   (one vote more than the necessary two-thirds to ratify a treaty)

Of the 57 who voted for the treaty:

   41 Republicans
   11 Democrats
    5 Others

Of the 27 who voted against the treaty:

    2 Republicans
   22 Democrats (mostly southerners)
    3 Others

Questions to Consider

Remember that you have a two-part task in this chapter. First, from the evidence, you must find the principal arguments for and against the United States' acquisition of the Philippines, and second, you must assess which of those arguments you believe to have been the most influential, supporting your belief with evidence. These tasks will require you to manipulate the evidence in a number of ways. In other words, once you have arranged the evidence (which is presented to you in the order in which the speeches or debates took place) in a way you feel will be helpful, it is very likely that you will have to modify the arrangement a number of times.

This will take considerable experimentation on your part. One way of arranging the evidence is by types of argument (economic, legal, cultural, and so forth). What were the *economic* arguments in favor of taking the Philippines? What economic arguments were made against the acquisition? You can do the same for the other types of arguments.

Another way of arranging the evidence is by specific topic. For example, there was considerable debate on the meaning of the Declaration of Independence and the Constitution, their relationship to territorial acquisitions, and whether the rights guaranteed by the Constitution were extended to residents of new territories.

Pull together all of the evidence dealing with those issues and analyze it. What points did each side make? Takes notes as you go along.

Other topics include:

1. How were the Filipinos depicted by each side? How did each depiction bolster the points made in debate?

2. How was Aguinaldo depicted? His revolt?

3. What were the arguments for and against the commercial possibilities of the islands?

Hence, the rearrangement of evidence by topic can give you clues to several other points for and against the treaty.

Finally, you may want to consider arranging the evidence according to the state or political affiliation of each senator. Were there any arguments made consistently by southern senators? By Democrats?

By arranging the evidence in these ways, you will find all or most of the principal arguments for and against the acquisition of the Philippines. Then you will be ready to assess which of the arguments were most important or most influential.

How should you do this? One way is to look for arguments that were repeated by several senators. We can surmise that they were important arguments, at least to the men who made them. Next look at the breakdown of the February 6 vote. By combining this information with that which you gained from analyzing the

Chapter 5
America's Rise to
World Power:
The Senate
Debate over the
Philippines, 1899

debates, you will be able to infer at least some of the influential arguments. For example, the twenty-two Democrats who voted against the treaty were mostly southerners. What arguments appear to have been most influential with them?

Another way to assess which arguments were the most important or influential is to examine the biographical sketches of the senators who spoke for and against the the acquisition of the Philippines. Admittedly some of these sketches are too brief to be of much help (for example, those of Mason, McLaurin, Bacon, Rawlins, Gear, Clay, Mallory, Berry, Money, Daniel, and Chilton). Other sketches, however, when paired with the respective speeches, will offer some good clues as to which arguments these senators found the most persuasive.

Epilogue

It would be naive to assume that the Senate debate took place in a vacuum. President McKinley applied political pressure and offers of patronage to try to secure ratification of the treaty. Indeed, McKinley even offered Senator George Frisbee Hoar (R, Massachusetts) the ambassadorship to England if Hoar would drop his opposition to the treaty. Hoar, one of the leaders of anticolonialism in the Senate, refused. It is impossible to measure the influence of McKinley's efforts.

Also, two days before the Senate voted, fighting broke out in the Philippines between United States troops and Filipinos under Aguinaldo, who had been led to believe that the United States was not interested in acquiring the lands and thus felt betrayed. Senators were aware of the fact that hostilities had broken out when they voted. Some observers believed that the incident convinced some senators that the United States must continue to occupy the Philippines in order to bring stability to the islands. But, as with McKinley's political moves, it is impossible to judge the influence that fighting in the Philippines had on the Senate vote.

Finally, at almost the last moment well-known anti-imperialist and titular head of the Democratic party William Jennings Bryan reversed his position and supported the treaty. Bryan defended his about-face by stating that it was necessary to make peace with Spain and that the issue of independence for the Philippines could be decided after the presidential election of 1900, in which Bryan expected to be the Democratic standard bearer as he had been in 1896. Some charged that Bryan's new stand on the treaty was a cynical attempt to use anti-imperialism as an issue in the upcoming presidential contest. Indeed, during the debate Senator Wolcott of Colorado accused antitreaty Democrats of just that. Many were disgusted with Bryan's apostasy, among them industrialist and leading anti-imperialist Andrew Carnegie, who later said of

Bryan, "I could not be cordial to him for years afterwards. He had seemed to me a man who was willing to sacrifice his country and his personal convictions for party advantage."

Carnegie's charge was probably unfair. Bryan wanted the United States to grant independence to the Philippines as soon as possible. To do so, however, he reasoned that the treaty first must be approved, thus formally ending the war with Spain and transferring its colonies to the United States. After that was done, Bryan hoped the Senate would approve a resolution favoring Philippine independence. Embracing that strategy, he tried to persuade Democrats, Populists, and "Silver Republicans" to vote for the treaty. Those votes probably were the difference.

Yet Bryan's strategy backfired. A resolution favoring Philippine independence was introduced by Georgia Senator Augustus Bacon and was taken up by the Senate immediately after the treaty's approval. The result was a tie vote that was broken by Vice-President Garret Hobart, who cast his vote against the Bacon Resolution and, therefore, against immediate Philippine independence.

President McKinley exulted over the Senate's ratification of the treaty. The president boasted that the Philippines would become

> a land of plenty and increasing possibilities; a people redeemed from savage and indolent habits, devoted to the arts of peace, in touch with the commerce and trade of all nations, enjoying the blessings of freedom, of civil and religious liberty, of education, and of homes, and whose children's children shall for ages hence bless the American republic because it emancipated their fatherland, and set them in the pathway of the world's best civilization.

Filipinos, however, showed a remarkable unwillingness to "bless the American republic." The Philippine insurrection against the United States lasted three bloody years. By the end of 1900 approximately 74,000 United States troops were in the Philippines. The conquerors suffered hundreds of casualties, but inflicted thousands on the rebels and even resorted to brutal torture, repression, and atrocities. By 1902 the Philippine insurrection had been crushed.

It has been argued that the acquisition of a colonial empire set the United States on an almost inexorable road toward involvement in world politics, problems, and wars. To those critics our actions in Eastern Europe, the Middle East, and Southeast Asia were but the logical extensions of our imperialistic adventures begun in 1898, adventures that robbed the resources of other nations and repressed the desires of other peoples. On the other hand, as one of the world's largest agricultural, commercial, and industrial nations, the United States could hardly avoid becoming embroiled in world affairs. Too, technological innovations in transportation and telecom-

Chapter 5
America's Rise to
World Power:
The Senate
Debate over the
Philippines, 1899

munications made the world seem smaller to its inhabitants and made nations' involvements in the affairs of others seem more logical and imperative.

To be sure, the United States has not always acted wisely or well in world affairs. But it is questionable whether the United States would have acted much differently if it had decided in 1899 not to pursue a policy of expansionism. Numerous impulses — economic, political, and intellectual — obliged Americans in the twentieth century to reassess their long-cherished isolation. The growing need for raw materials and worldwide consumers of manufactured goods made economic imperialism at least as important as the political acquisition of colonies. Yet as Americans ventured out into the world they often took with them notions of racial, cultural, and moral superiority that would ultimately undercut their own desires and self-image. Armed with hindsight, one can see many of the roots of America's opportunities and problems in the world in the 1899 Senate debate.

Chapter 6

Homogenizing a Pluralistic Culture: Propaganda During World War I

Although the United States by the early twentieth century had worldwide economic interests and even had acquired a modest colonial empire, many Americans wanted to believe that they were insulated from world affairs and impervious to world problems. Two great oceans seemed to protect the nation from overseas threats and problems, and the very enormity of the country and the comparative weakness of its neighbors appeared to secure it against all dangers. Let other nations waste their people and resources in petty wars over status and territory, Americans reasoned, but the United States should stand above such greed or insanity, and certainly should not wade in foreign mudpuddles.

To many Americans, European nations were especially suspect. For centuries European nations had engaged in an almost ceaseless round of armed conflicts, wars for national unity or territory or even religion or empire. Moreover, in the eyes of many Americans, these bloody wars appeared to have solved little or nothing, and the end of one war seemed to be but a prelude to the next. Ambitious kings and their plotting ministers seemed to make Europe the scene of almost constant uproar, an uproar that many Americans saw as devoid of reason and morality. Nor did it appear that the United States, as powerful as it was, could have any effect on the unstable European situation.

For this reason most Americans greeted news of the outbreak of war in Europe in 1914 with equal measures of surprise and determination to not become involved. They applauded

[165]

Chapter 6
Homogenizing a
Pluralistic
Culture:
Propaganda
During World
War I

President Woodrow Wilson's August 4 proclamation of neutrality, his statement (issued two weeks later) urging Americans to be impartial in thought as well as in deed, and his insistence that the United States continue neutral commerce with all the belligerents. Few Americans protested German violation of Belgian neutrality. Indeed, most Americans (naively, as it turned out) believed that the United States both should and could remain aloof from the conflict in Europe.

But many factors pulled the United States into the conflict that later became known as World War I. For one thing, America's economic prosperity to a large extent rested on commercial ties with Europe. United States trade with the Allies (England, France, Russia) exceeded $800 million in 1914, whereas trade with the Central Powers (Germany, Austria, Turkey) stood at approximately $170 million in that same year. Much of the trade with Great Britain and France was financed through loans from American banks, something President Wilson and Secretary of State William Jennings Bryan openly discouraged, since both believed those economic interests might eventually draw the United States into the conflict. Indeed, Wilson and Bryan probably were correct. Yet America's continued economic well-being virtually depended on that trade, and ultimately Wilson and Bryan had to back down.

A second factor pulling the United States into the war was the deep-seated feelings of President Wilson himself. Formerly a constitutional historian (Wilson had been a college professor and university president before entering the political arena as a reform governor of New Jersey), Wilson had long admired the British people and their form of government. Though technically neutral, the president strongly, although privately, favored the Allies and viewed a German victory as unthinkable. Moreover, many of Wilson's key advisers and the people close to him were decidedly pro-British. Such was the opinion of the president's friend and closest adviser Colonel Edward House, as well as that of Robert Lansing (who replaced Bryan as secretary of state) and Walter Hines Page (ambassador to England). These men and others helped to strengthen Wilson's strong political opinions and influence the president's changing position toward the war in Europe. Hence, while Wilson asked Americans to be neutral in thought as well as in deed, in fact he and his principal advisers were neither. When it appeared that the Central Powers might outlast their enemies, Wilson was determined to intercede.

A third factor affecting the United States' neutrality was the strong ethnic ties of many Americans to the Old World. Many Americans had been born in Europe and even a larger number were the sons and daughters of European immigrants (Tables 1 and 2). Although these people considered themselves to be, and were, Americans, some retained emotional ties to

TABLE 1 Foreign-Born Population, by Country of Birth*

Country of Birth	Total Foreign Born
England	813,853
Scotland	254,570
Ireland	1,037,234
Germany	1,686,108
Austria	575,627
Russia	1,400,495

* Both this and Table 2 were compiled from the United States census of 1920, the closest census to America's entrance into World War I (1917). The figures on Ireland include Northern Ireland, and the figures on Russia include the Baltic States.

TABLE 2 Native-Born Population of Foreign or Mixed Parentage, by Country of Origin

Country of Origin of Parents	Total Native-Born Children
England and Wales	1,864,345
Scotland	514,436
Ireland	3,122,013
Germany	5,346,004
Austria	1,235,097
Russia	1,508,604

Europe that they sometimes carried into the political arena — ties that could influence America's foreign policy.

Finally, as the largest neutral commercial power in the world, the United States soon became caught in the middle of the commercial warfare of the belligerents. With the declaration of war, Great Britain and Ger-

many both threw up naval blockades. Great Britain's blockade was designed to cut the Central Powers off from war material. American commercial vessels bound for Germany were stopped, searched, and often seized by the British navy. Wilson protested British policy many times, but to no effect. After all, the British navy was one of that nation's principal sources of military strength.

Germany's blockade was even more dangerous, partly because the vast majority of American trade was with England and France. In addition, however, Germany's chief method of blockading the Allies was the use of the submarine, a comparatively new weapon in 1914. Because of the nature of the submarine (lethal while underwater, not equal to other fighting vessels on the surface), it was difficult for the submarine to remain effective and at the same time adhere to international law, such as the requirement to give sufficient warning before sinking an enemy ship. In 1915, hoping to terrorize the British into making peace, Germany unleashed its submarines in the Atlantic with orders to sink all ships flying Allied flags. In March a German submarine sank the British passenger ship *Falaba.* Then on May 7, 1915, the British liner *Lusitania* was sunk with a loss of over one thousand lives, 128 of them American. Although Germany had published warnings in American newspapers specifically cautioning Americans not to travel on the *Lusitania* and although it was ultimately discovered

Chapter 6
*Homogenizing a
Pluralistic
Culture:
Propaganda
During World
War I*

that the *Lusitania* had gone down so fast (in only eighteen minutes) because the British were shipping ammunition in the hold of the passenger ship, Americans were shocked by the Germans' actions on the high seas. Most Americans, however, continued to believe that the United States should stay out of the war and approved of Wilson's statement, issued three days after the *Lusitania* went to the bottom, that "There is such a thing as a man being too proud to fight."

Yet a combination of economic interests, German submarine warfare, and other events gradually pushed the United States toward involvement. In early February 1917, Germany announced a policy of unrestricted submarine warfare against all ships — belligerent and neutral alike. Ships would be sunk without warning if found to be in what Germany designated forbidden waters. Later that month the British intercepted a secret telegram intended for the German minister in Mexico. In that telegram German foreign secretary Arthur Zimmermann offered Mexico a deal: Germany would help Mexico retrieve territory lost to the United States in the 1840s if Mexico would make a military alliance with Germany. Knowing the impact such a telegram would make on American public opinion, the British quickly handed the telegram over to Wilson, who released it to the press. From that point, United States involvement in World War I

was but a matter of time. On April 2, 1917, the president asked Congress for a declaration of war. On April 4 the Senate approved a war declaration (the vote was 82–6), and the House of Representatives followed suit two days later (with a vote of 373–50).[1] And so Americans became embroiled in a war that for three years they had sought so strenuously to avoid.

One week after the House approved the war declaration, President Wilson signed Executive Order 2594, which created the Committee on Public Information, designed to mobilize public opinion behind the war effort. Apparently there was considerable worry in the Wilson administration that the American public, which had supported neutrality and noninvolvement, would not rally to the war effort. That year the Bureau of the Census had estimated that approximately 4,662,000 people living in the United States had been born in Germany or one of the other Central Powers.[2] As Tables 1 and 2 show, the United States also contained a large

1. The fifty-six votes in the Senate and House against the declaration of war essentially came from three separate groups: senators and congressmen with strong German and Austrian constituencies, isolationists who believed the United States should not become involved on either side, and some Progressive reformers who maintained that the war would divert America's attention from political, economic, and social reforms.

2. No census had been taken since 1910, so this was a very rough guess. As shown in Table 1, it was much too high.

number of Irish-Americans, many of whom were vehemently anti-British and hence emotionally sided with the Central Powers. Could this heterogeneous society be persuaded voluntarily to support the war effort? Could Americans of the same ethnic stock as the enemies be rallied to the cause?

Further, there had been no decisive event to prompt the war declaration (some even thought the Zimmermann telegram was a British hoax). Would Americans support such a war with sufficient unanimity? No firing on Fort Sumter or blowing up of the battleship *Maine* had forced America's entrance into World War I. The *Lusitania* sinking had occurred two years before the war declaration. Without the obvious threat of having been attacked, would the American people stand together to defeat the faraway enemy? Could American isolationist and noninterventionist opinion, very strong as late as the presidential election of 1916, be overcome?

To head the Committee on Public Information, Wilson selected forty-one-year-old journalist and political ally George Creel. Creel rapidly established voluntary press censorship, which made the committee essentially the overseer of all war and war-related news. The committee also produced films, engaged some 75,000 lecturers (called "Four Minute Men") who delivered approximately 7.5 million talks, commissioned posters intended to stir up support for the war and sell war bonds (seven hundred poster designs were submitted and over nine million posters were printed in 1918 alone), and engaged in numerous other activities to blend this ethnically and ideologically diverse nation into a homogeneous nation in support of the country's war effort.

In this chapter you are asked to analyze the propaganda techniques of a modern nation at war. The evidence contains material sponsored or commissioned by the Committee on Public Information (posters, newspaper advertisements, selections of speeches by Four Minute Men) as well as privately produced works (musical lyrics and commercial films) that tended to parallel the committee's efforts. Essentially, then, the question you are to answer is: how did the United States mobilize public opinion in support of the nation's participation in World War I? In addition, what were the consequences, positive and negative, of this mobilization of public opinion?

The Method

For George Creel and the Committee on Public Information, the purposes of propaganda were very clear:

1. to unite a multiethnic, pluralistic society behind the war effort

2. to attract a sufficient number of men to the armed services and to elicit universal civilian support for those men

Chapter 6
Homogenizing a
Pluralistic
Culture:
Propaganda
During World
War I

3. to influence civilians to support the war effort by purchasing war bonds or by other actions (such as limiting personal consumption or rolling bandages)

4. to influence civilians to put pressure on other civilians to refrain from antiwar comments, strikes, antidraft activities, unwitting dispersal of information to spies, and other acts that could hurt the war effort

To achieve these ends, propaganda techniques had to be employed with extreme care. For propaganda to be effective, it would have to contain one or more of the following features:

1. a portrayal of American and Allied servicemen in the best possible light

2. a portrayal of the enemy in the worst possible light

3. a portrayal of the American and Allied cause as just and the enemy's cause as unjust

4. a message to civilians that they were being involved in the war effort in important ways

5. a communication of a sense of urgency to civilians

In this chapter you are given the following six types of World War I propaganda to analyze, some of it produced directly by the Committee on Public Information and some produced privately but examined by the committee:

1. popular songs performed in music halls or vaudeville houses. Although the Committee on Public Information did not produce this material, it could have discouraged performances of "unpatriotic" material.

2. newspaper and magazine advertisements produced directly by the Committee on Public Information.

3. posters, approved by the committee and used for recruiting, liberty loans, and other purposes.

4. an editorial cartoon, produced privately but generally approved by the committee.

5. a selection of speeches by Four Minute Men, volunteers engaged by the committee to speak in theaters, churches, and other gatherings. Their speeches were not to exceed four minutes in length — hence, their name. The committee published a newsletter that offered suggestions and material for speaking topics.

6. a review of the documentary film *Pershing's Crusaders,* 1918, and some advertising suggestions to theater owners concerning the film *Kultur.* The film industry was largely self-censored, but the committee could — and did — stop the distribution of films that, in its opinion, hurt the war effort. *Pershing's Crusaders* was a committee-produced film, whereas *Kultur* was a commercial production.

As you examine the evidence, you will see that effective propaganda operates on two levels. On the surface there is the logical appeal for support to help win the war. On another level, however, certain images and themes are employed to excite the emotions of the people for whom the propaganda is designed. As you examine the evidence, ask yourself the following questions:

1. For whom is this piece of propaganda designed?

2. What is this piece of propaganda trying to get people to think? To do?

3. What logical appeal is being made?

4. What emotional appeals are being made?

5. What might be the results, positive and negative, of these kinds of appeals?

In songs, speeches, advertisements, and film reviews, are there key words, important images? Where there are illustrations (advertisements, posters, cartoons), what facial expressions and images are used? Finally, are there any common logical and emotional themes running through American propaganda during World War I? How did the United States use propaganda to mobilize public opinion during World War I? What were some of the consequences, positive and negative, of this type of propaganda?

The Evidence

POPULAR SONGS

"Over There" (1917), by George M. Cohan

Johnnie, get your gun,
Get your gun, get your gun,
Take it on the run,
On the run, on the run.
Hear them calling you and me,
Every son of liberty.
Hurry right away,
No delay, no delay,
Make your daddy glad
To have had such a lad.

Chapter 6
Homogenizing a
Pluralistic
Culture:
Propaganda
During World
War I

Tell your sweetheart not to pine,
To be proud her boy's in line.
(repeat chorus twice)

Chorus
Over there, over there,
Send the word, send the word over there —
That the Yanks are coming,
The Yanks are coming,
The drums rum-tumming
Ev'rywhere.
So prepare, say a pray'r,
Send the word, send the word to beware.
We'll be over, we're coming over,
And we won't come back till it's over
Over there.

From Alfred E. Cornbise, War as Advertised: The Four Minute Men and America's Crusade, 1917–1918 *(Philadelphia: American Philosophical Society, 1984), p. 70.*

Untitled

*(To be sung to a variation
of the tune of
"My Country Tis of Thee")*

Come, freemen of the land,
Come meet the great demand,
True heart and open hand,
    Take the loan!
For the hopes that prophets saw,
For the swords your brothers draw,
For liberty and law
    Take the loan!

[172]

"Hello, Central! Give Me No Man's Land" (1918), Recorded by Al Jolson

When the gray shadows creep
And the world is asleep,
In the still of the night
Baby climbs down a flight.
First she looks all around
Without making a sound;
Then baby toddles up to the telephone
And whispers in a baby tone:

Chorus
Hello, Central! Give me No Man's Land,
My daddy's there, my mamma told me;
She tip-toed off to bed
After my prayers were said;
Don't ring when you get the number,
Or you'll disturb mamma's slumber.
I'm afraid to stand here at the 'phone
'Cause I'm alone,
So won't you hurry;
I want to know why mamma starts to weep
When I say, "Now I lay me down to sleep",
Hello, Central! Give me No Man's Land.
(*repeat chorus*)

Chapter 6
Homogenizing a
Pluralistic
Culture:
Propaganda
During World
War I

ADVERTISEMENTS

FIGURE 1 *(From James R. Mock and Cedric Larson,* Words That Won the War: The Story of the Committee on Public Information *(Princeton: Princeton University Press,* © 1939)*, after p. 64.)*

Spies *and* Lies

German agents are everywhere, eager to gather scraps of news about our men, our ships, our munitions. It is still possible to get such information through to Germany, where thousands of these fragments — often individually harmless — are patiently pieced together into a whole which spells death to American soldiers and danger to American homes.

But while the enemy is most industrious in trying to collect information, and his systems elaborate, he is *not* superhuman — indeed he is often very stupid, and would fail to get what he wants were it not deliberately handed to him by the carelessness of loyal Americans.

Do not discuss in public, or with strangers, any news of troop and transport movements, or bits of gossip as to our military preparations, which come into your possession.

Do not permit your friends in service to tell you or write you "inside" facts about where they are, what they are doing and seeing.

Do not become a tool of the Hun by passing on the malicious, disheartening rumors which he so eagerly sows. Remember he asks no better service than to have you spread his lies of disasters to our soldiers and sailors, gross scandals in the Red Cross, cruelties, neglect and wholesale executions in our camps, drunkenness and vice in the Expeditionary Force, and other tales certain to disturb American patriots and to bring anxiety and grief to American parents.

And do not wait until you catch someone putting a bomb under a factory. Report the man who spreads pessimistic stories, divulges — or seeks — confidential military information, cries for peace, or belittles our efforts to win the war.

Send the names of such persons, even if they are in uniform, to the Department of Justice, Washington. Give all the details you can, with names of witnesses if possible — show the Hun that we can beat him at his own game of collecting scattered information and putting it to work. The fact that you made the report will not become public.

You are in contact with the enemy today, just as truly as if you faced him across No Man's Land. In your hands are two powerful weapons with which to meet him — discretion and vigilance. *Use them.*

COMMITTEE ON PUBLIC INFORMATION
8 JACKSON PLACE, WASHINGTON, D. C.

George Creel, Chairman
The Secretary of State
The Secretary of War
The Secretary of the Navy

Contributed through Division of Advertising *United States Gov't Comm. on Public Information*

FIGURE 2   *(From Mock and Larson, p. 169.)*   *The Evidence*

Bachelor *of* Atrocities

IN the vicious guttural language of Kultur, the degree A. B.
means Bachelor of Atrocities.   Are you going to let the Prussian
Python strike at your Alma Mater, as it struck at the University
of Louvain?

The Hohenzollern fang strikes at every
element of decency and culture and taste
that your college stands for.   It leaves a
track so terrible that only whispered
fragments may be recounted.   It has
ripped all the world-old romance out of
war, and reduced it to the dead, black
depths of muck, and hate, and bitterness.

You may soon be called to fight.   But
you are called upon right now to buy
Liberty Bonds.   You are called upon to
economize in every way.   It is sometimes
harder to live nobly than to die nobly.
The supreme sacrifice of life may come
easier than the petty sacrifices of com-
forts and luxuries.   You are called to
exercise stern self-discipline.   Upon this
the Allied Success depends.

Set aside every possible dollar for the
purchase of Liberty Bonds.   Do it
relentlessly.   Kill every wasteful impulse,
that America may live.   Every bond
you buy fires point-blank at Prussian
Terrorism.

BUY U. S. GOVERNMENT BONDS FOURTH LIBERTY LOAN

Contributed through Division
of Advertising

United States Gov't Comm.
on Public Information

This space contributed for the Winning of the War by
A. T SKERRY, '84, and CYRILLE CARREAU, '04.

Chapter 6
Homogenizing a
Pluralistic
Culture:
Propaganda
During World
War I

FIGURE 3   *(From Mock and Larson, p. 98.)*

THE GERMAN IDEA

SHALL this war make Germany's word the highest law in the world?
Read what she expects.   Here are the words of her own spokesmen.
Then ask yourself where Germany would have the United States
stand after the war.

Shall we bow to Germany's wishes--assist German ambition?

No.   The German idea must be so completely crushed that it will
never again rear its venomous head.

It's a fight, as the President said, "to the last dollar, the last drop
of blood."

THE AMERICAN IDEA

The President's Flag Day Speech, With
Evidence of Germany's plans.   32
pages.
The War Message and the Facts Be-
hind It.   32 pages.
The Nation in Arms.   16 pages.
Why We Fight Germany.
War, Labor and Peace.

THE GERMAN IDEA

Conquest and Kultur.   160 pages.
German War Practices.   96 pages.
Treatment of German Militarism and
German Critics.
The German War Code.

COMMITTEE ON PUBLIC INFORMATION
8 JACKSON PLACE, WASHINGTON, D. C.

Contributed through Divi-
sion of Advertising, United
States Governm't Committee
on Public Information

George Creel, Chairman
The Secretary of State
The Secretary of War
The Secretary of the Navy

This space contributed for the Winning of the War by

The Publisher of

POSTERS

FIGURE 4 *(From* The James Montgomery Flagg Poster Book, *introduction by Susan E. Meyer (New York: Watson-Guptill Publications, © 1975). Courtesy of the Library of Congress.)*

Chapter 6
Homogenizing a
Pluralistic
Culture:
Propaganda
During World
War I

FIGURE 5 *(From Peter Stanley,* What Did You Do in the War, Daddy? *(Melbourne: Oxford University Press, © 1983), p. 55.)*

FIGURE 7 (*From* The James Montgomery Flagg Poster Book.)

FIGURE 7 (*From* The James Montgomery Flagg Poster Book.)

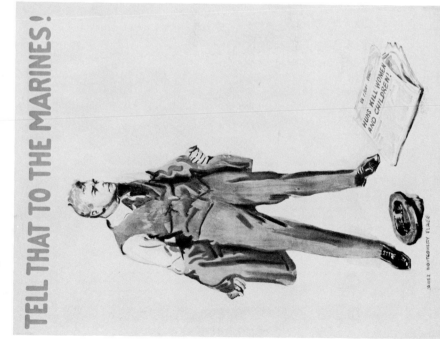

FIGURE 6 (*From* The James Montgomery Flagg Poster Book.)

[179]

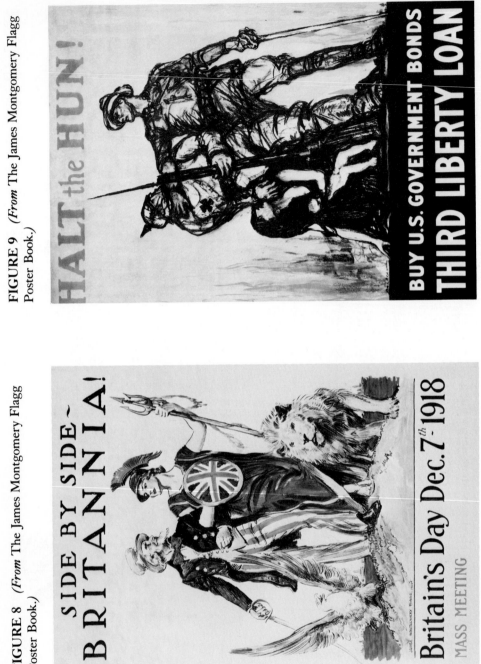

FIGURE 8 (*From* The James Montgomery Flagg Poster Book.)

FIGURE 9 (*From* The James Montgomery Flagg Poster Book.)

FIGURE 10   *(From Stanley, p. 65.)*   *The Evidence*

Chapter 6
Homogenizing a
Pluralistic
Culture:
Propaganda
During World
War I

FIGURE 11 *(From Joseph Darracott, ed.,* The First World War in Posters *(New York: Dover Publications, © 1974), p. 30.)*

Chapter 6
Homogenizing a
Pluralistic
Culture:
Propaganda
During World
War I

FIGURE 14 *(From Anthony Crawford,* Posters in the George C. Marshall Research Foundation *(Charlottesville: University of Virginia Press, © 1939), p. 30.)*

FIGURE 15 *(From Darracott, p. 40.)*

FIGURE 16 German-American Dr. Karl Muck, conductor of the Boston Symphony Orchestra, needed a police escort when he conducted a concert in March 1918 in New York City. *(From John Higham,* Strangers in the Land: Patterns of American Nativism, *1860–1925 (New Brunswick, N.J.: Rutgers University Press, 1955), after p. 210.)*

Selection of speeches by Four Minute Men from Alfred E. Cornbise, War as Advertised: The Four Minute Men and America's Crusade, *1917–1918 (Philadelphia: American Philosophical Society, 1984), pp. 72–73, 122, 60, and 27, respectively.*

SPEECH BY A
FOUR MINUTE MAN

Ladies and Gentlemen:

I have just received the information that there is a German spy among us — a German spy watching *us.*

Chapter 6
Homogenizing a
Pluralistic
Culture:
Propaganda
During World
War I

He is around, here somewhere, reporting upon you and me — sending reports about us to Berlin and telling the Germans just what we are doing with the Liberty Loan. From every section of the country these spies have been getting reports over to Potsdam — not general reports but details — where the loan is going well and where its success seems weak, and what people are saying in each community.

For the German Government is worried about our great loan. Those Junkers fear its effect upon the German *morale*. They're raising a loan this month, too.

If the American people lend their billions now, one and all with a hip-hip-hurrah, it means that America is united and strong. While, if we lend our money half-heartedly, America seems weak and autocracy remains strong.

Money means everything now; it means quicker victory and therefore less bloodshed. We are *in* the war, and now Americans can have but *one* opinion, only *one* wish in the Liberty Loan.

Well, I hope these spies are getting their messages straight, letting Potsdam know that America *is hurling back* to the autocrats these answers:

For treachery here, attempted treachery in Mexico, treachery everywhere — *one billion*.

For murder of American women and children — *one billion more*.

For broken faith and promise to murder more Americans — *billions and billions more*.

And then we will add:

In the world fight for Liberty, our share — *billions and billions and BILLIONS and endless billions*.

Do not let the German spy hear and report that *you* are a slacker.

PART OF A SPEECH BY A
FOUR MINUTE MAN

German agents are telling the people of this . . . race through the South that if they will not oppose the German Government, or help our Government, they will be rewarded with Ford automobiles when Germany is in control here. They are told that 10 negroes are being conscripted to 1 white man in order that the Negro race may be killed off; and that the reason Germany went into Belgium was to punish the people of that country for the cruel treatment of the negroes in the Congo.

POEM READ BY
FOUR MINUTE MEN

"It's Duty Boy"

My boy must never bring disgrace to his immortal sires —
At Valley Forge and Lexington they kindled freedom's fires,
John's father died at Gettysburg, mine fell at Chancellorsville;
While John himself was with the boys who charged up San Juan Hill.
And John, if he was living now, would surely say with me,
"No son of ours shall e'er disgrace our grand old family tree
By turning out a slacker when his country needs his aid."
It is not of such timber that America was made.
I'd rather you had died at birth or not been born at all,
Than know that I had raised a son who cannot hear the call
That freedom has sent round the world, its precious rights to save —
This call is meant for you, my boy, and I would have you brave;
And though my heart is breaking, boy, I bid you do your part,
And show the world no son of mine is cursed with craven heart;
And if, perchance, you ne'er return, my later days to cheer,
And I have only memories of my brave boy, so dear,
I'd rather have it so, my boy, and know you bravely died
Than have a living coward sit supinely by my side.
To save the world from sin, my boy, God gave his only son —
He's asking for MY boy, to-day, and may His will be done.

POEM READ BY
FOUR MINUTE MEN

Attention, Mr. Farmer Man, and listen now to me,
and I will try and show to you what I can plainly see.
Your Uncle Sam, the dear old man who's been so good to you,
is needing help and watching now to see what you will do.
Your Uncle's in the great world war and since he's entered in
it's up to every one of us to see that he shall win.
He's trying hard to "speed things up" and do it with a dash,
and so just now he's asking you to aid him with your cash.

[187]

*Chapter 6
Homogenizing a
Pluralistic
Culture:
Propaganda
During World
War I*

Remember, all he asks of you is but a simple loan,
and every patriot comes across without a single moan.
Should Uncle Sammy once get mad (he will if you get lax),
he then will exercise his right, and make you pay a tax.
Should Kaiser Bill and all his hordes, once get across the Pond,
d'ye think he'll waste his time on you, and coax to take a bond?
Why no, siree. He'd grab and hold most everything he saw.
He'd take your farm, your stock and lands, your wife and babies all.
He'd make you work, he'd make you sweat, he'd squeeze you till you'd groan.
So be a man, and come across. Let Uncle have that loan.

FILM REVIEW OF
PERSHING'S CRUSADERS

From Literary Digest, *June 8, 1918.*

Seeing Our Boys
"Over There"

MULTIFORM ARE THE WAR-ACTIVITIES of Uncle Sam. Whoever would have thought of him a year ago as an *impresario* in moving pictures? In a small way this has been one of his war-activities, but now he boldly challenges competition with the biggest and launches his "Pershing's Crusaders" for the benefit of the American Army, the American Navy, and the Allied War-Relief. The initial performance at the Lyric Theater, New York, brought out an audience that might have swelled to the dimensions of a Metropolitan Opera crowd if capacity had permitted. Mr. E. H. Sothern and our former Ambassador to Germany, Mr. James W. Gerard, were present to speak, but the pictures of the boys at the front were the thing, and the country will eagerly await the sight of her sons in their present environment here and "over there." As described by the *New York Tribune*, we learn that —

> Whoever took the pictures have not depended on the popularity of the subject alone, for they show a fine attention to detail that is most satisfying, when everything connected with the boys at the front is of vital interest.
> The pictures show "the mailed fist of the world," and altho this is merely symbolic, it is such a telling hit that it is impossible not to mention it. Germany and France are shown as tho modeled in clay, and then slowly, out of the center of

Germany, rises a volcano, and a huge mailed fist appears scattering mud and sand and lava over France.

The first part of the picture shows how plots, fires, strikes, etc., were fomented by German agents in America; how America is putting her hand to the plow to feed the Allies; the huge cantonments which have sprung up to house the Army; cutting the khaki clothes by machinery. Other subjects are: What American women are doing; how the army shoes are made; feeding America's Army; mighty ships in the building; supremacy in the air will strike down the German vultures; our Navy; camouflage of the sea; our own submarines; in the aviation camps; baptizing the boys ordered to the front; tenderness and skill at the dressing-stations; the sniper's job; the victor of yesterday and the victor of to-morrow, and Pershing's crusaders and their Allies, who will get the Kaiser.

FIGURE 17   *(From* The Moving Picture World, *September 28, 1918.)*

ADVERTISING AIDS FOR BUSY MANAGERS
"KULTUR."

William Fox Presents Gladys Brockwell in a Typical Example of the Brutality of the Wilhelmstrasse to Its Spy-slaves.

Cast.

Countess Griselda Von Arenburg,	Gladys Brockwell
Eliska	Georgia Woodthorpe
René de Bornay	William Scott
Baron von Zeller	Willard Louis
Archduke Franz Ferdinand	Charles Clary
Danilo	Nigel de Brullier
The Kaiser	William Burress
Emperor Franz Josef	Alfred Fremont

Directed by Edward J. Le Saint.

The Story: The Kaiser decides that the time is ripe for a declaration of war, and sends word to his vassal monarch of Austria. René de Bornay is sent by France to discover what is being planned. He meets the Countess, who falls in love with him. She sickens of the spy system and declares that she is done with it, but is warned that she cannot withdraw. She is told to secure René's undoing, but instead procures his escape and in her own boudoir is stood against the wall and shot for saving the man whom she loves better than her life.

Feature Gladys Brockwell as Countess Griselda Von Arenburg and William Scott as René de Bornay.

Program and Advertising Phrases: Gladys Brockwell, Star of Latest Picture, Exposing Hun Brutality and Satanic Intrigue.
How An Austrian Countess Gave Her All for Democracy.
She Was an Emperor's Favorite Yet She Died for World Freedom.
Story of an Emperor's Mistress and a Crime That Rocked the World.
Daring Exposure of Scandals and Crimes in Hun Court Circles.
Astonishing Revelations of Hun Plots to Rape Democracy.

Advertising Angles: Do not offer this as a propaganda story, but tell that it is one of the angles of the merciless Prussian spy system about which has been woven a real romance. Play up the spy angle heavily both in your newspaper work and through window cards with such lines as "even the spies themselves hate their degradation." Miss Brockwell wears some stunning and daring gowns in this play, and with these special appeal can be made to the women.

*Chapter 6
Homogenizing a
Pluralistic
Culture:
Propaganda
During World
War I*

Questions to Consider

The first three pieces of evidence are songs that were popular during World War I. Each song should be analyzed for its message. What was "Over There" urging young men to do? Why? What emotions were the lyrics trying to arouse? Both "Hello Central!" and the untitled song were directed at the home front. What where the sacrifices expected of Americans who did not go to war?

Next in the evidence are three advertisements (Figures 1–3) produced by the Committee on Public Information. How were the Germans portrayed in "Spies and Lies"? In "Bachelor of Atrocities"? In "The German Idea"? How could Americans counteract Germans and their actions? Were there any dangers inherent in the kinds of activities the CPI was urging on patriotic Americans?

In some ways poster art, which follows in the evidence, is similar to the art in editorial cartoons, principally because the artist has only one canvas or frame on which to tell his or her story. Yet the poster must be more arresting than the cartoon, must convey its message rapidly, and must avoid ambiguities or confusion. Posters were an extremely popular form of propaganda during World War I. Indeed, so popular were the posters of James Montgomery Flagg (1877–1960) that, along with other artists and entertainers, Flagg helped

sell $1,000 Liberty Bonds by performing (in his case painting posters) in front of the New York Public Library. The well-known "Tell That to the Marines" was created there.

As you examine the first four posters,[3] determine their intended audience. What emotional appeal did each make? What feelings did each poster seek to elicit? The eighth poster ("Side by Side") is quite different from its predecessors in this exercise. How is it different? What appeal was it making? The next two posters ("Halt the Hun" and "Remember Belgium") were intended to encourage American civilians to buy Liberty Bonds. What logical and emotional appeals were being made? How are the two posters similar? How did they use innuendos to make their point? See also the last poster presented in the evidence (Figure 15, "The Hun — his Mark"). How is that poster similar to the other two?

Each of the remaining four posters (Figures 11–14) was intended to elicit a different reaction from those who saw it. Yet they are remarkably similar in their logical and emotional appeals. What do these posters have in common? How are women portrayed in Figures 12–14?

The editorial cartoon from the

3. The first poster ("I Want YOU for the U.S. Army") by Flagg is the most famous American poster ever created. The idea was taken from a British poster by Alfred Leete, and Flagg drew himself as Uncle Sam. The poster is still used by the United States Army.

New York Herald (Figure 16) is self-explanatory. What emotions does the cartoon elicit? What actions, intended or unintended, might result from those emotions?

The four selections by the Four Minute Men are from the Committee on Public Information's *Bulletin,* which was distributed to all volunteer speakers (they also received a letter of commendation and a certificate from President Wilson after the war). What logical and emotional appeals were made in each selection?

No sound films were produced in the United States before 1927. Until that time a small orchestra or (more prevalent) a piano accompanied a film's showing. What dialogue there was — and there wasn't much — was done in subtitles. Therefore, the best means we have to learn about these films, short of actually viewing them, is to analyze movie reviews. The review presented in the evidence is of the film *Pershing's Crusaders,* a documentary produced by the Committee on Public Information in 1918.[4] Can you tell from the review what logical and emotional appeals were made in the film?

The advertising aids for the film *Kultur* (Figure 17) suggest a number of phrases and angles designed to attract audiences. What are the strongest emotional appeals that were suggested to theater owners? Do those same appeals also appear in the other evidence?

You must now summarize your findings and return to the central questions: How did the United States use propaganda to mobilize public opinion in support of our participation in World War I? What were the consequences, positive and negative, of the mobilization of public opinion?

Epilogue

The creation of the Committee on Public Information and its subsequent work shows that the Wilson administration had serious doubts concerning whether the American people, multiethnic and pluralistic as they were, would support the war effort with unanimity. And, to be sure, there was opposition to American involvement in the war, not only from socialist Eugene Debs and the left, but also from reformers Robert LaFollette, Jane Addams, and others. As it turned out, however, the Wilson administration's worst fears proved groundless. Americans of all ethnic backgrounds overwhelmingly supported the war effort, sometimes rivaling each other in patriotic ardor. How much of this unanimity can be attributed to patriotism and how much to the propaganda efforts of the Committee on Public Information will never really be known. Yet, for whatever reason, it can be said that the war

---

4. *Pershing's Crusaders* is in the National Archives in Washington, D.C.

Chapter 6
Homogenizing a
Pluralistic
Culture:
Propaganda
During World
War I

had a kind of unifying effect on the American people. Women sold Liberty Bonds, worked for such agencies as the Red Cross, rolled bandages, and cooperated in the government's efforts to conserve food and fuel. Indeed, even blacks sprang to the colors, reasoning, as did the president of Howard University, that service in the war might help blacks achieve long-withheld civil and political rights.

However, this homogenization was not without its price. Propaganda was so effective that it created a kind of national hysteria, sometimes with terrible results. Vigilante-type groups often shamefully persecuted German-Americans, lynching one German-American man of draft age for not having been in uniform (the man was physically ineligible, having only one eye) and badgering German-American children in and out of school. Many states forbade the teaching of German in schools, and a host of German words were purged from the language (sauerkraut became liberty cabbage, German measles became liberty measles, hamburgers became liberty steaks, frankfurters became hot dogs). The city of Cincinnati even banned pretzels from saloons. In such an atmosphere many Americans lived in genuine fear of being accused of spying or of becoming victims of intimidation or violence. In a society intent upon homogenization, being different could be dangerous.

During such hysteria one would expect the federal government in general and the Committee on Public Information in particular to have attempted to dampen the more extreme forms of vigilantism. However, it seemed as if the government had become the victim of its own propaganda. The postmaster-general (Albert Burleson), empowered to censor the mail, looking for examples of treason, insurrection, or forcible resistance to laws, used his power to suppress all socialist publications, all anti-British and pro-Irish mail, and anything that he believed threatened the war effort. One movie producer, Robert Goldstein, was sentenced to ten years in prison for releasing his film *The Spirit of '76* (about the American Revolution) because it portrayed the British in an unfavorable light.[5] Socialist party leader Eugene Debs was given a similar sentence for criticizing the war in a speech in Canton, Ohio. The left-wing union, Industrial Workers of the World (IWW), was broken. Freedom of speech, press, and assembly were violated countless times, and numerous lynchings, whippings, and tar and featherings occurred. Excesses by both government and private individuals were as effective in *forcing* homogeneity as were the voluntary efforts of American people of all backgrounds.

Once the hysteria had begun, it is doubtful whether even President Wil-

5. This gave rise to a court case with the improbable title *United States v. The Spirit of '76.*

son could have stopped it. Yet Wilson showed no inclination to do so, even stating that dissent was not appreciated by the government. Without the president to reverse the process, the hysteria continued unabated. Indeed, the movement toward homogenization continued after the war was over, climaxing in the Red Scare of 1919 and in increasing suspicion of "foreigners" and efforts to restrict their immigration.

As Americans approached the Second World War, some called for a revival of the Committee on Public Information. Yet President Franklin Roosevelt rejected this sweeping approach. The Office of War Information was created, but its role was a restricted one. Even so, Japanese-Americans were subjected to relocation and humiliation in one of the more shameful episodes of recent American history. In general, however, a different spirit pervaded the United States during World War II, a spirit generally more tolerant of American pluralism and less willing to stir Americans into an emotional frenzy.

And yet, the possibility that propaganda will create mass hysteria and thus endanger the civil rights of some Americans is present in every national crisis, especially in wartime. In the "total wars" of the twentieth century, in which civilians played as crucial a role as fighting men (in factories, in training facilities for soldiers, and in shipping soldiers and material to the front), the mobilization of the home front was a necessity. But could that kind of mobilization be carried too far?

Chapter 7

Stemming the Tide: Immigration and Nativism After World War I

The Problem

Years after impoverished immigrant Andrew Carnegie became a fabulously successful and wealthy American industrialist, philanthropist, and pillar of the community, he still recalled his childhood in his native Scotland, when his mother sang to him about faraway America:

> To the west, to the west, to the land of the free,
> When the mighty Missouri rolls down to the sea;
> Where a man is a man if he's willing to toil,
> And the humblest may gather the fruits of the soil;

> Where children are blessings and he who hath most
> Has aid for his fortune and riches to boast.
> Where the young may exult and the aged may rest,
> Away, far away, to the land of the West.

Carnegie's American experience, of course, was an exceptional one. Arriving in the United States as a youth (age thirteen) prior to the Civil War, he found work as a bobbin boy in a textile mill and then as a telegrapher in the Union army (he was incapacitated by sunstroke during the Battle of Bull Run). By saving his money and borrowing judiciously, Carnegie purchased a small iron company, which he ultimately built into one of the nation's largest and most successful industries. Believing that people had the obligation to use their money for the good of the community (Carnegie called it "stewardship"), he endowed libraries, schools, and concert halls, and became (along with oil baron John D. Rockefeller and banker J. P. Morgan) one of the most widely known figures of the Gilded Age. Truly, all the hopes his mother sang about seem to have come true.

Very few immigrants, however, were able to match Carnegie's success. Coming mostly from the small villages and rural areas of Europe, often with little more than their clothing and a few personal possessions, they found it impossible to acquire farmland on the fast-receding frontier. Instead, most immigrants huddled together in America's burgeoning industrial cities where opportunities for employment were greatest and where, with others of their respective ethnic groups, they could preserve their cultural heritage. Some achieved modest success and gradually bettered their lots, although many more ended their lives in America as they had begun them — in poverty, want, and insecurity.

The millions of men and women who immigrated to the United States during the nineteenth century formed one of the greatest mass migrations in human history. Like Carnegie, many came in search of economic opportunity. Others were drawn by the promise of religious toleration, political equality, or inexpensive farmland. And while these dreams were rarely realized, the dreams themselves continued to exert their power and drew still others to America's shores. Conversely, many immigrants were fleeing from conditions they found intolerable in their native countries: enforced army service and wars, religious and ethnic persecution, famine, and the conditions of peasantry. Indeed, the reasons for coming to America were many, and the number of immigrants who came seemed almost inexhaustible.

Collectively, the immigrants' contribution to American life was enormous. They provided the muscle that built the nation's canals and railroads. Immigrant women by the thousands found employment as domestic servants, thus allowing native upper- and middle-class women the time and opportunity to further their quest for "true womanhood." Immigrant men and boys swelled the ranks of the Union army as volunteers, draftees, and hired substitutes and were largely responsible for the numerical superiority that finally assured the North's victory in the Civil War. Immigrant men, women, and children provided most of the labor for America's industrialization, working long hours in

Chapter 7
Stemming the
Tide: Immigration
and Nativism
After World
War I

poor conditions for meager wages and thus assuring industrialists (like Carnegie, ironically) of high profits that could be used to expand their industries and further industrialize the nation. Undoubtedly the immigrants' collective legacy to modern industrial America was almost incalculable.

Cultural life was a different story altogether. While immigrants were permitted to retain their religious preferences and their folk traditions, in general they were expected to meld into the dominant American culture: learn English, accept American political traditions and institutions, adopt "American" values of hard work, thrift, and deferred gratification, and become almost indistinguishable from any other American on the streets. This forced some immigrants into a kind of cultural dualism (preserving their native culture while simultaneously adopting the basic components of the dominant American culture), but most accommodated to this dualism rather smoothly and successfully. In their minds they were Americans, but Americans who purposely retained some of their Old-World traditions. And occasionally a few segments of their Old-World traditions were absorbed into the dominant mainstream (a so-called traditional American Christmas, for example, is in fact a conglomeration of British, Dutch, German, Scandinavian, and central-European traditions). Indeed, seen against the ethnic and religious conflicts occurring in Europe, this dual process was a comparatively smooth one.

This is not to say, however, that all native Americans welcomed immigrants with open arms or saw cultural dualism as healthy. As early as the 1790s, the nation's reception of new arrivals was decidedly mixed. Federalists warned darkly of "wild Irishmen" and "French Jacobins" who, they believed, threatened American life. For his part, Thomas Jefferson, the Federalists' principal foe, feared that immigrants from Europe did not possess native American traditions of freedom, virtue, and republicanism. In the 1840s and 1850s anti-immigrant sentiment was extremely strong, largely because a high proportion of arrivals were Roman Catholics. Samuel F. B. Morse, the inventor of the telegraph, wrote a hysterial attack on Roman Catholic immigrants[1] in which he charged that there was a Jesuit plot to subvert American institutions:

> Will you be longer deceived by the pensioned Jesuits . . . ? Up! Up! I beseech you. Awake! To your posts! Let the tocsin[2] sound from Maine to

1. An American [Samuel F. B. Morse], *Immigrant Dangers to the Free Institutions of the United States Through Foreign Immigration* (New York: E. B. Clayton, 1835), p. 25. Morse (1791–1872) received his patent for the telegraph in 1840.

2. A tocsin is an alarm sounded on a bell; a warning.

Louisiana. Fly to protect the vulnerable places of your Constitution and Laws. Place your guards; you will need them, and quickly too. — And first, shut your gates. Shut the open gates. The very first step of safety is here.

In such a highly charged atmosphere, anti-immigrant feeling led to discrimination, persecution, and occasional violence. In fact, many immigrants found the very conditions they sought to escape as bad or even worse in the New World.

Anti-immigrant sentiment again became strong in the late nineteenth and early twentieth centuries. A combination of several factors contributed to this nativist fervor. The Bureau of the Census announced the "closing" of the American frontier in 1890, causing many to fear that immigrant hordes would have no opportunities and would wind up as paupers, criminals, and drains on America's resources. Those who investigated the urban slums in which many immigrants lived were shocked and repelled and could see no way of absorbing more people from the Old World. Fear of political radicalism and labor violence prompted some to question whether America should welcome troublemakers from elsewhere. Economic depressions caused others to wonder if more immigrants would simply mean fewer jobs for native Americans. Many American workers (some of them, ironically, former immigrants) feared that more arrivals would glut the labor market and drive wages down. Anti–Roman Catholic feeling was still strong and, since an increasing number of immigrants were Jews primarily from Russia and Poland,[3] was accompanied by a virulent anti-Semitism. At the same time, "scientific" notions of racial purity, mongrelization, and Social Darwinism were the vogue among many intellectuals, theologians, editors, and government officials. Together, these and other factors stoked nativist feeling to a high pitch around the turn of the century.

There were several efforts in the nineteenth century to restrict immigration, but except for the Chinese Exclusion Act of 1882, most were confined to weeding out "undesirables." In 1882 Congress passed the first comprehensive federal immigration law, denying admission to convicts, lunatics, idiots, and incapacitated persons likely to become public charges. In 1885 Congress prohibited the overseas recruitment of unskilled labor and in 1891 added polygamists

3. The shift in the source of American immigration was marked. Between 1881 and 1890, 72 percent of all immigrants came from northern and western Europe, whereas only 18.2 percent came from eastern, central, and southern Europe. Between 1901 and 1910, however, only 21.7 percent came from northern and western Europe while the proportion of eastern, central, and southern European immigrants had risen to 70.8 percent.

Chapter 7
Stemming the
Tide: Immigration
and Nativism
After World
War I

and "persons suffering from a loathsome or dangerous contagious disease" to the restrictions list. In 1903 anarchists, saboteurs, professional beggars, and epileptics were barred. Beginning in 1896 Congress made several attempts to impose literacy requirements on prospective immigrants, but all such efforts were blocked by presidential vetoes until 1917 when President Woodrow Wilson allowed a literacy test for immigrants to become law.[4]

Until World War I, however, most Americans seem to have believed that the solution to the problem was to "Americanize" the immigrants rather than restrict their entrance. Indeed, the idea of absorbing the immigrants into the American mainstream (known as the "melting pot" idea) was extremely strong. Public educators, the Daughters of the American Revolution, the Society of Colonial Dames, the Committee for Immigrants in America, various "Americanization Day" committees, the National Americanization Committee, the General Federation of Women's Clubs, and the United States Chamber of Commerce all endorsed plans to "Americanize" the immigrants and achieve

4. For a full discussion of immigration legislation see Stephan Thernstrom, ed., *Harvard Encyclopedia of American Ethnic Groups* (Cambridge, Mass.: Belknap Press, 1980), pp. 490–495. Even before 1882 some states, notably California, had passed immigration restriction laws.

the goal of cultural uniformity. Campaigns to teach immigrants to speak English and learn American history were widespread, and the motto "Many Peoples, But One Nation" was heard throughout the country.

But during and especially after the war, public opinion began to shift markedly away from absorbing the immigrants and toward restricting immigration altogether. As we have already seen, some native Americans had advocated immigration restrictions since the beginning of the republic. Until 1917–1921, however, that sentiment had never been held by a sufficient majority of native Americans to prompt Congress to act. Your task in this chapter is to assess the evidence and explain why American public opinion appears to have changed so rapidly.

The Method

Assessing shifts in public opinion is no easy task — and certainly not a very scientific one. Even pollsters and public opinion analysts, armed with an abundance of techniques, money, and computer assistance, cannot be very precise as to why public opinion changes but conclude only that it does change. Historians examining the past, of course, are at an even greater disadvantage.

Historians can, however, collect the material to which the public has access (newspapers, speeches, books, magazine articles, pamphlets, statistics, even surviving rumors) and arrange that material to determine which arguments are most often repeated. Then they can collect information on events and trends that might affect the issue under investigation. By combining the evidence, they can form a hypothesis about why public opinion shifted. To be sure, it will be only a guess; but it will be an educated guess, one made after a careful examination and analysis of the available evidence.

Suppose we follow the same process as the historians. How can we *verify* our hypothesis? In other words, how can we support our guess? This is a problem for historians, one that takes (and should take) a considerable amount of thought. Some historians verify their hypotheses by collecting more evidence. Does that evidence support or contradict the hypothesis? But when more evidence is not available, historians generally ask the following questions:

1. Does my hypothesis make sense? (Is it logical?)

2. Is it supported by the vast weight of the evidence? (Is there any alternative explanation that is supported by more evidence?)

3. Does my hypothesis "fit" with other things I know about the time period? (See Questions to Consider.)

4. Can I explain or account for the evidence that does not support my hypothesis? (Can I show why this evidence is not as important as the evidence that supports my hypothesis?)

5. Can my hypothesis withstand the criticisms of someone with an alternative hypothesis? (Can I defend my hypothesis?)

If the answers to these questions are satisfactory, historians usually feel that they have found a plausible hypothesis.

In this chapter, you are given a great variety of evidence drawn from a number of different and conflicting sources. Examine each piece of evidence closely. If that were the only piece of evidence available at the time, what effect would it have had on public opinion? Make brief notes as you go along.

All of the pieces of evidence will not lead to *one* answer. Instead, it will seem as if you have several pieces, all from different puzzles. Which of the puzzles is most important? In other words, which explanation is most reasonable for why public opinion concerning immigration shifted in the United States after World War I?

The Evidence

All tables from U.S. Bureau of the Census, Historical Statistics of the United States (Washington, D.C.: Government Printing Office 1975), p. 105.

TABLE 1 Immigrants, by Country: 1891–1925*

| | | | Europe | | | | | | | | | | | |
| | | | Northwestern Europe | | | | Central Europe | | | Eastern Europe | | Southern Europe | |
Year	All Countries	Total	Great Britain	Ireland	Scandi-navia	Other North-western	Germany	Poland	Other Central	U.S.S.R. and Baltic States	Other Eastern	Italy	Other Southern
1925	294,314	148,366	27,172	26,650	16,810	8,548	46,068	5,341	4,701	3,121	1,566	6,203	2,186
1924	706,896	364,339	59,490	17,111	35,577	16,077	75,091	28,806	32,700	20,918	13,173	56,246	9,150
1923	522,919	307,920	45,759	15,740	34,184	12,469	48,277	26,538	34,038	21,151	16,082	46,674	7,008
1922	309,556	216,385	25,153	10,579	14,625	11,149	17,931	28,635	29,363	19,910	12,244	40,319	6,477
1921	805,228	652,364	51,142	28,435	22,854	29,317	6,803	95,089	77,069	10,193	32,793	222,260	76,409
1920	430,001	246,295	38,471	9,591	13,444	24,491	1,001	4,813	5,666	1,751	3,913	95,145	48,009
1919	141,132	24,627	6,797	474	5,590	5,126	52	(†)	53	1,403	51	1,884	3,197
1918	110,618	31,063	2,516	331	6,506	3,146	447		61	4,242	93	5,250	8,471
1917	295,403	133,083	10,735	5,406	13,771	6,731	1,857		1,258	12,716	369	34,596	45,644
1916	298,826	145,699	16,063	8,639	14,761	8,715	2,877		5,191	7,842	1,167	33,665	46,779
1915	326,700	197,919	27,237	14,185	17,883	12,096	7,799		18,511	26,187	2,892	49,688	21,441
1914	1,218,480	1,058,391	48,729	24,688	29,391	25,591	35,734		278,152	255,660	21,420	283,738	55,288
1913	1,197,892	1,055,855	60,328	27,876	32,267	28,086	34,329		254,825	291,040	18,036	265,542	43,526
1912	838,172	718,875	57,148	25,879	27,554	22,921	27,788		178,882	162,395	20,925	157,134	38,249
1911	878,587	764,757	73,384	29,112	42,285	25,549	32,061		159,057	158,721	21,655	182,882	40,051

Year													
1910	1,041,570	926,291	68,941	29,855	48,267	23,852	31,283		258,737	186,792	25,287	215,537	37,740
1909	751,786	654,875	46,793	25,033	32,496	17,756	25,540		170,191	120,460	11,659	183,218	21,729
1908	782,870	691,901	62,824	30,556	30,175	22,177	32,309		168,509	156,711	27,345	128,503	32,792
1907	1,285,349	1,199,566	79,037	34,530	49,965	26,512	37,807		338,452	258,943	36,510	285,731	52,079
1906	1,100,735	1,018,365	67,198	34,995	52,781	23,277	37,564		265,138	215,665	18,652	273,120	29,975
1905	1,026,499	974,273	84,189	52,945	60,625	24,693	40,574		275,693	184,897	11,022	221,479	18,156
1904	812,870	767,933	51,448	36,142	60,096	23,321	46,380		177,156	145,141	12,756	193,296	22,197
1903	857,046	814,507	33,637	35,310	77,647	17,009	40,086		206,011	136,093	12,600	230,622	25,492
1902	648,743	619,068	16,898	29,138	54,038	10,322	28,304		171,989	107,347	8,234	178,375	14,423
1901	487,918	469,237	14,985	30,561	39,234	9,279	21,651		113,390	85,257	8,199	135,996	10,685
1900	448,572	424,700	12,509	35,730	31,151	5,822	18,507		114,847	90,787	6,852	100,135	8,360
1899	311,715	297,349	13,456	31,673	22,192	5,150	17,476		62,491	60,982	1,738	77,419	4,772
1898	229,299	217,786	12,894	25,128	19,282	4,698	17,111	4,726	39,797	29,828	1,076	58,613	4,633
1897	230,832	216,397	12,752	28,421	21,089	5,323	22,533	4,165	33,031	25,816	943	59,431	2,893
1896	343,267	329,067	24,565	40,262	33,199	7,611	31,885	691	65,103	51,445	954	68,060	5,292
1895	258,536	250,342	28,833	46,304	26,852	7,313	32,173	790	33,401	35,907	768	35,427	2,574
1894	285,631	277,052	22,520	30,231	32,400	9,514	53,989	1,941	38,638	39,278	1,027	42,977	4,537
1893	439,730	429,324	35,189	43,578	58,945	17,888	78,756	16,374	57,420	42,310	625	72,145	6,094
1892	579,663	570,876	42,215	51,383	66,295	21,731	119,168	40,536	76,937	81,511	1,331	61,631	8,138
1891	560,319	546,085	66,605	55,706	60,107	21,824	113,554	27,497	71,042	47,426	1,222	76,055	5,047

* For years ending June 30.
† Between 1899 and 1919, included with western Austria-Hungary, Germany, and Russia.

Chapter 7
Stemming the
Tide: Immigration
and Nativism
After World
War I

BOOK EXCERPTS

From Madison Grant, The Passing of the Great Race, *4th ed. (New York: Charles Scribner's Sons, 1922), pp. 16–18, 89–90; originally published, 1916.*

There exists to-day a widespread and fatuous belief in the power of environment, as well as of education and opportunity to alter heredity, which arises from the dogma of the brotherhood of man, derived in its turn from the loose thinkers of the French Revolution and their American mimics. Such beliefs have done much damage in the past and if allowed to go uncontradicted, may do even more serious damage in the future. Thus the view that the Negro slave was an unfortunate cousin of the white man, deeply tanned by the tropic sun and denied the blessings of Christianity and civilization, played no small part with the sentimentalists of the Civil War period and it has taken us fifty years to learn that speaking English, wearing good clothes and going to school and to church do not transform a Negro into a white man. Nor was a Syrian or Egyptian freedman transformed into a Roman by wearing a toga and applauding his favorite gladiator in the amphitheatre. Americans will have a similar experience with the Polish Jew, whose dwarf stature, peculiar mentality and ruthless concentration on self-interest are being engrafted upon the stock of the nation.

Recent attempts have been made in the interest of inferior races among our immigrants to show that the shape of the skull does change, not merely in a century, but in a single generation. In 1910, the report of the anthropological expert of the Congressional Immigration Commission gravely declared that a round skull Jew on his way across the Atlantic might and did have a round skull child; but a few years later, in response to the subtle elixir of American institutions as exemplified in an East Side tenement, might and did have a child whose skull was appreciably longer; and that a long skull south Italian, breeding freely, would have precisely the same experience in the reverse direction. In other words the Melting Pot was acting instantly under the influence of a changed environment.

What the Melting Pot actually does in practice can be seen in Mexico, where the absorption of the blood of the original Spanish conquerors by the native Indian population has produced the racial mixture which we call Mexican and which is now engaged in demonstrating its incapacity for self-government. The world has seen many such mixtures and the character of a mongrel race is only just beginning to be understood at its true value.

It must be borne in mind that the specializations which characterize the higher races are of relatively recent development, are highly unstable and when mixed with generalized or primitive characters tend to disappear. Whether we like to admit it or not, the result of the mixture of two races, in the long run, gives us a race reverting to the more ancient, generalized and lower type. The cross between a white man and an Indian is an Indian; the cross between a white man and a Negro is a Negro; the cross between a white man and a Hindu is a Hindu; and the cross between any of the three European races and a Jew is a Jew. . . .

The prosperity that followed the war attracted hordes of newcomers who were welcomed by the native Americans to operate factories, build railroads and fill up the waste spaces — "developing the country" it was called.

These new immigrants were no longer exclusively members of the Nordic race as were the earlier ones who came of their own impulse to improve their social conditions. The transportation lines advertised America as a land flowing with milk and honey and the European governments took the opportunity to unload upon careless, wealthy and hospitable America the sweepings of their jails and asylums. The result was that the new immigration, while it still included many strong elements from the north of Europe, contained a large and increasing number of the weak, the broken and the mentally crippled of all races drawn from the lowest stratum of the Mediterranean basin and the Balkans, together with hordes of the wretched, submerged populations of the Polish Ghettos. Our jails, insane asylums and almshouses are filled with this human flotsam and the whole tone of American life, social, moral and political has been lowered and vulgarized by them.

With a pathetic and fatuous belief in the efficacy of American institutions and environment to reverse or obliterate immemorial hereditary tendencies, these newcomers were welcomed and given a share in our land and prosperity. The American taxed himself to sanitate and educate these poor helots and as soon as they could speak English, encouraged them to enter into the political life, first of municipalities and then of the nation.

The native Americans are splendid raw material, but have as yet only an imperfectly developed national consciousness. They lack the instinct of self-preservation in a racial sense. Unless such an instinct develops their race will perish, as do all organisms which disregard this primary law of nature. Nature had granted to the Americans of a century ago the greatest opportunity in recorded history to produce in the isolation of a continent a powerful and racially homogeneous people and had provided for the experiment a pure race of one of the

[203]

*Chapter 7
Stemming the
Tide: Immigration
and Nativism
After World
War I*

most gifted and vigorous stocks on earth, a stock free from the diseases, physical and moral, which have again and again sapped the vigor of the older lands. Our grandfathers threw away this opportunity in the blissful ignorance of national childhood and inexperience.

From Samuel Gompers, Seventy Years of Life and Labor: An Autobiography, *Vol. I (New York: E. P. Dutton and Company, 1925), p. 171.*

Public opinion moved just as slowly to accept the proposals for restricting immigration as did the organized labor movement. Throughout the intervening years I continued my effort to secure an Immigration Restriction Law for the United States. The literacy test remained the accepted method for setting up the restrictive standards. The two members of Congress who became distinctively identified with the literacy test were Senator Henry Cabot Lodge and his son-in-law, Augustus P. Gardner.

So far as I remember, this is the only issue upon which I have ever found myself in accord with Senator Lodge. I made a number of trips to the Capitol and the White House. On the "Hill" we encountered the same organized opposition which blocked the way of our injunction regulation proposals. It came, of course, from organized employers, such as the National Association of Manufacturers which inaugurated a campaign of hostility.

TABLE 2 Unemployment, 1890–1925

Year	Unemployed	Percent of Civilian Labor Force
1925	1,453	3.2
1924	2,190	5.0
1923	1,049	2.4
1922	2,859	6.7
1921	4,918	11.7
1920	2,132	5.2
1919	546	1.4
1918	536	1.4
1917	1,848	4.6
1916	2,043	5.1
1915	3,377	8.5
1914	3,120	7.9
1913	1,671	4.3
1912	1,759	4.6
1911	2,518	6.7
1910	2,150	5.9
1909	1,824	5.1
1908	2,780	8.0
1907	945	2.8
1906	574	1.7
1905	1,381	4.3
1904	1,691	5.4
1903	1,204	3.9
1902	1,097	3.7
1901	1,205	4.0
1900	1,420	5.0
1899	1,819	6.5
1898	3,351	12.4
1897	3,890	14.5
1896	3,782	14.4
1895	3,510	13.7
1894	4,612	18.4
1893	2,860	11.7
1892	728	3.0
1891	1,265	5.4
1890	904	4.0

Chapter 7
Stemming the
Tide: Immigration
and Nativism
After World
War I

TABLE 3   Labor Union Membership, by Affiliation: 1897–1934*

Year	Total Union Membership (1,000), BLS	American Federation of Labor		Independent or Unaffiliated Unions, Total Membership (1,000), Wolman†
		Number of Affiliated Unions, BLS	Total Membership (1,000), BLS	
1934	3,728	109	3,045	683
1933	2,857	108	2,127	730
1932	3,226	106	2,532	694
1931	3,526	105	2,890	636
1930	3,632	104	2,961	671
1929	3,625	105	2,934	691
1928	3,567	107	2,896	671
1927	3,600	106	2,813	787
1926	3,592	107	2,804	788
1925	3,566	107	2,877	689
1924	3,549	107	2,866	683
1923	3,629	108	2,926	703
1922	3,950	112	3,196	754
1921	4,722	110	3,907	815
1920	5,034	110	4,079	955
1919	4,046	111	3,260	786
1918	3,368	111	2,726	642
1917	2,976	111	2,371	605
1916	2,722	111	2,073	649
1915	2,560	110	1,946	614
1914	2,647	110	2,021	626
1913	2,661	111	1,996	665
1912	2,405	112	1,770	635
1911	2,318	115	1,762	556
1910	2,116	120	1,562	554
1909	1,965	119	1,483	482
1908	2,092	116	1,587	505
1907	2,077	117	1,539	538
1906	1,892	119	1,454	438
1905	1,918	118	1,494	424
1904	2,067	120	1,676	391
1903	1,824	113	1,466	358
1902	1,335	97	1,024	311
1901	1,058	87	788	270
1900	791	82	548	243
1899	550	73	349	201
1898	467	67	278	189
1897	440	58	265	175

* Includes Canadian members of labor unions with headquarters in U.S.   BLS = U.S. Bureau of Labor Statistics.
† Leo Wolman, *Ebb and Flow in Trade Unionism* (New York: National Bureau of Economic Research, 1936).

BOOK EXCERPTS

From Carl C. Brigham, A Study of American Intelligence *(Princeton, N.J.: Princeton University Press, 1922), pp. 197, 202, 210.*

OUR study of the army tests of foreign born individuals has pointed at every step to the conclusion that the average intelligence of our immigrants is declining. This deterioration in the intellectual level of immigrants has been found to be due to two causes. The migrations of the Alpine and Mediterranean races have increased to such an extent in the last thirty or forty years that this blood now constitutes 70% or 75% of the total immigration. The representatives of the Alpine and Mediterranean races in our immigration are intellectually inferior to the representatives of the Nordic race which formerly made up about 50% of our immigration. In addition, we find that we are getting progressively lower and lower types from each nativity group or race. . . .

. . . Careless thinkers are prone to select one or two striking examples of ability from a particular group, and then rest confidently in the belief that they have overthrown an argument based on the total distribution of ability. The Fourth of July orator can convincingly raise the popular belief in the intellectual level of Poland by shouting the name of Kosciusko from a high platform, but he can not alter the distribution of the intelligence of the Polish immigrant. All countries send men of exceptional ability to America, but the point is that some send fewer than others. . . .

The steps that should be taken to preserve or increase our present intellectual capacity must of course be dictated by science and not by political expediency. Immigration should not only be restrictive but highly selective. And the revision of the immigration and naturalization laws will only afford a slight relief from our present difficulty. The really important steps are those looking toward the prevention of the continued propagation of defective strains in the present population. If all immigration were stopped now, the decline of American intelligence would still be inevitable. This is the problem which must be met, and our manner of meeting it will determine the future course of our national life.

From Clinton Stoddard Burr, America's Race Heritage *(New York: The National Historical Society, 1922), pp. 231–232.*

Meanwhile the American people must be on the alert to guard against a repetition of the old methods of seduction by which the anti-restrictionists have been so successful in the past. We are still going to hear reproachful oratory in de-

Chapter 7
Stemming the
Tide: Immigration
and Nativism
After World
War I

fense of the "strong-hearted and ambitious characters who have torn themselves up by the roots, leaving home, family and friends, to travel to the uncertainty of a new life in a new land" — when, as a matter of fact, from the testimony of all our unprejudiced representatives on the other side of the Atlantic, the emigrants who are now coming from Eastern and Southern Europe are for the most part the weakest and poorest material in Europe, usually traveling on money they have begged from relatives and friends or organizations in America.

It is true that the period lasting from January 1, 1920, to June 30, 1920, saw a marked proportional increase of the number of immigrants from Northwestern Europe as compared with the number from Southern and Eastern Europe. And there was a great rush of persons returning to Southern and Eastern Europe. This must be regarded, however, as merely the continuation of a transitory period incident to post-bellum conditions.

Yet it only needs a cessation of immigration to save America for Nordic humanity. It would take but two or three decades of emigration to scatter the majority of the some 8,000,000 Alpines and Mediterraneans to their homelands. They are remarkably devoted to the countries of their origin. On the other hand, our Jewish population is probably permanent. It is problematical whether many orthodox Jews would emigrate to Palestine, in the event that the latter domain becomes economically established.

During the last six months of the year 1920 there was a gradual change in the class of immigration we had received after the Armistice of 1918, and by December, the very month which marks the anniversary of the Pilgrim landing at Plymouth Rock, it had become apparent that not only was our immigration stream returning to a pre-war condition, both as to quantity as well as quality, but that the deluge would be measured only by the numbers of ships available. Thus, May of 1921 witnessed the enactment of practically the same emergency laws that had passed Congress in the previous administration, but had been pocket-vetoed by President Wilson at that time.

The Republican administration is pledged to devise a new restrictive immigration policy. It has begun well, all things considered, and the Democrats have proved their intention to make the immigration problem a national, not a party question.

The Japanese feel that they have been discriminated against, as compared to so-called white nationalities. Therefore, why not "kill two birds with one stone" by keeping out not only Japanese, but also Southern and Eastern Europeans of low standards?

[208]

At the present time selection of our immigrants by nationality is the only efficacious method, perhaps, to reduce the proportion of the lower racial elements in our population. Yet it may be sooner than most people imagine that our incoming immigrants will be minutely examined by a corps of eugenics experts, who will make certain beyond the shadow of a doubt that we shall "carry on" the heritage left to us by our pioneer Nordic forefathers.

From Frank Julian Warne, The Immigrant Invasion *(New York: Dodd, Mead and Company, 1913), pp. 289–290, 295–296, 316.*

Those who are desirous of settling the immigration question solely from the point of view of the best interests of the country are quite frequently side-tracked from the only real and fundamental argument into the discussion of relatively unimportant phases of it. The real objection to immigration at the present time lies not in the fact that Slavs and Italians and Greeks and Syrians instead of Irish and Germans and English are coming to the United States. Nor does it lie in the fact that the immigrants are or become paupers and criminals. The real objection has nothing to do with the composition of our immigration stream, nor with the characteristics of the individuals or races composing it. It is more than likely that the evils so prominent to-day would still exist if we had received the Slavs and Italians fifty years ago and were receiving the English and Irish and Germans at the present day.

The real objection to immigration lies in the changed conditions that have come about in the United States themselves. These conditions now dominate and control the tendencies that immigration manifests. At the present time they are giving to the country a surplus of cheap labour — a greater supply than our industries and manufacturing enterprises need. In consequence this over-supply has brought into play among our industrial toilers the great law of competition. This economic law is controlled by the more recent immigrant because of his immediate necessity to secure employment and his ability to sell his labour at a low price — to work for a low wage. Against the operation of this law the native worker and the earlier immigrant are unable to defend themselves. It is affecting detrimentally the standard of living of hundreds of thousands of workers — workers, too, who are also citizens, fathers, husbands. . . .

When any one suggests the restriction of immigration to those who believe in throwing open wide our gates to all the races of the world, the conclusion is immediately arrived at that the proposer has some personal feeling in the matter and that he is not in sympathy with the immigrant. As a matter of fact the

Chapter 7
Stemming the
Tide: Immigration
and Nativism
After World
War I

restriction of immigration is herein suggested not alone from the point of view of the future political development of the United States, but also from that of the interest and welfare of the immigrant himself and his descendants. It is made in order to prevent them from becoming in the future an industrial slave class in America and to assist them in throwing off in their European homes the shackles which now bind them and are the primary cause of their securing there so little from an abundant world.

One of the strongest arguments in the past of the liberal immigrationist is that the downtrodden and oppressed of Europe are fleeing from intolerable economic, political, and religious conditions into a land of liberty and freedom which offers opportunities to all. It may be very much questioned if these immigrants are finding here the hoped-for escape from oppression and servitude and exploitation, for since the newer immigration began in the eighties there has come to dwell in America a horrible modern Frankenstein in the shape of the depressing conditions surrounding a vast majority of our industrial toilers. But even granting that the immigrants coming to us do better their condition, a very pertinent question is as to the effect the prevention of this immigration would have upon the countries from which it comes. If we grant that the immigrants are able-bodied, disposed to resent oppression and are striving to better their condition, Are they not the very ones that should remain in their European homes and there through growing restlessness and increasing power change for the better the conditions from which they are fleeing? As it is now, instead of an improvement in those conditions the stronger and more able-bodied — the ones better able to cope with them and improve them — are running away and leaving behind the less able and weaker members, who continue to live under the intolerable conditions. . . .

The alternative is to restrict immigration so that we can catch our breath and take an inventory of what we already have among us that must imperatively be raised to a higher standard of living and a safer citizenship.

Our decision means a choice between two conditions. By continuing our present policy we choose that which is producing a plutocratic caste class of idle nobodies resting upon the industrial slavery of a great mass of ignorant and low standard of living toilers. By restricting immigration we influence the bringing about of a condition that will give to a large body of citizens a decent and comfortable standard of living. This desired result is to be obtained by a more just distribution of wealth through wages and prices and dividends.

FACT SHEET

August 5–8, 1920. In West Frankfort, Illinois, mobs burned the homes of foreigners, clubbed and stoned immigrants on the streets. Five hundred state police were called out to restore order.

May 1920. Henry Ford launched anti-Jewish propaganda campaign.

1920. Georgia politician Tom Watson won a seat in the United States Senate. The major plank in his campaign was anti-Catholicism.

1919. Alabama state legislature passed a convent inspection law.

September 1920. Five thousand immigrants per day passed through Ellis Island, New York.

1918. "The Protocols of the Elders of Zion" (a document created by the anti-Semitic Russian secret police, purporting to "prove" a Jewish plot existed for world domination) first appeared in the United States.

1919–1920. Postwar economic recession afflicted the United States. Agricultural depression began in 1920.

October 1915. The new Ku Klux Klan was founded by William Simmons in Atlanta, Georgia. It grew rapidly in the South and Midwest.

1921. Nicola Sacco and Bartolomeo Vanzetti, immigrants and admitted anarchists, were convicted of murdering a guard during a robbery in Massachusetts. The case was followed throughout the nation. The men appealed their convictions several times, but were executed in 1927.

1919. The Eighteenth Amendment to the Constitution, which prohibited the manufacture, sale, and transportation of intoxicating liquors, was ratified.

1914. *The Menace* (an anti-Catholic weekly) had a circulation of nearly 1.5 million.

Ku Klux Klan. "We believe that the American stock, which was bred under highly selective surroundings . . . and should not be mongrelized . . . automatically and instinctively developed the kind of civilization which is best suited to its own healthy life and growth; and this cannot be safely changed except by ourselves and along the lines of our own character."

Chapter 7
Stemming the
Tide: Immigration
and Nativism
After World
War I

1917. Beginning of the Bolshevik Revolution in Russia. The United States refused to recognize the Bolshevik government.

1919. Red Scare in the United States. Fearing infiltration and influence, Attorney General A. Mitchell Palmer was extremely active in "hunting suspicious persons."

BOOK EXCERPTS

From John R. Commons, Races and Immigrants in America, *2nd ed. (New York: Augustus M. Kelley, 1967), pp. xxiii–xxvi, xxix; originally published by Macmillan, 1907.*

The alternatives are, indeed, not simple. Labor unionism brings its conflicts and problems. But, on the whole, with capitalism organized in combinations, speaking through lawyers, lobbyists, managers, superintendents, and foremen of its own choosing, no beginning, even, of a settlement can be seen until labor organization is free also to choose and speak through agents of its own choosing. In general, the heads of labor organizations are more cautious and faithful to agreements than the rank and file. They occupy exposed positions between the attacks of capitalists in front and of radicals behind. The great majority of them, so far, have shown patriotism and caution. To displace them with revolutionists will not make it easier for the nation to deal with organized labor. But, with immigration restricted, American business will learn its responsibility to give as careful, efficient attention to its department of personal relations with employees as it does to its engineering, production, sales and credit departments, and can be expected to be equally successful. . . .

The stabilization of employment is the first important task of business and the nation, and an evident reason why it does not come to the front is unregulated immigration. This is America's convenient reserve army of the unemployed, and its operation in prosperity and depression is shown in the following pages. With the possibility of falling back on immigrants, business does not plan ahead, spread out, and dovetail its work so as to utilize to best advantage the workers already here. The problem, of course, is not simple and easy. It requires thought and serious attention. But it is not even thought about when business can look to the easier way of taking on and laying off immigrants. . . .

. . . Americanization is a special problem only because fresh immigrants pour in each year. It ceases to be a special problem in the second generation. Some progress has been made. After four vetoes of a literacy test by three presidents, in 1897, 1913, 1915, and 1917, Congress adopted the test in 1917, over the last veto. All of the numerous restrictions on immigration, except the Chinese exclusion law, are *not restrictive* but *selective*. They have not limited immigration, but have improved it. The next steps needed are real restrictions.

From Peter Roberts, The New Immigration *(New York: Arno, 1970), pp. 347–348; originally published by Macmillan, 1912.*

The foreigners have many undesirable qualities, and chief among these is their love for drink. Wherever the immigrants live in colonies, the number of saloons in these localities is large. These drinking dens are scenes of vice and debauchery. They are responsible, either directly or indirectly, for 60 per cent of the crime committed by them. But in every state of the Union laws regulating the liquor traffic are in vogue, and the executive power is in the hands of men of native birth. In the state of Pennsylvania, the right to grant licenses is in the hands of the judges of the Courts of Quarter Sessions, and in no section of the country has the power been more abused. These cultured and capable men, in many counties, have given licenses to foreigners to sell intoxicants regardless of the needs of the towns, the sentiment of decent people, or the welfare of the communities. This shameful abuse of power is due to two causes, greed and politics: the greed of men in the brewery business is limitless and they have the ears of the court; the cunning of politicians who use saloons as centers of influence to control the foreign vote is equally selfish. But with very rare exceptions the men on the bench, in the brewery business, and in politics, dominated by these motives, are native-born. The Keystone state places the power of granting licenses in the hands of judges for the purpose of regulating the liquor traffic according to the well-being of industrial communities. These men have the power to limit the number of licenses given foreigners or other men catering to their appetite for strong drink. They saw at every session of the court how the immigrants were debauched by liquor and how appalling was their crime record because of intoxicants; and yet without consideration to their oath of office, without regard to their patriotic duty, and in the teeth of the demands of the Christian conscience, they issue the right to sell liquor to these men at the rate of one license per hundred people — men, women, and children. Can we blame the foreigners for their jamborees, their lawlessness, and their vice under conditions of this kind? They are much like children, and should be treated as such in the question of drink. If the governments of the several states in the immi-

TABLE 4 Immigrants by Major Occupation Group, 1899–1930

Year	Total	Professional, Technical, and Kindred Workers	Farmers and Farm Managers	Managers, Officials, and Proprietors, Exc. Farm	Clerical, Sales, and Kindred Workers	Craftsmen, Foremen, Operatives, and Kindred Workers	Private Household Workers	Service Workers, Exc. Private Household	Farm Laborers and Foremen	Laborers, Exc. Farm and Mine	No Occupation
1930	241,700	8,585	8,375	4,620	14,414	32,474	29,073	6,749	13,736	18,080	105,594
1929	279,678	8,792	8,309	4,709	15,354	36,437	31,841	6,820	19,849	27,873	119,694
1928	307,255	9,332	8,773	5,287	16,344	42,765	28,751	8,846	24,161	37,904	125,092
1927	335,175	9,883	10,324	5,772	20,140	42,394	31,344	10,070	23,698	55,989	125,561
1926	304,488	9,203	9,720	5,374	19,086	38,682	30,587	14,340	17,390	45,199	114,907
1925	294,314	8,942	13,875	5,508	15,363	36,927	26,924	15,399	16,022	36,610	118,744
1924	706,896	20,926	20,320	15,668	27,373	123,923	51,680	29,621	27,492	112,344	277,909
1923	522,919	13,926	12,503	12,086	17,931	87,899	52,223	22,244	25,905	86,617	191,585
1922	309,556	9,696	7,676	9,573	10,055	40,309	44,531	22,340	10,529	33,797	131,050
1921	805,228	12,852	22,282	18,286	18,922	109,710	102,478	24,298	32,400	162,859	301,141
1920	430,001	10,540	12,192	9,654	14,054	55,991	37,197	18,487	15,257	83,496	173,133
1919	141,132	5,261	3,933	4,247	6,524	21,671	6,277	11,571	4,412	18,922	58,314
1918	110,618	3,529	2,583	3,940	4,239	17,501	7,816	6,367	4,538	15,142	44,963
1917	295,403	7,499	7,764	8,329	10,554	38,660	31,885	11,784	22,328	52,182	104,418
1916	298,826	9,024	6,840	8,725	9,907	36,086	29,258	10,989	26,250	56,981	104,766
1915	326,700	11,453	6,518	10,728	9,377	45,591	39,774	11,976	24,723	49,620	116,940
1914	1,218,480	13,454	14,442	21,903	17,933	149,515	144,409	19,621	288,053	288,935	320,215
1913	1,197,892	12,552	13,180	19,094	15,173	139,091	140,218	17,609	320,105	223,682	297,188
1912	838,172	10,913	7,766	14,715	13,782	107,893	116,529	13,580	184,154	137,872	231,070
1911	878,587	11,275	9,709	15,416	14,723	128,717	107,153	11,051	176,003	158,518	246,022
1910	1,041,570	9,689	11,793	14,731	12,219	121,847	96,658	8,977	288,745	216,909	260,002
1909	751,786	7,603	8,914	11,562	8,467	75,730	64,568	5,849	171,310	176,490	221,293
1908	782,870	10,504	7,720	16,410	11,523	106,943	89,942	10,367	138,844	147,940	242,677
1907	1,285,349	12,016	13,476	20,132	12,735	169,394	121,587	13,578	323,854	293,868	304,709
1906	1,100,735	13,015	15,288	23,515	12,226	156,902	115,984	10,439	239,125	228,781	285,460
1905	1,026,499	12,582	18,474	27,706	12,759	159,442	125,473	5,849	142,187	290,009	232,018
1904	812,870	12,195	4,507	26,914	11,055	133,748	104,937	6,400	85,850	212,572	214,692
1903	857,046	6,999	13,363	15,603	7,226	110,644	92,686	11,482	77,518	321,824	199,701
1902	648,743	2,937	8,168	9,340	3,836	71,131	69,913	6,298	80,562	243,399	153,159
1901	487,918	2,665	3,035	8,294	3,197	57,346	42,027	5,352	54,753	162,563	148,686
1900	448,572	2,392	5,433	7,216	2,870	54,793	40,311	4,406	31,949	164,261	134,941
1899	311,715	1,972	3,973	6,815	2,473	38,608	34,120	4,580	17,343	92,452	109,379

gration zone had restricted the number of licenses granted foreigners to one to every five hundred persons, the disgraceful orgies common in foreign colonies would not be witnessed, the heinous crimes committed in drink would not be as common, and the liquor laws of each commonwealth would be better enforced.

NEWSPAPER ARTICLE

From Kenneth Roberts, "Plain Remarks on Immigration for Plain Americans," Saturday Evening Post, *Vol. 193, February 12, 1921.*

IMMIGRATION has grown to such proportions that immigration experts are stating coldly but firmly that it has become a matter of life and death for the American people. Representatives of the United States in every part of Europe — many of whom have hitherto been in favor of allowing almost anyone to go to America — have become universally aware of the danger. During the year 1920 American officials in Europe were, for the first time, brought into direct contact with the countless myriads of foreigners who were determined to reach America by fair means or foul. It has set them determinedly against immigration, as it would set anyone whose private interests in the matter were not more important than the interests of America at large. They are frightened to-day. You can hear them all over Europe.

"Our immigration laws," they say, "are worse than useless. We must have new ones. Immigration must be stopped. This is a matter of life and death for America. Immigration must be handled in America by people who know what this immigration means. The people who are handling it don't know anything about it, because they haven't seen it at its source and cannot see what is coming."

The men who are saying these things are in many instances the men who, early in 1920, were saying the America was a nation of immigrants and that the person who advocated stopping the flow of immigrants was advocating cutting off the flow of blood into our national veins, or bunk to that effect. In other instances they are men who have for years foreseen the inevitable results of unrestricted immigration. But now they are as one in saying that immigration must be limited to the irreducible minimum. . . . "It's easy to be sentimental and see plenty of reasons why it shouldn't be stopped; but America has got to stop it! This isn't a matter of sentiment; it's a matter of life and death for our people!" . . .

BUSINESS men of the type who have hitherto advocated unrestricted immigration are becoming frightened at the alarming changes that the present enor-

[215]

Chapter 7
Stemming the
Tide: Immigration
and Nativism
After World
War I

mous immigration is working beneath their very eyes. They are going in increasing numbers to the State Department and demanding that it be stopped. Many big employers of labor, for the first time in our history, are declaring that America cannot handle the numbers that are coming. . . .

. . . But the consuls cannot stop these people; for under the present interpretation of the immigration laws they are allowed the right of appeal before the immigration officials in a United States port. A consul can tell a person that he is excludable under the law, and that he probably will be excluded if he goes to America; but he has no right to withhold a visé from that person if the person demands it, unless the person is a Bolshevik or an anarchist or a habitual criminal. A consul, through the machinery which has been built up in Europe, knows when prospective immigrants are idiots, insane, tuberculous, contract laborers, prostitutes or persons likely to become public charges, but he's got to give them a visé if they demand it. This puts our consuls in the embarrassing position of having degenerate, offensive, undesirable products of the sink holes of Europe step into their presence and tell them what to do. The consuls can and do warn the immigration officials in America of the arrival of these menaces; but in spite of that between thirty and fifty per cent of them are allowed to enter. This is because they have friends or relatives in the United States, and the friends and relatives bring such pressure to bear that the immigration laws, weak as they are, are ignored, and the scum floats in with the flood. . . .

. . . News flashes like wireless messages from slum to slum and from city to city. For example, after the Bolshevik push against Poland in the summer of 1920 a number of Hebrews from Poland fled across the line into Czecho-Slovakia. They were a tiny part of the three million Polish Hebrews who wanted to go to America. So they went to the American consulate in Prague and asked to be allowed to travel to America although they had failed to obtain a visé on the passports from the American consulate in Poland. The American consul at Prague cabled to the State Department asking for permission to do this, and the State Department cabled its assent for a limited period. These persons were allowed to go. The word flashed back to Poland, and at the expiration of a few days trainloads of Hebrews began pouring into Prague from Poland and besieging the American consul for similar permission. They didn't get it, however.

I repeat that the desire throughout Europe to emigrate to America is so strong that the immigrants will practice any chicanery to break through the weak spots in an immigration law.

TABLE 5 Foreign-Born Population, by Country of Birth, 1870–1930

Country of Birth	Total Foreign Born						
	1930	1920	1910	1900	1890	1880	1870
All countries	14,204,149	13,920,692	13,515,886	10,341,276	9,249,560	6,679,943	5,567,229
Northwestern Europe	3,728,050	3,830,094	4,239,067	4,202,683	4,380,752	3,494,484	3,124,638
England	809,563	813,853	877,719	840,513	909,092	664,160	555,046
Scotland	354,323	254,570	261,076	233,524	242,231	170,136	140,835
Wales	60,205	67,066	82,488	93,586	100,079	83,302	74,533
Northern Ireland	178,832 }	1,037,234	1,352,251	1,615,459	1,871,509	1,854,571	1,855,827
Ireland (Eire)	744,810 }						
Norway	347,852	363,863	403,877	336,388	322,665	181,729	114,246
Sweden	595,250	625,585	665,207	582,014	478,041	194,337	97,332
Denmark	179,474 }	189,154	181,649	153,690	132,543	64,196	30,107
Iceland	2,764 }						
Netherlands	133,133	131,766	120,063	94,931	81,828	58,090	46,802
Belgium	64,194	62,687	49,400	29,757	22,639	15,535	12,553
Luxembourg	9,048	12,585	3,071	3,031	2,882	12,836	5,802
Switzerland	113,010	118,659	124,848	115,593	104,069	88,621	75,153
France	135,592	153,072	117,418	104,197	113,174	106,971	116,402
Central and Eastern Europe	5,897,799	6,134,845	6,014,028	4,136,646	3,420,629	2,187,776	1,784,449
Germany	1,608,814	1,686,108	2,311,237	2,663,418	2,784,894	1,966,742	1,690,533
Poland	1,268,583	1,139,979	937,884	383,407	147,440	48,557	14,436
Czechoslovakia	491,638	362,438					
Austria	370,914	575,627	845,555	432,798	241,377	124,024	70,797
Hungary	274,450	397,283	495,609	145,714	62,435	11,526	3,737
Yugoslavia	211,416	169,439					
U.S.S.R.	1,153,628 }						
Latvia	20,673 }	1,400,495 }	1,184,412	423,726 }	182,644	35,722	4,644
Estonia	3,550 }						
Lithuania	193,606	135,068 }					
Finland	142,478	149,824	129,680	62,641 }			
Romania	146,393	102,823	65,923	15,032			
Bulgaria	9,399	10,477	11,498				
Turkey in Europe	2,257	5,284	32,230	9,910	1,839	1,205	302
Southern Europe	2,106,295	1,911,213	1,525,875	530,200	206,648	58,265	25,853
Greece	174,526	175,976	101,282	8,515	1,887	776	390
Albania	8,814	5,608					
Italy	1,790,429	1,610,113	1,343,125	484,027	182,580	44,230	17,157
Spain	59,362	49,535	22,108	7,050	6,185	5,121	3,764
Portugal	73,164	69,981	59,360	30,608	15,996	8,138	4,542
Other Europe	16,255	5,901	12,871	2,251	12,579	3,786	1,678
Danzig	1,483	2,049					
Europe, not specified	14,772	3,852	12,871	2,251	12,579	3,786	1,678
Asia	275,665	237,950	191,484	120,248	113,396	107,630	64,565
Armenia	32,166	36,628 }					
Palestine	6,137	3,203 }	59,729				
Syria	57,227	51,901 }					
Turkey in Asia	46,654	11,019 }					
China	46,129	43,560	56,756	81,534	106,701	104,468	63,042
Japan	70,993	81,502	67,744	24,788	2,292	401	73
India	5,850	4,901	4,664	2,031	2,143	1,707	586
Korea							
Philippines							
Other Asia	10,509	5,236	2,591	11,895	2,260	1,054	864
America	2,102,209	1,727,017	1,489,231	1,317,380	1,088,245	807,230	551,335
Canada–French	370,852	307,786	385,083	395,126	302,496 }		
Canada–Other	915,537	817,139	819,554	784,796	678,442 }	717,157	493,464
Newfoundland	23,980	13,249	5,080				
Cuba	18,493	14,872	15,133	11,081 }	23,256 {	6,917	5,319
Other West Indies	87,748	64,090	32,502	14,354 }		9,484	6,251
Mexico	641,462	486,418	221,915	103,393	77,853	68,399	42,435
Central America	10,514	4,912	1,736	3,897	1,192	707	301
South America	33,623	18,551	8,228	4,733	5,006	4,566	3,565
All other	77,876	73,672	43,330	31,868	27,311	20,772	14,711
Africa	8,859	5,781	3,992	2,538	2,207	2,204	2,657
Australia	12,816	10,914	9,035	6,807	5,984	4,906	3,118
Azores	35,611	33,995 }	18,274	9,768	9,739	7,641	4,434
Other Atlantic Islands	9,467	10,345 }					
Pacific Islands	4,527	3,712	2,415	2,013	3,369	1,953	910
Country not specified	1,588	3,589	2,687	2,546	479		954
Born at sea	5,008	5,336	6,927	8,196	5,533	4,068	2,638

Chapter 7
Stemming the
Tide: Immigration
and Nativism
After World
War I

Questions to Consider

In this chapter you are asked to explain why American public opinion on the subject of immigration shifted so dramatically between roughly 1915 and 1924. Several types of evidence have been provided.

As you look over the various pieces of evidence, you will notice that the evidence is not presented in any logical order. Instead, the evidence is given to you randomly, much as you would find it if you had collected it yourself. Hence your first task is to try to put the evidence into some logical order.

There are a number of ways evidence can be arranged:

1. chronologically

2. by type (for example, all the statistics grouped together)

3. by the main argument presented

4. by linkages you establish (for example, a newspaper article concerning labor may be grouped with statistics on labor, unemployment, or union membership)

Moreover, each problem you confront (not just in United States history, but everywhere) will require a different arrangment of the available evidence. One problem might best be solved by grouping the evidence by main argument. Yet this might not work for another problem. Therefore, some experimentation will be necessary.

Examine each piece of evidence carefully. What is each piece trying to tell you? For example, immigrants had lived for years in the mining town of West Frankfort, Illinois. Yet in the 1920s mobs tried to burn them out. What else was happening in 1920 that might have contributed to this behavior? Look through the evidence to try to establish some linkages. Origin of immigrants? The economy? Unemployment?

Samuel Gompers was a well-known and respected leader of organized labor (he helped found the American Federation of Labor) and was himself an immigrant who came to American in 1863. How did he feel about immigration? Why? Did other writers agree with him? Can you establish linkages with some of the statistics? With some of the other facts presented?

The Ku Klux Klan was founded in 1915 (it was not related to the earlier organization by the same name). How did that organization stand on immigration? Why? Again, can you make linkages with other writers? With statistics? With other facts?

As you examine each piece of evidence and try to link it with other pieces, you will see that you have been putting the evidence in order. Once you have arranged the evidence and established important linkages, you will notice that there were many arguments in favor of restricting immigration. From the evidence presented, can you put those arguments in rank order (from the most influential to the least)? One method that will help is to see which piece or pieces of evidence have the most linkages with other pieces. That evidence may well be the key. Make notes as you go along, and refer back to them as you summarize, make linkages, reorder, and then analyze.

Epilogue

Responding to prevailing public opinion as well as to a variety of cries for immigration restrictions, Congress in 1921 passed its first general exclusion bill. If it had been approved by President Woodrow Wilson, the act would have limited the immigration of each nationality to 3 percent of that nationality's population in the United States in 1910. Although Wilson refused to sign the bill, his successor Warren G. Harding approved the measure on May 19, 1921.

But exclusionists were not satisfied and, sensing a receptive public opinion, pushed through the National Origins Act in 1924, which completely prohibited Oriental immigration and limited the total number of European immigrants to 2 percent of each nationality's U.S. population as of 1890. The shift from 1910 to 1890 strongly weighted immigration in favor of people from Britain, Ireland, and Germany and against those southern and eastern Europeans (principally Italians, Greeks, and Russians) who began to arrive in large numbers in the latter years of the nineteenth century. The exclusionists had won.

Yet public opinion is neither constant nor predictable. The rise of fascism in Europe in the 1930s caused Americans to reassess policies based on discrimination and racism. If the United States were to protect itself and its way of life, the support of all Americans of all origins would be necessary and valuable. Hence most Americans smiled and agreed with President Franklin Roosevelt when he began an address to the Daughters of the American Revolution with the greeting, "Fellow immigrants. . . ."[5] World War II and the cold war further served to draw Americans together against what they perceived to be their common enemies.

In the Hart-Celler Act of 1965 Congress finally abolished national quotas for immigrants. That law placed an annual ceiling of 290,000 on immigrants, with 120,000 of that figure assigned to the Western Hemisphere and 170,000 to the Eastern

5. Franklin Roosevelt could get away with that greeting. His family had arrived in America in the 1640s (long before most of the ancestors of the Daughters of the American Revolution) and had achieved considerable wealth and power by the time of the American Revolution.

Chapter 7
Stemming the
Tide: Immigration
and Nativism
After World
War I

Hemisphere. A limit of 20,000 immigrants was placed on immigrants from any one nation.

Still, in some ways the residue of the controversy over immigration remained. As the United States is currently confronted with another wave of "new immigrants," this time from Latin America and Southeast Asia, many of the older fears are resurfacing. And the extent to which immigrants should be encouraged to retain their respective languages, religious practices, and culture, or should be required to conform to the American "mainstream," is once again being debated by legislators, public school teachers, and the rest of the American populace, all of us (as Franklin Roosevelt observed) "fellow immigrants."

Chapter 8

Surviving the Great Depression

"Hard times," one historian called it — an experience that left an invisible scar on a generation of Americans, according to another. Both historians were referring to the Great Depression, which persisted through nearly the entire decade of the 1930s, leaving millions of Americans jobless, hungry, and homeless. Estimates of the number of unemployed during those years vary (even today, young people entering the work force for the first time, women reentering the job market, and blacks seeking jobs are often underreported in the unemployment statistics). Nevertheless, between one-fourth and one-third of all American workers were unable to find jobs in 1932, and there is no doubt that by that year the depression was deep, severe, and worldwide. In the United States, the difference between the economic indicators in 1929 and 1932 was startling: $8.7 billion in

profits became a $5.6 billion deficit, the gross national product was cut in half, exports fell nearly 80 percent, and farm income was down 63 percent. By 1932 4,377 banks had failed.

The newly elected Herbert Hoover was at first bewildered and somewhat defensive about the rapid downward spiral of the nation's economy. Like many Americans, Hoover believed in the basic soundness of capitalism, advocated the values of an older individualism, and maintained that the role of the federal government in the economy should be quite limited. Nevertheless, Hoover was a compassionate man, unlike some of the members of his cabinet. As private relief sources dried up, the president authorized public-works projects and some institutional loans, at the same time vetoing other relief bills and trying to convince the nation that prosperity would return soon. Americans turned out at the polls in record numbers for the election of 1932 — and voted for the Democratic candidate Franklin D. Roosevelt in equally record numbers.

We know how the government reacted to the spreading economic calamities after March 1933 — Congress rapidly passed an assortment of programs collectively known as the New Deal. Calling together a group of experts (mainly professors and lawyers) to form a "brains trust," the newly elected president acted quickly to try to restore the confidence of the nation. In his fireside radio chats as well as in his other speeches, Roosevelt consistently reassured the American public that the country's economic institutions were sound. In the meantime Congress met in an emergency session to begin the difficult process of providing immediate relief for the needy and legislation for longer-term recovery. The First and Second Agricultural Adjustment Acts were intended to aid farmers by discouraging overproduction; the National Recovery Act was part of a wide-ranging effort to provide public-works projects for the unemployed and establish fair practice codes for business and industry. Young people were the subject of special attention — the National Youth Administration helped finance the educations of many students, and the Civilian Conservation Corps provided work camps for thousands of unemployed young men.

Eleanor Roosevelt was equally ac-tive in her efforts to mitigate the effects of the depression. With boundless energy, she traveled throughout the country, observing conditions first-hand and reporting to her husband. Three groups — blacks, young people, and women — were the primary focus of her concern. Eleanor Roosevelt was one of the few New Dealers deeply committed to black civil rights; she championed both individuals and the movement whenever she could. Young people had easy access to Mrs. Roosevelt, and women found her sympathetic to their pleas for inclusion in work relief projects. Her nontraditional behavior as First Lady was controversial and inspired many unflattering jokes and cartoons, but for millions of Americans Eleanor Roosevelt was the heart of the New Deal efforts to overcome the depression.

Aimed at relief, recovery, and (sometimes) reform of the American economy, New Deal programs alleviated but did not solve the problems that had spread across the nation with the depression. How did average people react to the depression? What did they think about what was happening? Were their lives changed by the depression? If so, how did they cope with these changes? In this chapter you will first learn how to do oral history. Then you will examine several interviews conducted by Studs Terkel for his book about the depression. This examination will help you sharpen your analytical skills before you conduct your own interview. Finally, you will interview a person who was a child or a young adult during the 1930s. Try to find out what that person's experiences were, and then analyze the degree to which his or her account supports or contradicts what historians believe were the major effects of the Great Depression upon the lives of "ordinary" Americans.

The Method

Historians are often frustrated because they are unable to ask specific questions of the participants in a historical event — questions that are not answered in their surviving diaries, letters, and other documents. Further, many people, especially the poor, the uneducated, and the members of minority groups, did not leave written records and are thus often overlooked by historians.

But when historians are dealing with the comparatively recent past, they do have an opportunity to ask questions by using a technique called oral history. Oral history — interviewing famous and not-so-famous people about their lives and the events they observed or participated in — can greatly enrich our knowledge of the past. It can aid the historian in capturing the "spirit of an age" as seen through the eyes of average citizens, and it often bridges the gap

between impersonal forces (wars, epidemics, depressions) and the personal and individual responses to them. Furthermore, oral history allows the unique to emerge from the total picture: the conscientious objector who would not serve in the army, the woman who did not marry and devote herself to raising a family, and so forth.

Oral history is both fascinating and challenging. It seems easy to do, but is really rather difficult to do well. There is always the danger that the student may "lead" the interview by imposing his or her ideas on the subject. Equally possible is that the student may be led away from the subject by the person being interviewed. Still other problems sometimes arise: the student may miss the subtleties in what is being said, or may assume that an exceptional person is representative of many people. Yet oral history, when used carefully and judiciously along with other sources, is an invaluable tool that helps one to re-create a sense of our past.

Recently much attention has been paid — and rightly so — to protecting the rights and privacy of human subjects. For this reason, the federal government requires that the interviewee consent to the interview and be fully aware of how the interview is to be used. The interviewer must explain the purpose of the interview, and the person being interviewed must sign a release form (for samples, see Figures 1–3). Although these requirements are intended to apply mostly to psychologists and sociologists, historians who employ oral history are included as well.

The Great Depression of the 1930s presents an almost matchless opportunity for the oral historian. Most Americans over the age of sixty-five (11.3 percent of the total population in 1980) even today have vivid memories of the depression. Of course those memories vary, depending on the age, socioeconomic status, race, sex, and region of the individual. But together the recollections of a number of people should give us an accurate picture of the depression and how the people responded to it. Not only will this approach to the past bring your reading about the depression to life, but it may also present a few surprises not contained in what you have read.

FIGURE 1   **Sample Unconditional Release.** *(From Collum Davis, Kathryn Back, and Kay MacLean,* Oral History: From Tape to Type *(Chicago: American Library Assn.,* © *1977), p. 14.)*

Tri-County Historical Society

    For and in consideration of the participation by *Tri-County Historical Society* in any programs involving the dissemination of tape-recorded memoirs and oral history material for publication, copy-right, and other uses, I hereby release all right, title, or interest in and to all of my tape-recorded memoirs to *Tri-County Historical Society* and declare that they may be used without any restriction whatsoever and may be copyrighted and published by the said *Society*, which may also assign said copyright and publication rights to serious research scholars.

    In addition to the rights and authority given to you under the preceding paragraph, I hereby authorize you to edit, publish, sell and/or license the use of my oral history memoir in any other manner which the *Society* considers to be desirable and I waive any claim to any payments which may be received as a consequence thereof by the *Society*.

PLACE *Indianapolis, Indiana*

DATE   *July 14, 1975*

Harold S. Johnson
(Interviewee)

Jane Rogers
(for *Tri-County Historical Society*   )

FIGURE 2 Sample Conditional Release. *(From Davis et al., p. 15.)*

<u>Tri-County Historical Society</u>

    I hereby release all right, title, or interest in and to all or any part of my tape-recorded memoirs to <u>Tri-County Historical Society</u>, subject to the following stipulations:

    That my memoirs are to be closed until five years following my death.

PLACE *Indianapolis,*
       Indiana

DATE *July 14, 1975*

    Harold S. Johnson
    (INTERVIEWEE)

    Jane Rogers
    (for *Tri-County Historical Society*)

FIGURE 3 Form Developed by a Large U.S. History Survey Class at the University of Tennessee, Knoxville, 1984

This form is to state that I have been inter- viewed by _____ on _____
          (Interviewer)   (date)
on my recollections of the Great Depression and life in the 1930's. I understand that this interview will be used in a class project at the University of Tennessee, and that the results will be saved for future historians.

_____
Signature

_____
Date

---

[226]

FIGURE 4   An Oral History Deed of Gift. *(From Betty McKeever Key,* Exploring Oral History *(Baltimore: Maryland Historical Society, © 1979), p. 39.)*

The Oral History Collection of the Maryland Historical Society is composed of taped interviews with significant Maryland citizens who can give first-hand accounts of some aspect of Maryland history which would otherwise go unrecorded. Interviews are obtained from well-known leaders in the state and also from those who probably do not appear in any other historical record. The goal is to supplement and enhance the collections of conventional library-archival material held by the Library of the Maryland Historical Society.

You have been asked to give an interview to one of our interviewers.

A tape recording of your interview will be made by the interviewer. In some cases a verbatim transcript will be made. In every case an abstract will be made of the tape. Tapes, abstracts and transcriptions will be deposited at the Maryland Historical Society.

These materials will be made available for research by qualified scholars, for educational use, for scholarly publications and other related purposes.

I, _____, have read the above,
          (Interviewee, please print or type)
and, in view of the historical and scholarly value of this information, I knowingly and voluntarily permit the Maryland Historical Society the full use of this information. I hereby grant and assign all my rights of every kind whatever pertaining to this information, whether or not such rights are now known, recognized, or contemplated, to the Maryland Historical Society.

_____   _____
        Date   Interviewee

_____   _____
        Date   Interviewer

_____   _____
        Date   Maryland Historical Society

Interview Date(s) _____   Subject _____

                                                          Md.Hi.1978

Instructions for Interviewers

1. Establish the date, time, and place of the interview well in advance. You may wish to call and remind the interviewee a few days before your appointment.

2. Clearly state the purpose of the interview *at the beginning.* In other words, explain why the class is doing this project.

3. Prepare for the interview by carefully reading background information about the depression and by writing down and arranging the questions you will be asking to guide the interview.

4. It is usually a good idea to keep most of your major questions broad and general so the interviewee will not simply answer with a word or two ("How did you spend your leisure time?"). Specific questions like "How much did it cost to go to the movies?" are useful for obtaining more details.

5. Avoid loaded questions such as "Everybody liked Eleanor Roosevelt, didn't they?" Instead, keep your questions neutral — "What did you think about Eleanor Roosevelt and the things she did?"

6. If any of your questions involve controversial matters, it is better to ask them toward the end of the interview, when the interviewee is more comfortable talking with you.

7. Always be courteous, and be sure to give the person enough time to think, remember, and answer. Never argue, even if he or she says something with which you strongly disagree. Remember that the purpose of the interview is to find out what *that person* thinks, not what you think.

8. Always take notes, even if you are tape-recording the interview. Notes will be helpful in clarifying unclear portions of the tape and will be essential if the recorder malfunctions or the tape is accidentally erased.

9. Many who use oral history believe that the release forms should be signed at the beginning of the interview, while others insist that this often inhibits the person who is to be interviewed, and therefore should not be done until the end of the session. Although students who are only using the material for a class exercise are not always held strictly to the federal requirements, it is still better to obtain a signed release. Without such a release the tape cannot be heard and used by anyone else (or deposited in an oral history collection), and the infor-

mation the tape contains cannot be published or made known outside the class-room.

10. Try to write up the results of your interview as soon as possible after the interview has been completed. Even in rough form, these notes will help you to capture the "sense" of what was said, as well as the actual information that was presented.

A Suggested Interview Plan

Remember that the person you have chosen to interview is a *person*, with feelings, sensitivities, and emotions. If you intend to tape-record the interview, ask permission first. If you believe that a tape recorder will inhibit the person you have selected, then leave it at home and rely on your ability to take notes.

The following suggestions may help you get started. To begin with, people usually remember the personal aspects of their lives more vividly than they remember national or international events. That is a great advantage in this exercise, because what you are attempting to find out is how this person lived during the depression. Begin by getting some important data on the interviewee:

1. name

2. age in 1930

3. race, sex

4. where the person lived in the 1930s and what that area was like then

5. family background (what the interviewee's parents did for a living; number of brothers, sisters; whether interviewee considered himself/herself rich, middle class, poor)

6. educational background

Then move to the aspects of the person's life that will flesh out your picture of the 1930s.

1. What did this person do for a living?

2. Was the person ever unemployed during the depression? What did he or she do?

3. If the interviewee was young during the depression, what about his or her parents?

[229]

4. How did the person spend leisure time? If single, what were the dating and courtship practices like?

5. How important was the family? The church? The school? Other institutions?

The above questions will give you a fairly good idea of how the person lived during the 1930s. You should supplement these with questions of your own, formed to help clarify the points above. For example,

1. Did the person know other people worse off than he or she was? Did the person help them? If so, in what ways?

2. Was the person's life of the 1920s altered by the depression? How?

3. Did the person go to the movies often? What did he/she see? What about the radio and radio programs? How much did it cost to see a movie in the 1930s? How much was a coke or a soda?

Finally, review some of the basic legislation of the New Deal and the significant events of the era. Then, as a class or in small groups, develop some questions about these programs and events. For example,

1. Did the person ever get employment through programs like the WPA or CCC? If not, did the interviewee know others who did?

2. Does the person remember any new unions or efforts to unionize local industries during the 1930s? Were there any major strikes?

Such questions might well be tailored to different geographic and economic locations — farming, mining, urban, small town, South, West, Midwest, Northeast.

INTERVIEWS

From Studs Terkel, Hard Times *(New York: Pocket Books, 1978), pp. 139–142, 123–124, 104–105, 445–449, 62–63, and 148–150, respectively.*

HANK OETTINGER, *A Linotype Operator*
I came from a very small town in northern Wisconsin. It had been ravaged by the lumber barons. It was cut-over land, a term you hear very often up there. It was a one industry town: tourist business. During the winter, there was nothing.

A lot of people who suffered from the Depression — it was new to them. It wasn't new to me. I was number ten in a family of eleven. My father, who had one leg, worked in a lumber mill for a while. Lost it, held a political job for a while, Registrar of Deeds. Lost it. Ninety-two percent of the people in the county were on welfare in the early years of the Depression.

We could have gone on relief, but my father refused. Foolish pride. He would not accept medical care, even. I had, oh God, a beautiful set of teeth. To have one filled was $2 at the time, I think. Oh, my gosh, my teeth just went. Eventually, I got to work and saved most of them. But the fact that he wouldn't even accept medical relief — stubborn Dutchman! . . .

I remember seeing a hunger march to City Hall. It was a very cold, bitter day. My boss was looking out of the window with me. I didn't know what the hell it was. He says, "They ought to lock the bastards up." I thought to myself: Lock them up for what? All of a sudden, the printing business like everything else went kerplop. I was laid off in '31. I was out of work for over two years. I'd get up at six o'clock every morning and make the rounds. I'd go around looking for work until about eight thirty. The library would open at nine. I'd spend maybe five hours in the library.

The feeling among people was beautiful. Supposing some guy was a hunter. He'd go out and get a hold of some ducks or some game, they'd have their friends over and share it. . . .

I had it drilled in me: there are no such things as classes in America. I awoke one day. I was, by this time, working for a newspaper in Waukesha. They had a picture of this farm woman, standing in the window of her home and the dust had completely covered everything, and there was a dead cow. And here, at the bottom of the same page, they had a picture of Bernard Baruch. He had made some big deal in the stock market and was on somebody's yacht. I looked at one picture and then the other. No classes in America.

I was making sixty-seven cents an hour as a linotype operator. At about $27 a week, I was a big shot. I was rolling. And gradually got involved in the union movement. The printers played a big role in the early days of the CIO. This may seem unusual, a high class craft union went along with John L. Lewis against the old aristocracy of labor.

The union man today under forty knows absolutely nothing about the struggles. They don't want to upset the wonderful applecart they have. We used to sing, in the organizing days of the CIO, "Solidarity Forever." The Communists were active in it. Hell, we'd even sing "The Internationale" on occasion.

Could I get a young printer today, who drives a big Buick, who has a home in the suburbs — could I get him to sing "Arise, ye prisoners of starvation"?

DOROTHE BERNSTEIN, *A Waitress*

I went into an orphan home in 1933. I was about ten. I had clean clothes all the time, and we had plenty to eat. We'd go through the park when we walked to school. Railroad tracks came somewhere. The picture's like it was yesterday.

The men there waited for us to go through and hand them our lunches. If we had something the dietitian at the home would prepare that we didn't like. We'd give them the little brown paper bags.

Today I tell my daughters: be careful of people, especially a certain type that look a certain way. Then we didn't have any fear. You'd never think that if you walked by people, even strangers: gee, that person I got to be careful of. Nobody was really your enemy. These were guys who didn't have work. Who'd probably work if there was work. I don't know how they got where they were going or where they ended up. They were nice men. You would never think they would do you bodily harm. They weren't bums. These were hard luck guys.

On Fridays, we used to give 'em our lunch, all of us. They might be 125 of us going to school, carrying the same brown paper bag, with mashed sardine sandwiches and mayonnaise on it. This was thirty some years ago. I still don't eat a sardine. (Laughs.) . . .

People talk about the good old times. These can't be the good old times when men wanted to work and couldn't work. When your kids wanted milk and you had to go scratch for it. I remember one girl friend I went to store with. She was real ashamed because they had food stamps. I remember how apologetic she was to me. It kind of embarrassed her. She said, "You want to wait outside?"

Louise was a Bohemian girl. Her mother had a grocery store that they lived behind. Louise used to do the books, and there was always owing. You never said to the people: "Do you have the money to pay me?" They would say, "Write it in the book." And you wrote it in the book, because this was their family food, and they had to have it. It wasn't that you were giving it away. Eventually, you'd be paid.

I never knew any real millionaires who were diving out of windows. I would read it like it was fiction. Who had that kind of fantastic money? They would kill themselves because of loss of it? To me, it's easier and nicer to scratch a little bit and get up.

You know, when you get down so low that you can't get any lower, there's no place else to go but up. You do either one of two things: you either lay down and die, or you pull yourself up by your bootstraps and you start over.

CLIFFORD BURKE, *A Retired Man Who Does Volunteer Work in a Black Neighborhood*

The negro was born in depression. It didn't mean too much to him, The Great American Depression, as you call it. There was no such thing. The best he could be is a janitor or a porter or shoeshine boy. It only became official when it hit the white man. If you can tell me the difference between the depression today and the Depression of 1932 for a black man, I'd like to know it. Now, it's worse, because of the prices. Know the rents they're payin' out here? I hate to tell ya.

We had one big advantage. Our wives, they could go to the store and get a bag of beans or a sack of flour and a piece of fat meat, and they could cook this. And we could eat it. Steak? A steak would kick in my stomach like a mule in a tin stable. Now you take the white fella, he couldn't do this. His wife would tell him: Look, if you can't do any better than this, I'm gonna leave you. I seen it happen. He couldn't stand bringing home beans instead of steak and capon. And he couldn't stand the idea of going on relief like a Negro. . . .

I never applied for PWA or WPA, 'cause as long as I could hustle, there was no point in beating the other fellow out of a job, cuttin' some other guy out. . . .

ELSA PONSELLE, *Elementary School Principal*

I began to teach in December, 1930, and I was paid until June, 1931. When we came back, the city had gone broke. We kept on teaching, of course. I didn't go hungry and had a place to live. My father provided me with enough money to get by. But it was another thing for the men who were married and had children.

They began to pay us with warrants, which carried six percent interest. A marvelous investment. But not for the teachers who had to take them for pay. They had to peddle those warrants for what they could get. It was a promise to pay when the city got some money. We didn't think we'd ever get paid, but the businessmen knew better. . . .

The Depression hit other members of my family. My brother, a tailor, like my father, was working one day every three months. He had a wife and two children. We were able to help him out. My sister-in-law came to me one day and said: "You want to hear something really funny? Johnny came home and said he had to bring some canned goods to school for the poor children. Where the hell is he gonna find kids poorer than we are?" We protected the kids from any idea that they were deprived. . . .

Do you realize how many people in my generation are not married? Young teachers today, they just naturally get married. All the young men are around. There were young men around when we were young. But they were supporting mothers.

It wasn't that we didn't have a chance. I was going with someone when the Depression hit. We probably would have gotten married. He was a commercial artist and had been doing very well. I remember the night he said, "They just laid off quite a few of the boys." It never occurred to him that he would be next. He was older than most of the others and very sure of himself. This was not the sort of thing that was going to happen to *him*. Suddenly he was laid off. It hit him like a ton of bricks. And he just disappeared. . . .

. . . The rich, then, had an instinct for self-preservation. They didn't flaunt their money, if you remember. They didn't have fancy debutante parties, because it was not the thing to do. They were so God-damned scared they'd have a revolution. They damn near did, too, didn't they? Oooohhh, were they scared! What's more scared than a million dollars?

The Depression was a way of life for me, from the time I was twenty to the time I was thirty. I thought it was going to be forever and ever and ever. That people would always live in fear of losing their jobs. You know, *fear*. And, yet, we had, in a way, a wonderful time. We were young. . . .

How can you talk about the Depression without talking about F.D.R.? I remember when he was at the Chicago Stadium and all of us ran from school to get there. He came in on his son's arm. We didn't realize that he was really and truly crippled until we saw the braces. He got up there and the place just absolutely went up in smoke. What was tremendous about him was — with all the adoration — his sense of humor. He acted as though he didn't take himself seriously.

And Eleanor. Eleanor. I think she's the greatest thing that ever happened to anybody. I think of the way they talked about her, about her looks, about her voice. I used to get so rabid. Why I didn't have high blood pressure, I don't know.

[234]

MARY OWSLEY, *A Farm Woman Who Was Born in Kentucky and Moved to Oklahoma in 1929*

There was thousands of people out of work in Oklahoma City. They set up a soup line, and the food was clean and it was delicious. Many, many people, colored and white, I didn't see any difference, 'cause there was just as many white people out of work than were colored. Lost everything they had accumulated from their young days. And these are facts. I remember several families had to leave in covered wagons. To Californy, I guess.

See, the oil boom come in '29. People come from every direction in there. A coupla years later, they was livin' in everything from pup tents, houses built out of cardboard boxes and old pieces of metal that they'd pick up — anything that they could find to put somethin' together to put a wall around 'em to protect 'em from the public.

I knew one family there in Oklahoma City, a man and a women and seven children lived in a hole in the ground. You'd be surprised how nice it was, how nice they kept it. They had chairs and tables, and beds back in that hole. And they had the dirt all braced up there, just like a cave.

Oh, the dust storms, they were terrible. You could wash and hang clothes on a line, and if you happened to be away from the house and couldn't get those clothes in before that storm got there, you'd never wash that out. . . . These storms, when they would hit, you had to clean house from the attic to ground. Everything was covered in sand. Red sand, just full of oil.

The majority of people were hit and hit hard. They were mentally disturbed you're bound to know, 'cause they didn't know when the end of all this was comin'. There was a lot of suicides that I know of. From nothin' else but just they couldn't see any hope for a better tomorrow. I absolutely know some who did. Part of 'em were farmers and part of 'em were businessmen, even. They went flat broke and they committed suicide on the strength of it, nothing else.

A lot of times one family would have some food. They would divide. And everyone would share. Even the people that were quite well to do, they was ashamed. 'Cause they were eatin',' and other people wasn't.

My husband was very bitter. That's just puttin' it mild. He was an intelligent man. He couldn't see why as wealthy a country as this is, that there was any sense in so many people starving to death. . . .

JOE MORRISON, *A Coal Miner*

Once I counted the people that I gave a lift to from Detroit to southern Indiana. It was fourteen people that I give a lift to that day. One was a woman with three children. Detroit was a one-industry town. When auto went down, everything went down. If there was a job in the auto plant, there'd be two hundred men for that job. (Laughs.)

In '30 and '31 you'd see freight trains, you'd see hundreds of kids, young kids, lots of 'em, just wandering all over the country. Looking for jobs, looking for excitement. . . . The one thing that was unique was to see women riding freight trains. That was unheard of, never had been thought of before. But it happened during the Depression. Women gettin' places by ridin' freight trains. Dressed in slacks or dressed like men, you could hardly tell 'em. Sometimes some man and his wife would get on, no money for fare.

You'd find political discussions going on in a boxcar. Ridin' a hundred miles or so, guys were all strangers, maybe two or three knew each other, pairs. There might be twenty men involved. They would discuss politics, what was happening. What should be done about this, that and so forth.

Questions to Consider

The first four pieces of evidence (Figures 1–4) consist of three sample release forms and a form for an oral history deed of gift. Why might some people want to close their memoirs until after their deaths? Of what value might it be to a neighborhood, town, or state to accumulate an oral history collection?

If there is no one in your family who is over sixty-five years old, how will you go about finding someone to interview for this project? If you do have older relatives, what would be the special advantages of interviewing them? Would there be any disadvantages? Which do you think might be the most difficult part(s) of the interview you will be conducting? Why?

There is a great deal of literature about conducting oral history interviews, and the Instructions for Interviewers lists some of the most helpful hints from the literature. It is particularly important to prepare interview questions in advance and to avoid leading your interviewee by asking loaded questions. The interview plan presented in the evidence is in the form of suggestions — something to get you started. How can you learn more about the New Deal programs and their impact? About what your interviewee thought about the Roosevelts?

The last section of evidence consists of brief excerpts from a book called *Hard Times: An Oral History of the Depression.* The author, Studs Terkel, was a young law school student at the beginning of the Great

Depression. He lived with his parents in Chicago until the mid-1930s, when he gave up the idea of being a lawyer, became a radio script writer, and worked odd jobs. Eventually he turned to journalism, interviewing ordinary people about their experiences. The excerpts included in the evidence are from interviews with a variety of people who lived in different parts of the country. As you study each excerpt, note the specific points emphasized by the person being interviewed. Then try to find patterns in their experience as a whole — what do these patterns tell you about people's feelings, perceptions, and reactions to the depression?

For example, try to identify the socioeconomic class (upper, middle, lower) to which these people belonged at the time of the depression. (The occupations, such as waitress, coal miner, and teacher, listed after their names indicate the occupations they had at the time they were interviewed.) Some, like Hank Oettinger, Clifford Burke, and Elsa Ponselle, tell you directly, but others, like Dorothe Bernstein, Mary Owsley, and Joe Morrison, give you only indirect clues to their backgrounds.

At least four of the six people mention specific personal effects the depression had on them. What were those effects? Furthermore, Morrison, Owsley, and Oettinger came from regions that were especially hard hit by the depression. Why were their regions hit so hard? Is there anything in the evidence to indicate how the depression affected women and blacks? How did those interviewed react to other people and their hardships? How did their communities react? Finally, several of the people interviewed compared conditions during the depression with conditions at the present time. What conclusions did they reach?

Epilogue

"People talk about the good old times," Dorothe Bernstein told Studs Terkel. "These can't be the good old times when men wanted to work and couldn't work." In spite of her conclusion, however, the popularity of sentimental television shows like "The Waltons" and 1930s collectible items like "depression glass" and Shirley Temple dolls indicates that many Americans may well be nostalgic for the "good old days."

Yet for Americans who lived through the depression, the fear of a recurring depression lingered on even after World War II. After the war, women and blacks were relegated to low-level jobs and marginal positions in both educational institutions and the work place as middle-class white men concentrated on climbing the professional and corporate ladders. The 1950s American dream centered on the traditional nuclear family, inhabiting a ranch-style suburban house

[237]

fully equipped with a modern kitchen, a television set, and two cars. The cold war added a new fear — atomic warfare — to the old economic anxieties, and the conservative swing in national politics was matched by the conservative mood in high schools and on college campuses across the nation. It would not be until the 1960s, when a new generation came of age, that Americans (especially women, blacks, and young people) would begin to raise real questions about our country and its postdepression values.

Chapter 9

The United States and the Cold War: Salt of the Earth (1954)

The Problem

By the end of the Second World War in 1945, the lives and collective mentality of Americans were quite different than they had been prior to 1941. Waging war had required almost the total mobilization of the country, an effort organized and directed by a federal government that continued to grow in size and power. Government contracts to large manufacturers for war materials had acted both to stimulate the economy and to increase the size and profits of America's largest corporations. On the agricultural front, the need to feed our own servicemen and servicewomen, those of our allies, and our civilian population had accelerated the mechanization of the farm as well as the consolidation of once-independent family farms into large agribusinesses.

For blacks and women, World War II was both an opportunity and a challenge. With over 16 million men in military service (over 10 percent of the nation's total population), blacks and women were able to obtain civilian defense jobs in unprecedented numbers. Over six million women entered the labor force during the war, many securing jobs previously held exclusively by males. For many women, working outside the home provided a new sense of self-worth and independence, feelings that did not disappear after the war. Almost 900,000 blacks, both men and women, served in the armed forces, and over one million blacks migrated from the South to take industrial jobs in other sections of the nation. Hence both black servicemen and service-women, and civilians used the Second World War to better their situations

Chapter 9
*The United States
and the Cold
War:* Salt of the
Earth *(1954)*

and, by 1945, were in the process of pushing for political and social rights to complement their economic gains. And having just triumphed over the extreme racism of Nazi Germany, many white Americans were sympathetic to black aspirations, seeking to place the United States on a higher moral plane than that of its former foe.

Probably the greatest change confronting Americans at the end of World War II was the nation's new position of leadership in world affairs. The United States had acquired enormous industrial and military might (supplemented by the atomic bomb), and many Americans were anxious that the country not retreat into isolationism but rather use its power to build a better postwar world. As President Franklin Roosevelt's close adviser Harry Hopkins remembered, "We really believed in our hearts that this was the dawn of the new day we had all been praying for and talking about for so many years."

This optimism, however, was soon tempered by the realities of the postwar world. Two major superpowers had emerged from World War II: the United States and the Soviet Union. Allies in the war against Germany, the two superpowers nevertheless harbored feelings of mutual suspicion and distrust. To many Americans, including the new president Harry Truman, Russian Communists were dedicated to the overthrow of capitalism and "democracy" and intent on world domination. To the Soviets, whose

nation had been invaded twice in the twentieth century, the United States and its western allies posed an immediate threat. To counter any future invasion, the Soviet Union sought to dominate nations in Eastern Europe. Furthermore, both powers resorted to widespread espionage activities.

Both the United States and the Soviet Union took actions that collectively increased tension and a sense of cold war between the two great powers. These actions shocked Americans out of their postwar idealistic hopes, plummeting them into an era of fear, suspicion, hysteria, and anticommunism. Each Communist victory was seen as a great tragedy for what Americans came to call the "free world." Each captured Soviet spy only increased apprehensions and gave birth to the fear that the Communists were everywhere — in the government, in businesses important to national security, in schools, in scientific research centers, in Hollywood. By 1949, when Communist leader Mao Zedong triumphed in China, America had entered into a second Red Scare, similar to the paranoia that gripped the United States after World War I. The media carried the near-hysterical charges of the House Committee on Un-American Activities (HUAC), Senator Joseph McCarthy, and others that Communist agents and spies were actively trying to subvert nearly every aspect of American life.

This second Red Scare affected almost every aspect of Americans' behavior and collective thought. Most states joined the federal government in requiring loyalty oaths and establishing loyalty review boards, many of which flagrantly disregarded the constitutional safeguards of those under suspicion. Worse, a growing number of private individuals (some historians have called them "loyalty sleuths") added to the alarm by hunting "subversives" on their own. Almost anyone was a potential target.[1]

What did it take for someone to be accused of subversion? In 1947 United States attorney general Tom C. Clark issued a list of "subversive organizations" thought to be dominated by or sympathetic to communists. Although most of the listed organizations conformed to neither criterion (several were leftist but not Communist), membership or former membership in any of them could be the basis for suspicion. In the 1930s, during the depths of the depression and the rise of fascism in Europe, a number of people had joined leftist organizations, but generally they abandoned those societies after World War II. However, former memberships often returned to haunt people during the second Red Scare. People having friends or associates who had been accused of subversion and people

who obstructed, criticized, or refused to cooperate with anti-Communist investigations also came under suspicion. In short, a person could be accused on the most trivial and insubstantial "evidence." Many were.

In such an atmosphere, when accusations could cost a person his or her job, ruin a career, or mean the loss of friends, it is not surprising that people generally embraced extreme patriotism, conformity, and a collective mentality that strongly encouraged a "don't be different, don't make waves" approach to living. A few people resisted, but the vast majority went along, afraid either of a Communist menace or of being destroyed by someone's accusation against them, no matter how groundless. Government employees and teachers were but two groups under continual investigation. In reality, everyone — from businesspeople to actors, actresses, and writers — were deeply affected and afraid.

The period of the second Red Scare was a confusing one for the American film industry, largely centered in Hollywood, California. On one hand, filmmakers had traditionally opposed censorship from outside the industry, preferring instead to allow Hollywood to police itself as to language, sexual material, and sociopolitical opinions. On the other hand, many people in the film community felt strongly that leftists within that community were such a threat to the United States and the independence of the film industry that these people must be rooted out by any means possible. Therefore,

1. Young screen actress Nancy Davis was rumored to be the subject of such an investigation. She appealed for help to Screen Actors Guild president Ronald Reagan, claiming that there was no truth to the accusations against her. Reagan offered her the assistance of his office.

Chapter 9
The United States
and the Cold
War: Salt of the
Earth *(1954)*

when the House Committee on Un-American Activities in 1947 undertook an investigation of communism in Hollywood, many producers and prominent actors (including Walt Disney, Robert Taylor, Gary Cooper, and Ronald Reagan) cooperated with the committee, offering examples of leftist activity in the film industry and names of men and women thought to have Communist affiliations.

The House Committee on Un-American Activities, formed in 1938 as a temporary committee to investigate fascist and Communist activities in the United States, had long been eager, as one of its members put it, "to track down the footprints of Karl Marx in movieland." Republican victories in the congressional elections of 1946 had given that party control of both the House of Representatives and the Senate and, as a result, the chairs of all congressional committees. The chairmanship of HUAC thus fell to J. Parnell Thomas of New Jersey, a man determined to purge Hollywood of all Communist and leftist influence. Under Thomas, the committee held closed hearings in Los Angeles in May 1947 and, amid much ballyhoo, open hearings in Washington in October.

At the Washington hearings, some of the witnesses who had received HUAC subpoenas refused to cooperate with the committee, invoking their rights under the First Amendment and refusing to give information on their own affiliations or the affiliations of others. Mostly screenwriters, some

undoubtedly Communists, some former Communists, and others simply liberal in their sociopolitical opinions, these uncooperative witnesses were dubbed the "Hollywood Ten," were judged by Chairman Thomas to be in contempt of Congress, and were later sentenced by a grand jury to a one-year term in the federal penitentiary.[2]

While the HUAC hearings were confusing and, moreover, failed to uncover any Communist conspiracy to mold American public opinion through movies, an aroused public opinion forced Hollywood executives to take steps to bar "suspicious" people from the film industry. In November 1947 fifty motion picture executives held a two-day meeting at the Waldorf-Astoria Hotel in New York, at which they established an informal but highly effective blacklist that prevented "suspicious" people from finding jobs in films. No studio would hire a blacklisted writer, director, producer, actor, or actress, nor would any film be distributed in which

2. The Hollywood Ten were screenwriters Dalton Trumbo, Albert Maltz, Alvah Bessie, Samuel Ornitz, Ring Lardner, Jr., Lester Cole, and John Howard Lawson; writer and producer Adrian Scott; directors Edward Dmytryk and Herbert Biberman. Two of them, Maltz and Lardner, had won Academy Awards for screenplays, and Trumbo was probably the best-paid screenwriter in Hollywood. Although each member of the Hollywood Ten was sentenced to one year in prison, most were released after serving half of their terms. At the hearings, the Hollywood Ten all invoked their rights under the First Amendment (freedom of speech) rather than under the Fifth Amendment (freedom from self-incrimination).

a blacklisted person had taken part. Some careers were permanently ruined; other men and women were unable to find work in films for years; still others, like screenwriter Carl Foreman, were forced to leave the United States in order to continue their film work. As actor and strong anti-Communist John Wayne said, "I'll never regret having helped run [Carl] Foreman out of the country."[3]

Unable to find anything in Hollywood, a number of blacklisted film artists banded together in 1951 to form their own production company. As one of their supporters exclaimed, "The blacklisted! They're like gold laying in the streets. We'll make good pictures and we'll make money." The new company immediately went out in search of stories that would make good film plots, financial backing, and other blacklisted artists to join the initial company members.

The key figures in the new company were Herbert Biberman, Paul Jarrico, and Michael Wilson. Biberman had been born in Philadelphia in 1900, educated at the University of Pennsylvania, at Yale, and in Europe, and had spent some time in his family's textile business before going into the theater and films. From 1935 to 1947 he worked in Hollywood as director, screenwriter, and sometimes co-producer of low-budget films. Jarrico was a screenwriter who longed to produce films, and had as part of his credits the screenplays to *Tom, Dick and Harry, Thousands Cheer, Song of Russia,* and *Las Vegas Story.* Undoubtedly the most talented of the trio was Michael Wilson. A native of Oklahoma, Wilson became involved in leftist causes while attending the University of California, Berkeley. Moving to Hollywood in 1940, he worked mostly on scripts for William Boyd ("Hopalong Cassidy") westerns before joining the Marines during World War II. Returning to Hollywood after the war, Wilson shared an Academy Award for the screenplay *A Place in the Sun* (1951) and was nominated for another Oscar for his screenplay *Five Fingers* (1952). When HUAC returned to its investigation of the film industry in 1951, Wilson was named an "unfriendly witness" for refusing to answer the committee's questions and was blacklisted.

At the time that the new company was searching for good stories, a strike had been called in Bayard, New Mexico, against the New Jersey Zinc Company by Local 890 of the Mine, Mill and Smelter Workers Union, a local whose membership was largely composed of Mexican-Americans.[4]

3. Before Foreman was blacklisted and forced to leave Hollywood, he and Stanley Kramer collaborated on the film *High Noon,* considered by many to be a film classic and the first "adult" western. The film was released early in 1952 and won the New York Film Critics' award for best picture of 1952.

4. The militant Mine, Mill and Smelter Workers Union had been expelled from the Congress of Industrial Organizations (CIO) in 1950 for alleged Communist influence, a fact that had undoubtedly influenced Jarrico and Wilson's choice of their subject.

Chapter 9
*The United States
and the Cold
War:* Salt of the
Earth *(1954)*

Jarrico went to New Mexico to investigate, and subsequently Wilson spent several weeks in the area talking with striking miners and their families. They returned with a fascinating story that they were determined would be their new company's first film. Prohibited from picketing by a court-issued injunction, the miners gave over the picket line to their wives and children, who kept the strike alive.[5] It was, Jarrico and Wilson agreed, to be a story of miners and the giant company, of Mexican-Americans and Anglos, and of miners and their families. The movie was to be shot in New Mexico with the miners and their families playing themselves and a pieced-together film crew of blacklisted and nonunion cameramen and technicians. Only two professional actors were in the film: blacklisted Will Geer, who played the unsympathetic sheriff, and Mexican star Rosaura Revueltas.

The decision to make a film based on the story of a strike waged mostly by Mexican-Americans made it almost inevitable that the movie would clash with the climate of opinion of the early 1950s. Hostility to Mexican-Americans, which had been strong for many years, had increased markedly during the depression of the

1930s, when Mexicans, many illegal aliens willing to work for low wages, secured jobs that Anglos thought belonged to them. In 1953 the federal government initiated Operation Wetback, a program designed to find and deport illegal Mexican aliens. At the same time, the conservative shift in public opinion during the late 1940s adversely affected the image of organized labor in the American mind. In 1947 a Republican Congress passed over the veto of President Truman the Taft-Hartley Act, which severely restricted the actions of organized labor and gave more power to employers who dealt with unions. In light of all these developments, a film about unionized Mexican-American miners was bound to be controversial.

In spite of technical and financial difficulties and continued threats of violence, the shooting of the film, by then titled *Salt of the Earth,* was completed in 1953. Editing the film and adding the sound track proved even more difficult because leaders of the various Hollywood unions tried to close all facilities to the makers of *Salt of the Earth.* Even after the film was ready for showing, no company would distribute it and the head of the International Alliance of Theatrical and Stage Employees Union (IATSE) refused to allow projectionists to show the movie. After some preview showings in Chicago, the film was shown in a New York theater, opening in March 1954, and in a drive-in theater in New Mexico. After that, *Salt of the*

---

5. Under the terms of the 1947 Taft-Hartley Act, the United States attorney general can request a federal judge to issue an injunction prohibiting strikers from picketing if the attorney general believes that the industry being struck is important to national security.

Earth was forgotten by almost everyone except those who had made it.

In this chapter you have been provided with several pieces of evidence:

1. a speech discussing *Salt of the Earth* by Representative Donald L. Jackson (R, Calif., and a member of HUAC) from the *Congressional Record* of March 19, 1953;

2. letters by certain individuals in government, organized labor, and the film industry concerning the movie;

3. portions of the film's screenplay, copyright © 1953 by Michael Wilson and used by permission; and

4. some reviews and news stories about the film from *Newsweek* magazine.

Your task in this chapter is to examine and analyze the evidence to understand how the controversy surrounding *Salt of the Earth* and the movie itself can be seen as a reflection of the times in which the film was made. Like literature, poetry, art, music, and other creative forms, a film can be understood as a product of the time in which it was produced. So also can the public *reactions* to films and other artistic endeavors be understood as the products of those same times. In this chapter, therefore, you will be using the evidence to re-create the public mood of the early 1950s, when *Salt of the Earth* was made and when the public first reacted to it.

The Method

In addition to entertaining large audiences and thereby making money, commercial films almost always contain messages for the viewers. Sometimes explicitly stated, sometimes partially hidden through the uses of metaphor or allegory, these messages are always the products of the times in which the films are created and therefore form the central core or meaning of each film. For example, the film *Drums Along the Mohawk* (released in 1939 and starring Henry Fonda and Claudette Colbert) was ostensibly a story about the trials of a family on the American frontier in the 1770s. In this case, the frontier was a metaphor for America in the 1930s, its ideals and institutions endangered by the rise of totalitarianism in Europe and Asia. The message was clear: To save themselves and their way of life, Americans would have to be prepared to meet the attacks of the ruthless barbarians who sought to destroy them. So while the film *Drums Along the Mohawk* seemed to be a story about American settlers and their Indian foes, the real message of the movie was lost on almost no one.

Films, therefore, can generally be seen on two levels. On one level is the story being told, the unfolding of events. On another level, however, is the message the film is trying to convey. What is the filmmaker trying to communicate to his or her audience?

Chapter 9
The United States
and the Cold
War: Salt of the
Earth *(1954)*

How does the filmmaker hope the audience will react to the film? Like a good book, a good film will leave its audience with much to think about.

To a historian, the audience reaction to a particular film and its message is as important a piece of evidence as the film itself. In addition to box office receipts and audience behavior in the theaters (applause, boos, and so forth), movie reviews and news stories about a particular film, although not always precise or reliable, often are good indications of the public's reaction to a specific movie. How did the public react to a particular film? What can that reaction tell us about the collective mentality of the times in which the film was made and shown?

Begin by reading the material excerpted from the *Congressional Record* of March 19, 1953, and the letters and news stories about the film *Salt of the Earth.* Representative Jackson's speech was delivered and these letters and stories were written before anyone had actually seen the controver-

sial movie and indeed even before it was finished. Why, then, was there so much controversy? What does this tell you about the time in which the film was made?

Next examine the excerpts from the screenplay for *Salt of the Earth.* What is the central story line? Are there important subplots? More crucial, what is the message (or messages) of the film? How, therefore, is the film a product of the time in which it was made?

Finally, analyze the five reviews of *Salt of the Earth* (the piece in *Variety,* a weekly newspaper that caters to the entertainment industry, is not a review per se but can be treated as such). On what points do the reviewers agree? On what points do they disagree? How do the reviews either confirm or deny statements made about the film in the earlier news stories and in the material from the *Congressional Record*? How does all this evidence shed light on the collective mentality of Americans in the 1950s?

The Evidence

SPEECH AND CORRESPONDENCE FROM THE *CONGRESSIONAL RECORD*

Excerpted from the Congressional Record, *83rd Cong., 1st Sess., March 19, 1953, Vol. 99, pt. 2, pp. 2126–2127.*

REPRESENTATIVE DONALD L. JACKSON *(R, Calif.)*

Mr. Speaker, there has been considerable interest in the House and throughout the country generally with respect to a moving picture being made in Silver

City, N. Mex., under the auspices of a number of witnesses who have in the past refused under oath to affirm or deny their alleged membership in the Communist Party.

I have asked all major studios, the Hollywood A. F. of L. [American Federation of Labor] Film Council, the Secretaries of State and Commerce, and the Attorney General of the United States to submit suggestions as to what legal steps can be taken, following upon a proper finding that the picture is indeed designed to inflame racial hatreds, toward stopping the export of this picture abroad to the detriment of United States policy and interests abroad.

I wish I could have waited for all of the replies to these inquiries before inserting any in the *Record*. However, as a member of the Committee on Un-American Activities I am leaving tomorrow for Los Angeles where the committee opens hearings on next Monday. I am inserting those answers which I have received to this time from Roy M. Brewer, chairman, Hollywood A. F. of L. Council, Mr. Howard Hughes, of RKO, the Secretary of Commerce and the Assistant Secretary of State. I will insert other replies following my return to Washington.

I hope that a legal method can be found by which the completion of this picture in the United States and its export to foreign nations can be stopped pending a legal finding as to its contents and purposes.

(The letters referred to follow.)

Los Angeles, Calif., March 18, 1953.

Donald L. Jackson,
House of Representatives,
Washington, D.C.:

The Hollywood AFL Film Council assures you that everything which it can do to prevent the showing of the Mexican picture, Salt of the Earth will be done. However, an investigation discloses that at this time there is no work being done on this picture in Hollywood nor by any Hollywood persons except those who have been involved in one way or another in pro-Communist activities. The best information seems to indicate that final shots of this picture are to be taken in Mexico and it is probable that processing of film is being done there. The film council will solicit its fellow members in the theaters to assist in the prevention of showing of this picture in any American theaters, but the extent to which we can as a union take action in such a matter is limited by reason

Chapter 9
The United States
and the Cold
War: Salt of the
Earth *(1954)*

of the restrictive features in the Taft-Hartley Act which continues to be a burden on loyal American unions. Thank you for your interest.

Sincerely,
Roy M. Brewer,
Chairman, Hollywood AFL Council.

March 18, 1953.

Congressman Donald L. Jackson,
House Office Building,
Washington, D.C.

Dear Congressman Jackson:

In your telegram you asked the question, "Is there any action that industry and labor in motion picture field can take to stop completion and release of picture and to prevent showing of film here and abroad?"

My answer is "Yes." There is action which the industry can take to stop completion of this motion picture in the United States. And if the Government will act immediately to prevent the export of the film to some other country where it can be completed, then this picture will not be completed and disseminated throughout the world where the United States will be judged by its content.

According to newspaper reports, photography of this motion picture has been finished at Silver City, N. Mex.

However, completion of photography of a motion picture is only the first step in production.

Before a motion picture can be completed or shown in theaters, an extensive application of certain technical skills and use of a great deal of specialized equipment is absolutely necessary.

Herbert Biberman, Paul Jarrico, and their associates working on this picture do not possess these skills or this equipment.

If the motion picture industry — not only in Hollywood, but throughout the United States — will refuse to apply these skills, will refuse to furnish this equipment, the picture cannot be completed in this country.

Biberman and Jarrico have already met with refusal where the industry was on its toes. The film processing was being done by the Pathe Laboratories, until the first news broke from Silver City.

But the minute Pathe learned the facts, this alert laboratory immediately refused to do any further work on this picture, even though it meant refunding cash paid in advance.

Investigation fails to disclose where the laboratory work is being done now. But it is being done somewhere, by someone, and a great deal more laboratory work will have to be done by someone, before the motion picture can be completed.

Biberman, Jarrico, and their associates cannot succeed in their scheme alone. . . .

If the picture industry wants to prevent this motion picture from being completed and spread all over the world as a representative product of the United States, then the industry and particularly that segment of the industry listed above, needs only to do the following:

Be alert to the situation.

Investigate thoroughly each applicant for the use of services or equipment.

Refuse to assist the Bibermans and Jarricos in the making of this picture.

Be on guard against work submitted by dummy corporations or third parties.

Appeal to the Congress and the State Department to act immediately to prevent the export of this film to Mexico or anywhere else.

Sincerely,

Howard Hughes.

The Secretary of Commerce,
Washington, March 16, 1953.

The Honorable Donald L. Jackson,
House of Representatives,
Washington, D.C.

Dear Mr. Jackson:

This is in reply to your letter of February 26, 1953, in which you inquire whether effective legislation exists to prevent the exportation of finished prints of the motion picture Salt of the Earth, now in this country. You have stated further that this film presents a distorted and untrue picture of life in this country, and if shown abroad would serve anti-American purposes.

The Export Control Act (63 Stat. 7) authorizes the President (who, in turn, has authorized the Secretary of Commerce) to prohibit or curtail exports of any articles, materials, or supplies to the extent necessary (1) to safeguard the domestic economy from supply shortages, (2) to safeguard the national security

Chapter 9
*The United States
and the Cold
War:* Salt of the
Earth *(1954)*

insofar as it might be affected by exports of strategic commodities, and (3) to further our foreign policy. At the present time, exposed motion picture film is not on our list of controlled commodities and may, therefore, be exported to all countries except those of the Soviet bloc without our specific authorization. Shipments of film to the Soviet bloc would, however, now require our approval.
. . .

[*The secretary of commerce then noted that the government would ordinarily put all of one commodity, such as motion pictures, under export control, but that the government could single out a particular film if it wished.*]

I am not expressing an opinion as to whether such action should be taken since, as you are aware, it would necessitate a foreign policy determination with respect to which I should have to obtain advice from the Secretary of State, and possibly the President. It is my understanding that you have already written to Secretary Dulles in this connection, and also that regarding the alien agent aspect of this matter, referred to in your letter, you have written to the Attorney General.

Sincerely yours,

Sinclair Weeks,
Secretary of Commerce.

Department of State,
Washington, March 18, 1953.

The Honorable Donald L. Jackson,
House of Representatives.

My Dear Don:

Reference is made to your letter of February 26, 1953, regarding the motion picture, Salt of the Earth, now being produced in New Mexico. The background material which you have furnished relative to the content of this film and the circumstances of its production would apparently justify your concern as to its effect if released abroad.

A study of the existing legislation which might be employed to prevent the export of this film indicates that there are two principal relevant acts. Section 5b, of the Trading With the Enemy Act, would apparently offer control over the export of any item. The history of this legislation did not contemplate its use as a means of censorship. Its terms, however, are broad and general in nature and can be employed to prohibit any type of export. This act is administered by the Treasury Department. . . .

[*The assistant secretary of state then reviewed the Export Control Act, which he also thought was applicable. Finally, he pointed out that the Foreign Agents Registration Act of 1938, administered by the Department of Justice, might be used to stop distribution of the film.*]

The problem, therefore, apparently would be to determine the source of the funds used in the production of this picture and whether or not they are acting under order, request, or direction of a foreign principal, and a subsequent ruling by the Attorney General on the basis of his findings.

It would appear that the laws and regulations outlined above represent the acts which could be best employed to prevent the foreign distribution of this film.

I would like to discuss this with you.

Sincerely yours,

Thruston B. Morton,
Assistant Secretary
(For the Secretary of State).

NEWS STORIES

Excerpted from a review in Newsweek, *March 2, 1953, pp. 27–28.*

Reds in the Desert

Silver City is a rough-hewn mining town lying amidst the piñon- and juniper-dotted hills of southwestern New Mexico. In its 75 years, it has survived the raids by Geronimo's Apaches, the antagonisms of its Mexican-American and "Anglo" citizens, and the sometimes violent strikes in its valuable lead, copper, and zinc mines.

Last week, Silver City's 8,000 citizens were up in arms over a new chapter being added to the town's history. Cause of the trouble was "Salt of the Earth," a movie being made in and around town.

What gave Silver City the jimjams was not only the film's content — parts of which began leaking out last week — but the background of the people

Chapter 9
The United States
and the Cold
War: Salt of the
Earth *(1954)*

making it. Of the two-dozen professionals involved — actors, technicians, writers — fully half had been identified by Hollywood labor unions as persons named under oath as Communists or confirmed fellow travelers, or people who refused to answer Congressional questions by standing on the Fifth Amendment. . . .

Love Story. Production on "Salt of the Earth" began last month. Quietly, sets representing a jail, the "collar" of an underground mine, and battered shacks were constructed on a ranch owned by Alford Roos — an elderly eccentric who professes Mohammedanism and is the inventor of a money-manufacturing machine. The Fierro Café, a union hangout, was converted into an indoor sound stage.

A spokesman described the movie as a "love story" dealing with "the changed relationship of a husband and wife as they become involved in union activities." . . .

Two scenes, however, made Silver City's blood run hot and cold. One showed a deputy sheriff, who had arrested a Mexican-American, brutally pistol-whipping the man's small child. The other showed women and children jammed into the local jail. Mexican-Americans and "Anglos" in Silver City were certain that south of the border these scenes could only create ill.

Civic leaders calmed Silver City hot-heads who wanted to "run the Reds out of town." But in Hollywood, the studio unions were up in arms. Roy Brewer, chairman of the AFL Film Council, said: "Hollywood has gotten rid of these people and we want government agencies to investigate carefully." . . .

From Newsweek, *March 9, 1953, p. 39.*

Red Salt

The Communist-tinged movie "Salt of the Earth" being filmed at Silver City, N.M., encountered new difficulties last week (*Newsweek,* March 2). Immigration authorities picked up their Mexican star Rosaura Revueltas and held her for deportation proceedings. Then, Cathedral Films demanded a change in the title on the ground that it already had been used for a religious picture. And this week a citizens' delegation stopped a camera crew from shooting a street scene in Silver City.

Excerpted from a review in Newsweek, *March 16, 1953, p. 43.*

Silver City Troubles

The trials and tribulations of the "Salt of the Earth" company, making a movie whose thesis was that Latin Americans were persecuted in the United States, ballooned into violence last week.

In Silver City, N.M., the film's principal locale, people had grumbled about the Communist-dominated International Union, of Mine, Mill, and Smelter Workers, which was backing the project, and about the producers, writers, and technicians, most of whom had either served jail terms or run into Hollywood trouble for refusing to affirm or deny their Communist affiliations.

But in nearby Central, grumbling fomented action. When a movie crew attempted to shoot a few street scenes, citizens turned out to block it. They told the moviemakers to get out and stay out.

In another nearby town, Bayard, action was rougher. A committee met the crew and told it to leave. The crew refused and a fight broke out. Earl Lett, a 42-year-old druggist, spotted big, blond Clinton Jencks, international representative of the IUMMSW.

"I grabbed him by the coat so he couldn't get away and let him have it," said Lett. "It" was a black eye.

Bullets by Night. A few hours later, Jencks filed an assault and battery charge against Lett and then led reporters to a parking lot. He pointed to four bullet holes in his car and said it had happened in the early morning hours when no one was around.

On Tuesday night, 100 Silver City people met and set a deadline. A delegation was sent to the union with the message: "Get out of town in twelve hours or go out in black boxes." The deadline passed without any more trouble. But state troopers were called in to prevent bloodshed.

The next night, a secret meeting was held at the home of the Rev. John P. Linnane of St. Vincent de Paul Church, who had warned against violence. Present were another Catholic priest, representatives of the film company, two peace officers, and two townspeople. One of the townspeople was a saloon-keeper who had been hearing ugly talk from his customers. Some people were planning, he said, to take the law into their own hands. There was a sudden increase in the sale of guns, too. The film company agreed to wind up its work by Saturday, a promise which it kept. . . .

Chapter 9
The United States
and the Cold
War: Salt of the
Earth *(1954)*

SCREENPLAY

Screenplay from Herbert Biberman, Salt of the Earth: The Story of a Film *(Boston: Beacon Press, 1965), pp. 315–373.*

Salt of the Earth,
Screenplay by Michael Wilson

[*The film begins with a pregnant woman, Esperanza Quintero, doing her chores outside her home, one of many small wooden shacks along a dirt road. She has chopped wood, built a fire under a large tub of water, and is scrubbing clothes and then hanging them on the line to dry.*]

ESPERANZA'S VOICE: This is our home. The house is not ours. But the flowers . . . the flowers are ours.

EXT., ZINC TOWN. VISTA SHOT, DAY.

We see several small stores, a gas station, scattered frame and adobe shacks, and in deep b.g., a Catholic church.

ESPERANZA'S VOICE: This is my village. When I was a child, it was called San Marcos.

FULLER VISTA SHOT, INCLUDING THE MINE ON A HILLTOP.

The mine dominates the town like a volcano. Its vast cone of waste has engulfed most of the vegetation on the hill and seems to threaten the town itself.

ESPERANZA'S VOICE: The Anglos changed the name to Zinc Town. Zinc Town, New Mexico, U.S.A.

EXT., CHURCH CEMETERY. MEDIUM SHOT, DAY.

An ancient graveyard beside a Catholic church.

ESPERANZA'S VOICE: Our roots go deep in this place, deeper than the pines, deeper than the mine shaft.

EXT., COUNTRYSIDE. LONG PAN SHOT, DAY.

We see great scudding clouds and the jagged skyline of a mountain spur. The mountain is scarred and pitted by old diggings. The lower slope is a skirt of waste, the grey powdery residue of an abandoned mine.

ESPERANZA'S VOICE: In these arroyos my great grandfather raised cattle before the Anglos ever came.

CLOSE SHOT: A SIGN ATTACHED TO A FENCE.

It reads:

PROPERTY OF DELAWARE ZINC, INC.

VISTA SHOT: THE ZINC MINE IN THE DISTANCE.

ESPERANZA'S VOICE: The land where the mine stands — that was owned by my husband's own grandfather.

CLOSER SHOT, FEATURING THE MINE HEAD.

At closer range we see the head frame, power house and Administration Building.

ESPERANZA'S VOICE: Now it belongs to the company. Eighteen years my husband has given to that mine.

[*The scene shifts to the interior of the zinc mine where Esperanza's husband, Ramón, is fixing and lighting dynamite charges and then running rapidly to escape the blast. Next the camera shows the primitive but neat and clean interior of the Quintero home where Esperanza is ironing. Her son, Luís, thirteen, and her daughter, Estella, five, are looking at a cake she has baked. Meanwhile, a group of angry miners led by Ramón have gone to the mine administration building. They complain to Chief Foreman Barton about the dangers of igniting dynamite when working alone. Barton is unsympathetic and tells the miners that if they will not do the job the company will hire someone else.*]

RAMÓN: Who? A scab?[6]

BARTON: An American.

He exits. Ramón stands there, taut.

[*At the Quintero home that evening, Luís asks his father if there will be a strike. Ramón ignores the question. Esperanza tells Ramón that they are behind on their monthly payments for the radio and that the store has threatened to repossess it.*]

Ramón's forehead falls against his upraised palm, as if to say it's too much to bear. The little girl looks at him gravely.

6. Scab is a derogatory term for a nonunion worker, often someone brought in by management to take the place of a striking union worker.

Chapter 9
The United States
and the Cold
War: Salt of the
Earth *(1954)*

ESPERANZA: We're only one payment behind. I argued with her. It isn't right.

RAMÓN (*softly, imploring heaven*): It isn't right, she says. Was it right that we bought this . . . this instrument?

He rises, holding Estella.

RAMÓN: But you had to have it, didn't you? It was so nice to listen to.

ESPERANZA (*quietly*): I listen to it. Every night. When you're out to the beer parlor.

Ignoring this mild rebuke, Ramón crosses to the radio. CAMERA PANS with him. He glares at the console, mimicking an announcer's commercial.

RAMÓN: "No money down. Easy term payments." I tell you something: this installment plan, it's the curse of the working man.

He slams his coffee cup down on the console, sets his daughter down and goes to the kitchen. Esperanza quickly polishes the console where he struck it.

INT., KITCHEN. MEDIUM CLOSE SHOT.

Ramón strips to the waist, pours some water from the tub on the stove into a pan on the drainboard. Esperanza appears in the doorway, watching him, her heart sinking. Her fingers go to her lips in a characteristic gesture.

ESPERANZA: Where you going?

RAMÓN: Got to talk to the brothers.

Esperanza bites her finger, trying to hide her disappointment. Ramón bends over the pan to wash. He has not noticed the cake. Esperanza picks it up quickly, hides it in a cupboard. Ramón splashes his face and neck with water, looks up in irritation.

RAMÓN: This water's cold again.

ESPERANZA: I'm sorry. The fire's gone out.

She begins to stoke the stove.

RAMÓN: Forget it.

ESPERANZA: Forget it? I chop wood for the stove five times a day. Every time I remember. I remember that across the tracks the Anglo miners have hot water. In pipes. And bathrooms. Inside.

RAMÓN (*bitterly*): Do you think I like living this way? What do you want of me?!

He reaches for a towel. Esperanza hands him one.

ESPERANZA: But if your union . . . if you're asking for better conditions . . . why can't you ask for decent plumbing, too?

Frustrated, evasive, Ramón turns away, buttoning his shirt.

RAMÓN: We did. It got lost in the shuffle.

ESPERANZA: What?

RAMÓN (*shrugging*): We can't get everything at once. Right now we've got more important demands.

ESPERANZA (*timidly*): What's more important than sanitation?

RAMÓN (*flaring*): The safety of the men — that's more important! Five accidents this week — all because of speed-up. You're a woman, you don't know what it's like up there.

She bows her head without answering and picks up the heavy tub of water on the stove. Unassisted, she lugs it to the dishpan in the sink and fills it. Ramón begins to comb his hair, adding in a more subdued tone:

RAMÓN: First we got to get equality on the job. Then we'll work on these other things. Leave it to the men.

ESPERANZA (*quietly*): I see. The men. You'll strike, maybe, for your demands — but what the wives want, that comes later, always later.

RAMÓN (*darkly*): Now don't start talking against the union again.

ESPERANZA (*a shrug of defeat*): What has it got me, your union?

Ramón looks at her in amazement, not with anger, but with deep concern.

RAMÓN: Esperanza, have you forgotten what it was like . . . before the union came? (*Points toward parlor.*) When Estella was a baby, and we couldn't even

[257]

Chapter 9
The United States
and the Cold
War: Salt of the
Earth *(1954)*

afford a doctor when she got sick? It was for our families! We met in grave-yards to build that union!

ESPERANZA (*lapsing into despair*): All right. Have your strike. I'll have my baby. But no hospital will take me, because I'll be a striker's wife. The store will cut off our credit, and the kids will go hungry. And we'll get behind on the payments again, and then they'll come and take away the radio . . .

RAMÓN (*furiously*): Is that all you care about? That radio? Can't you think of anything except yourself?

ESPERANZA (*breaking*): If I think of myself it's because you never think of me. Never. Never. Never . . .

[*Esperanza breaks into tears, and Ramón stalks out of the house, heading for the beer parlor in Zinc Town. He is followed by his son, Luís. The miners are drinking beer and discussing the unsuccessful union negotiations with the company. They point out the in-justice of the rule that Mexicans must work alone when setting dynamite charges while Anglos work in pairs. Finally, someone notices Luís, who reminds his father that it is Esperanza's Saint's Day.[7] Ramón hastily arranges a serenade for his wife.*]

EXT., QUINTERO COTTAGE. FULL SHOT, NIGHT.

The lights come up in the parlor. The front door opens, revealing Esperanza and Estella. They smile, remaining in the open doorway as the serenaders go into a final chorus. The song ends in laughter and applause. They swarm into the house.

INT., PARLOR. FULL SHOT, NIGHT.

A merry bedlam, with Esperanza receiving her guests. Sal Ruiz starts up a bawdy folk song on his guitar. He is urged on by Charley Vidal's wild falsetto. Antonio lugs a case of beer into the house and immediately starts uncapping it, passing foaming bottles to everyone. The women gather around Esperanza, embracing her, wishing her a happy birthday in English and Spanish. Ramón is the last to enter.

CLOSER ANGLE, FEATURING ESPERANZA AND RAMÓN

confronting one another in the center of the room. Ramón gazes at her in si-lence, repentant. She returns his gaze, for the moment oblivious of her guests, who gracefully withdraw from the situation. Esperanza's eyes fill with tears, she smiles tremulously, and her fingers go to her lips.

---

7. One's Saint's Day is celebrated like a birthday.

ESPERANZA: I . . . I must get dressed.

She flees from the room. Ramón follows her, gesturing to men to keep on with their singing.

INT., BEDROOM. TWO SHOT: RAMÓN AND ESPERANZA.

He puts his arms around her, tentatively. Her forehead falls against his shoulder.

ESPERANZA: I did not mean to weep again. Why should I weep for joy?

RAMÓN: I'm a fool.

ESPERANZA: No, no . . .

She raises her head, brushing her cheek against his.

ESPERANZA: Was it expensive, the beer?

RAMÓN: Antonio paid for it.

ESPERANZA: Forgive me . . . for saying you never thought of me.

RAMÓN (*with effort*): I did forget. Luís told me.

Grateful for his honesty, she pulls his head down, kisses him. He returns her kiss passionately.

[*A few days later, Esperanza is again in her yard doing the family's laundry. She is approached by a group of miners' wives.*]

ESPERANZA'S VOICE: The Anglo miners have bathrooms and hot running water, Consuelo said, why shouldn't we?

ESPERANZA (*sighing*): I know. I spoke to Ramón about it — only a week ago.

RUTH: And what did he say?

ESPERANZA: They dropped it from their demands.

CONSUELO (*sighs*): *Es lo de siempre.*[8]

TERESA (*the militant*): We got to make them understand — make the men face up to it. (*To Ruth*) Show her the sign.

---

8. "That's how it always is."

Chapter 9
*The United States
and the Cold
War:* Salt of the
Earth *(1954)*

ANOTHER ANGLE: THE GROUP

as Ruth lifts up a placard, hitherto unseen, which she has been holding at her side. It reads:

WE WANT SANITATION NOT DISCRIMINATION

CONSUELO: We'll make a lot of signs like this. Then we'll get all the wives together and go right up to the mine.

ESPERANZA: To the mine?

TERESA: Sure. Where they're negotiating. In the company office. We'll go up there and picket the place.

CONSUELO: Then both sides will see we mean business.

ESPERANZA (*thunderstruck*): A picket line? Of . . . of ladies?

RUTH: Sure. Why not?

Luz flings a pair of damp pants on the clothes line without hanging them up.

LUZ: You can count me in.

ESPERANZA (*scandalized*): Luz!

LUZ: Listen, we ought to be in the wood choppers' union. Chop wood for breakfast. Chop wood to wash his clothes. Chop wood, heat the iron. Chop wood, scrub the floor. Chop wood, cook his dinner. And you know what he'll say when he gets home (*Mimics Antonio*), "What you been doing all day? Reading the funny papers?"

The women laugh softly, all except Esperanza.

TERESA: Come on, Esperanza — how about it? We got to.

ESPERANZA: No. No. I can't. If Ramón ever found me on a picket line . . . (*Her voice trails off*).

CONSUELO: He'd what? Beat you?

ESPERANZA: No . . . No . . .

[*Suddenly the women hear the mine whistle giving five short blasts — the signal that an accident has occurred. Women and children rush toward the mine and, after an agonizing delay, they discover that Kalinsky, one of the few Anglos in the mine, has been*

[260]

injured in a dynamite blast set by Ramón. After an angry exchange of words about safety practices, the foreman orders the miners back to work. But they refuse to return, and later that night hold a meeting at the union hall. Some of the women, including Esperanza, quietly enter the hall and sit along the side.]

ESPERANZA'S VOICE: The meeting was nearly over when we came in. Charley Vidal was making a speech. He said there was only one issue in this strike — equality. But the mine owners would stop at nothing to keep them from getting equality. . . .

THE HALL. FULL SHOT, FEATURING CHARLEY.

ESPERANZA'S VOICE: He said the bosses would try to split the Anglo and Mexican-American workers and offer rewards to one man if he would sell out his brother. . . . There was only one answer to that, Charley said — solidarity. The solidarity of working men.

Charley concludes his speech

CHARLEY VIDAL: To all this, brothers, there is only one answer, the solidarity of working men!

He sits down to loud applause which comes up over sound track. Sal Ruiz rises, bangs his gavel.

GROUP SHOT: THE WOMEN.

Ruth and Teresa nudge Consuelo, trying to get her to rise — but Consuelo, frightened, clings to her sleeping infant. Ruth grabs the baby and Teresa practically pushes Consuelo to her feet.

WIDER ANGLE, SHOOTING PAST SAL, INCLUDING WOMEN.

Charley Vidal plucks at Sal's sleeve, points in the direction of the women.

SAL: Yes? You ladies have an announcement?

CONSUELO (*haltingly*): Well — it's not an announcement, I guess. The ladies wanted me to . . .

VOICE FROM THE FLOOR: Louder!

SAL: Consuelo, will you speak from over here?

Painfully self-conscious, Consuelo moves toward camera in f.g. She faces the men and begins again, nervous, but trying to speak louder.

Chapter 9
*The United States
and the Cold
War:* Salt of the
Earth *(1954)*

CONSUELO: The ladies have been talking about sanitation . . . and we were thinking . . . if the issue is equality, like you say it is, then maybe we ought to have equality in plumbing too . . .

CLOSE GROUP SHOT: MINERS.

Some appear resentful of the women's intrusion; others seem amused. Antonio whispers something to Alfredo. Alfredo laughs. Frowning, Ramón looks around at Esperanza, as he might look at a woman who entered church uncovered.[9]

CONSUELO'S VOICE: I mean, maybe it could be a strike demand . . . and some of the ladies thought — it might be a good idea to have a ladies auxiliary! Well, we would like to help out . . . if we can . . .

FULL SHOT: THE HALL, FEATURING CONSUELO.

Consuelo hurries back to her seat.

CAMERA HOLDS.

We hear mild, scattered applause, and then a male falsetto giggle sets off a wave of laughter. Ruiz rises, grins sheepishly.

SAL: I'm sure I can speak for all of the brothers. We appreciate the ladies offering to help, but it's getting late and I suggest we table it. The chair will entertain a motion to adjourn.

FIRST MINER (*from the floor*): Move to adjourn!

SECOND MINER: Second!

SAL: So ordered.

He brings down his gavel, and the meeting ends. Some of the miners break for the door, others begin to mill about. Ruth and Consuelo walk to the front of the hall. Now, in quick succession we see four vignettes:

TWO SHOT: SAL AND CONSUELO.

He meets her near the speaker's table, flings out his arms in a helpless gesture.

SAL: Why didn't you check with me? It's embarrassing!

TWO SHOT: RUTH AND FRANK.[10]

9. Women were required to cover their heads as a sign of respect when inside a Catholic church.
10. Frank Jenkins is the union's paid official.

She leans across the speaker's table before Frank can rise and remarks acidly:

RUTH: Why didn't you support her? You're the worst of the lot.

FRANK: But honey . . .

RUTH: Or why don't you just put a sign outside? "No dogs or women allowed!"

[*The miners go on strike and set up a long picket line outside the mine to prevent the company from bringing in strikebreakers. The sheriff and his deputies are also present outside the mine. The union distributes food rations to the miners' wives, and one day an old lady, Mrs. Salazar, whose husband had been killed in an earlier strike, joins the picketers. After this, the miners' wives form a ladies auxiliary to serve coffee and food to the men on the picket line. The strikers hold firm in spite of the company's efforts to divide them and bring in scabs. Only one miner, Sebastian Prieto, goes over to the company side. After a confrontation with Prieto, Ramón is arrested, beaten, and jailed. Esperanza's baby is born and baptized after Ramón is released from jail. After the baptism the men play poker at the Quinteros' home while the women listen to the radio.*]

INT., PARLOR: AT THE POKER TABLE.

Frank is shuffling the cards. Esperanza is seen crossing the bedroom in b.g.

SAL (*to Ramón*): And another thing. Your attitude toward Anglos. If you're gonna be a leader . . .

RAMÓN (*cutting in*): What attitude?

SAL: You lump them all together — Anglo workers and Anglo bosses.

RAMÓN (*indicating Frank*): He's a guest in my house, isn't he?

SAL: Sure. But you want the truth? You're even suspicious of him.

RAMÓN: Maybe. I think he's got a few things to learn about our people.

There is a rather uneasy pause. Esperanza is seen re-crossing from bedroom to kitchen, the baby in her arms. Frank continues shuffling.

FRANK: Go on. Spill it.

RAMÓN (*slowly*): Well, you're the organizer. You work out strike strategy — and most of the time you're dead right. But when you figure everything the rank-and-file's to do, down to the last detail, you don't give *us* anything to think about. You afraid we're too lazy to take initiative?

[263]

Chapter 9
*The United States
and the Cold
War:* Salt of the
Earth *(1954)*

FRANK (*defensively*): You know I don't think that.

RAMÓN: Maybe not. But there's another thing . . . like when you came in tonight — (*indicates picture*) — I heard you ask your wife, "Who's that? His grandfather?"

CLOSE SHOT: PORTRAIT OF JUÁREZ.

RAMÓN'S VOICE: That's Juárez — the father of Mexico. If I didn't know a picture of George Washington, you'd say I was an awful dumb Mexican.

BACK TO GROUP.

CHARLEY (*softening the blow*): I've never seen it fail. Try to give Ramón a friendly criticism and he throws it right back in your face.

FRANK: No. He's right. I've got a lot to learn.

ANTONIO: Now we've got that settled, deal the cards.

Frank deals. Sal grins at Frank.

SAL: If it makes you feel any better, he's got even less use for women.

BACK TO KITCHEN. FULL SHOT.

Esperanza sits on a stool near the stove, her back to camera and the other women, nursing the baby. Teresa and Consuelo are sampling the sandwiches they have made.

CONSUELO: What are they talking about in there?

RUTH (*from the doorway*): Discussing each other's weaknesses.

LUZ (*mock surprise*): I didn't know they had any.

RUTH (*looking o.s.*): Right now, Ramón's on the receiving end.

TERESA: Let's break up that game.

BACK TO MEN AT POKER TABLE.

FRANK (*earnestly to Ramón*): If the women are shut off from life in the union . . .

ANTONIO: Bet your hand!

Ruth enters scene with coffee for the men. The other women, save Esperanza, trail in behind her. Frank is so intent on his point that he ignores Ruth's presence.

FRANK: We can't think of them just as housewives — but as allies. And we've got to treat them as such.

RUTH (*snorts*): Look who's talking! The Great White Father, and World's Champion of Women's Rights.

FRANK: Aw, cut it out, Ruth.

RUTH (*to Ramón*): Me, I'm a camp follower — following this organizer from one mining camp to another — Montana, Colorado, Idaho. But did he ever think to organize the women? No. Wives don't count in the Anglo locals either.

[*The men and women begin to dance when suddenly the sheriff's deputies arrive to repossess the radio. Ramón resists but Esperanza blocks him.*]

ESPERANZA: Let them take it!

RAMÓN: Over my dead body.

ESPERANZA: I don't want your dead body. I don't want you back in jail either.

RAMÓN: But it's *yours*. I won't let them . . .

ESPERANZA (*savagely, in Spanish*): Can't you see they want to start a fight so that they can lock you *all* up at one time?

Slowly, Ramón goes lax, and Esperanza relaxes her hold on him. The deputies pick up the heavy console, lug it toward the front door. The Quinteros' guests are glum and silent. The deputies leave, closing the door behind them.

RAMÓN (*bitterly*): What are you so sad about?

He crosses to a shelf, picks up a dusty guitar and tosses it to Sal.

RAMÓN: Let's hear some real music for a change.

Sal grins. He begins to improvise. . . .

Chapter 9
The United States
and the Cold
War: Salt of the
Earth *(1954)*

[*As the strike continues into its sixth month, the miners' families begin to go hungry. Stores refuse credit to the strikers but in the seventh month of the strike contributions begin to arrive from other unions as well as from Spanish-speaking people in all parts of the country.*]

CAMERA PULLS BACK SLOWLY TO DISCLOSE

two women at a mimeograph machine.

CAMERA PANS SLOWLY AROUND

the union hall, disclosing other women at work — cutting stencils, filing papers, sealing envelopes, etc. Several small children romp and climb over the benches.

ESPERANZA'S VOICE: But that was not all — we women were helping. And not just as cooks and coffee makers. A few of the men made jokes about it, but the work had to be done — so they let us stay.

MEDIUM SHOT, FEATURING ESPERANZA

standing behind a desk, sealing envelopes. The infant Juanito lies on an improvised pallet beside her, hemmed in by piles of leaflets. Estella is licking stamps.

ESPERANZA'S VOICE: No one knew how great a change it was, till the day of the crisis . . .

FULL SHOT: THE UNION HALL.

The Sheriff, a U.S. Marshall, and several deputies appear suddenly in the entrance to the hall. They cross the room to Sal Ruiz' desk. The Sheriff is grinning broadly.

ESPERANZA'S VOICE: That was the day when the Sheriff and the Marshall came. The Sheriff was smiling — so we knew he brought bad news.

CLOSER ANGLE: GROUP AT TABLE.

Sal takes the paper, reads it gravely. The Sheriff grins triumphantly and leaves, followed by his entourage.

[*The mining company had obtained a court injunction under the Taft-Hartley Act ordering the strikers to stop picketing. If they refused they could be fined or jailed. Men and women pack the meeting in the union hall that evening. There seems to be no way out of the dilemma.*]

FULL SHOT: THE UNION HALL. ANOTHER ANGLE.

In near f.g. Chairman Ruiz is on his feet, pounding his gavel. In b.g. we can see Teresa Vidal waving for recognition. The chair recognizes her. Teresa has advanced to the speakers' table in f.g. Though obviously scared, she is not as inarticulate or halting as Consuelo had been.

> TERESA: Brother Chairman, if you read the court injunction carefully you will see that it only prohibits *striking miners* from picketing. (*A pause.*) We women are not striking miners. We will take over your picket line.

We hear a stirring, then a raucous male laugh.

> TERESA: Don't laugh. *We* have a solution. You have none. Brother Quintero was right when he said we'll lose fifty years of gains if we lose this strike. Your wives and children too. But this we promise — if the women take your places on the picket line, the strike will *not* be broken, and no scabs will take your jobs.

There is silence in the hall now. Teresa starts to walk back to her seat when Sal's voice checks her.

> SAL: If that's a motion . . . only members of the union can make a motion.

Sal glances at Charley Vidal, who sits beside him. Charley hesitates. Teresa glares at her husband. Charley takes a deep breath, yells:

> CHARLEY: I so move!

> VOICE (*from the floor*): Second!

> SAL (*uneasy*): You've heard the motion. The floor is open for debate.

> MINER: If we allow our *women* to help us, we'll be the joke of the whole labor movement!

> ANOTHER MINER: Look, brother, our women are ours, our countrywomen! Why shouldn't they help us?

THE HALL. ANOTHER ANGLE.

We see miners with their heads together in heated argument, grimaces and gestures of disapproval, individual miners rising to address the chair.

ANOTHER ANGLE, FEATURING LUZ MORALES.

Eyes flashing, she addresses the men.

Chapter 9
The United States
and the Cold
War: Salt of the
Earth *(1954)*

ESPERANZA'S VOICE: And Luz asked which was worse, to hide behind a woman's skirt, or go down on his knees before the boss?

ANOTHER ANGLE, FEATURING GONZALES.

GONZALES: We haven't counted enough on our women. The bosses haven't counted on them at all.

ANOTHER ANGLE, FEATURING CHARLEY VIDAL.

CHARLEY: Will the bosses win *now* because we have no unity between the men and their wives and sisters?

ANOTHER ANGLE, FEATURING A MINER AND HIS WIFE.

A husky miner named José Sánchez can be seen goading his wife to speak. The frightened woman finally obeys.

ESPERANZA'S VOICE: And Carlotta Sánchez said she didn't think picketing was proper for ladies. It wasn't nice. Maybe even a sin.

ANOTHER ANGLE, FEATURING GONZALES AND RAMÓN.

GONZALES: I say give the sisters a chance . . .

Gonzales' voice fades, and Ramón rises, glancing angrily at Gonzales, and begins to speak.

RAMÓN: And what will happen when the cops come, and beat our women up? Will we stand there? Watch them? No. We'll take over anyway, and we'll be right back where we are now. Only worse. Even *more* humiliated. Brothers, I beg you — don't allow this.

Ramón sits down. There is scattered applause from the men. Someone calls the question.

[*After quarreling over whether the women could vote on a union question, the miners adjourn the union meeting and reconvene as a community mass meeting in which every adult has a vote. The majority of women vote to take over the picket line but the men are divided. The motion carries, 103–85.*]

ESPERANZA'S VOICE: And so they came, the women . . . they rose before dawn and they came, wives, daughters, grandmothers. They came from Zinc Town and the hills beyond, from other mining camps, ten, twenty, thirty miles away . . .

[268]

CLOSER VIEW: THE PICKET LINE.

The women march in an orderly, determined fashion. There is no gaiety. Teresa and Mrs. Salazar are in charge. They are as bold and self-assured as two drill sergeants. Most of the women are dressed for the occasion — wearing shirts, jeans and sneakers or saddle shoes.

> ESPERANZA'S VOICE: By sun-up there were a hundred on the line. And they kept coming — women we had never seen before, women who had nothing to do with the strike. Somehow they heard about a women's picket line — and they came.

MEDIUM LONG SHOT: MINERS ON HILLSIDE.

On the steep wooded slope above the picket post the varsity squats on its collective haunches. The men smoke, watching the picket line with mingled awe and apprehension.

> ESPERANZA'S VOICE: And the men came too. They looked unhappy. I think they were afraid. Afraid the women wouldn't stand fast — or maybe afraid they would.

THE HILLSIDE. ANOTHER ANGLE, HIGHER UP THE SLOPE.

Several miners stand here with their families. They, too, look unhappy. Jenkins and his wife are among them.

> ESPERANZA'S VOICE: But not all the women went to the picket post. Some were forbidden by their husbands. (*A pause.*) I was one of these.

[*Sheriff Vance and his deputies try to frighten off the women by driving trucks at the picket line, but the women will not leave. The officials then fire tear gas into the line but the wind blows it back toward the trucks. Finally, the deputies begin hitting the women but they fight back. At this point Esperanza hands the baby to Ramón and runs to join the other women.*]

CLOSER ANGLE: THE PICKET POST.

Luz Morales is climbing Vance's back, clinging to his arms. Another woman clutches at his gun hand, trying to prevent him from drawing his pistol. Esperanza comes running up. She stops for a second, slips off her right shoe. Vance knocks the other woman down, pulls his revolver from his holster. Esperanza whacks him over the wrist with her shoe, knocking the weapon out of his hand. Luz digs into his hair with both hands.

Chapter 9
The United States
and the Cold
War: Salt of the
Earth *(1954)*

BACK TO RAMÓN ON HILLSIDE,

helpless, speechless, holding the baby. Suddenly he runs out of scene. Luís grabs Estella's hand, follows.

ANOTHER PART OF THE HILL: THE LOWER SLOPE.

Charley and Frank are watching the action. Ramón comes running into scene.

RAMÓN: Why are you standing there? Do something!

CHARLEY (*looking o.s.*): Relax.

RAMÓN: But women are getting hurt! We've gotta take over!

CHARLEY: They're doing all right.

FRANK (*grins, looks at baby*): Anyway, looks like you've got your hands full.

Completely frustrated, Ramón looks down at the tiny bundle in his arms.

[*The women continue to staff the picket line in spite of continual harassment by the sheriff and his deputies. Finally, the superintendent of the mines, Mr. Alexander, arrives in his Cadillac.*]

ALEXANDER (*to Sheriff*): Well?

SHERIFF (*hopelessly*): I've tried everything but shootin' 'em down.

ALEXANDER: You haven't tried locking them up!

SHERIFF (*doubtfully*): You want 'em *all* arrested?

ALEXANDER: No, just the ring leaders. The fire-eaters. And the ones with big families . . . (*to Barton*) Barton — where's that boy?

BARTON (*waves, shouts*): Hey, you — c'mere.

Sebastian Prieto, the fingerman, leaves a group of deputies in b.g. and comes over. The Sheriff glances at him with contempt, then starts toward the picket line, Prieto and the deputies moving with him.

[*Prieto points out the key women in the strike, including Esperanza, and they are arrested. Once in jail, the women begin chanting and demanding food, cots, and baths. In the meantime, the men must do the housework and care for the children.*]

EXT., QUINTERO BACK YARD. FULL SHOT, DAY.

The shot matches the earlier scene of Luz and Esperanza — but now Ramón and Antonio are hanging out the wash. Estella and the little Morales boy are there. Ramón sees them playing in the baskets.

RAMÓN: Will you kids get out of those baskets!

There are two large wicker baskets beside the fence: one contains Juanito, the other a mountain of damp clothes. As he works, Antonio calls from across the fence:

ANTONIO (*in Spanish*): How goes it?

RAMÓN (*in Spanish*): It never ends.

He snaps out a damp undershirt, hangs it up. Suddenly he explodes:

RAMÓN: Three hours! Just to heat enough water to wash this stuff! (*A pause. He goes on working.*) I tell you something. If this strike is ever settled — which I doubt — I don't go back to work unless the company installs hot running water for us. (*Another pause.*) It should've been a union demand from the beginning.

ANTONIO: Yeah.

We hear the baby wail. Ramón walks over to the basket, puts the nipple of the bottle back in Juanito's mouth. Then he resumes his chores. Antonio muses as he works.

ANTONIO: It's like Charley Vidal says — there's two kinds of slavery, wage slavery and domestic slavery. The Woman Question, he calls it.

RAMÓN: The woman . . . *question?*

ANTONIO: Question, question — the problem, what to do about 'em.

RAMÓN (*cautious*): So? What does he want to do about 'em?

ANTONIO: He says give 'em equality. Equality in jobs, equality in the home. Also sex equality.

RAMÓN (*a long pause*): What do you mean — sex equality?

ANTONIO: You know . . . . (*Leers, shifts into Spanish.*) What's good for the goose is good for the gander.

Chapter 9
*The United States
and the Cold
War:* Salt of the
Earth *(1954)*

CLOSE SHOT: RAMÓN

with a clothespin in his mouth, mulling over this concept. His imagination runs away with him. He scowls thoughtfully.

ANTONIO'S VOICE: He's some organizer, that Charley. He can organize a wife right out of your home.

Ramón bites viciously on a clothespin and hangs up a pair of diapers.

[*The sheriff soon releases the women picket leaders, who return to the Quintero home to plan the next day's picket line. Ramón is angry and leaves for the beer hall. When he returns late that night, he and Esperanza argue about the strike, its chances for success, and her role in it.*]

ESPERANZA: Ramón . . . we're not getting weaker. We're stronger than ever before. (*He snorts with disgust.*) *They're* getting weaker. They thought they could break our picket line. And they failed. And now they can't win unless they pull off something big, and pull it off fast.

RAMÓN: Like what?

ESPERANZA: I don't know. But I can feel it coming. It's like . . . like a lull before the storm. Charley Vidal says . . .

RAMÓN (*exploding*): Charley Vidal says! (*He rises, flinging rifle aside.*) Don't throw Charley Vidal up to me!

ESPERANZA: Charley's my friend. I need friends. (*She looks at him strangely.*) Why are you afraid to have me as your friend?

RAMÓN: I don't know what you're talking about.

ESPERANZA: No, you don't. Have you learned nothing from this strike? Why are you afraid to have me at your side? Do you still think you can have dignity only if I have none?

RAMÓN: You talk of dignity? After what you've been doing?

ESPERANZA: Yes. I talk of dignity. The Anglo bosses look down on you, and you hate them for it. "Stay in your place, you dirty Mexican" — that's what they tell you. But why must you say to me, "Stay in *your* place." Do you feel better having someone lower than you?

[272]

RAMÓN: Shut up, you're talking crazy.

But Esperanza moves right up to him, speaking now with great passion.

ESPERANZA: Whose neck shall I stand on, to make me feel superior? And what will I get out of it? I don't want anything lower than I am. I'm low enough already. I want to rise. And push everything up with me as I go . . .

RAMÓN (*fiercely*): Will you be still?

ESPERANZA (*shouting*): And if you can't understand this you're a fool — because you can't win this strike without me! You can't win *anything* without me!

He seizes her shoulder with one hand, half raises the other to slap her. Esperanza's body goes rigid. She stares straight at him, defiant and unflinching. Ramón drops his hand.

[*The women return to the picket line in the morning and the men, except Ramón, go deer hunting rather than stay around the mine. Suddenly the sheriff and his deputies arrive to evict the Quinteros and begin to remove their possessions from the company-owned house. Men, women, and children gather to watch the eviction — helpless and frustrated. Small boys throw clods of dirt at the deputies.*]

CLOSER ANGLE, FEATURING RAMÓN AND ESPERANZA.

Ramón is calmer now, but alert, planning, thinking. He looks around at their gathering forces — not yet impressive, but growing every moment. He almost smiles with slow realization.

RAMÓN (*half to himself*): This is what we've been waiting for.

ESPERANZA (*anxious, puzzled*): What are you saying?

RAMÓN: This means they've given up trying to break the picket line. (*A pause.*) Now we can *all* fight together — all of us.

Suddenly he draws Esperanza close, whispers something in her ear. She nods, turns swiftly to several other women, huddles with them a moment.

CAMERA PANS

with the women as they enter the yard, swooping down to pick up household belongings on their way.

EXT., FRONT YARD. FULL SHOT.

Other women, seeing what Esperanza and her sisters are up to, swiftly join them in the yard, begin to pick up furniture and carry it back into the house by way of the rear door. Deputies emerging from the house, loaded down with furniture and bric-a-brac, find themselves passing women loaded with objects they have just deposited in the yard. One of the deputies stops in close f.g., staring at the women in slack-jawed bafflement. Ramón glances at Mrs. Salazar. He winks. Mrs. Salazar smiles. It is the first time we have seen her smile.

BACK TO YARD, FEATURING SHERIFF.

His deputies are hopelessly dispersed. Half of them are chasing the boys, while the furniture-moving contingent is out-numbered by women crowding into the yard. The Sheriff wheels right and left in helpless exasperation. He spots Ramón near the front fence, strides over to him.

SHERIFF (*bellowing*): Now see here, Quintero! These women are obstructin' justice. You make 'em behave, savvy?

RAMÓN: I can't do nothing, sheriff. You know how it is — they won't listen to a man any more.

SHERIFF (*blustering*): You want me to lock 'em up again?

RAMÓN (*smiles*): You want 'em *in* your lock-up again?

The Sheriff stalks off, fuming.

[*More and more miners arrive at the Quintero home, and the sheriff and his men leave. A short distance away the sheriff meets with the mining company officials, who have been watching the confrontation.*]

SHERIFF: Got any more ideas?

ALEXANDER[11] (*defensively, passing the buck*): I don't make policy.

He looks at Hartwell.[12] Hartwell puffs on a cigarette. After a long pause he says:

HARTWELL: I'll talk to New York. Maybe we better settle this thing. (*Another puff.*) For the present.

BACK TO QUINTERO YARD. FULL SHOT.

11. Alexander is the local head of Delaware Zinc, Inc., the company that owns the mine.
12. Hartwell is the company official from the New York office.

Part of the milling throng has already dispersed; those who remain are carrying the last of the Quinteros' possessions back into the house. We see Luís jump the fence and run toward his mother in f.g. She gives him a fierce hug.

MEDIUM SHOTS AT FRONT GATE.

Ramón approaches Mrs. Salazar. He takes the baby from her arms. Estella enters the gate, dragging the portrait of Juárez. Solemnly she lifts up the portrait. Ramon takes it. He walks back toward the porch, Estella at his side.

THE YARD, SHOOTING FROM THE PORCH.

Esperanza and Luís stand on the porch steps in f.g. Reaching them, Ramón turns, looks back at his friends, some of whom are still in the yard. They seem to be waiting for him to speak.

> ESPERANZA'S VOICE: We did not know then that we had won the strike. But our hearts were full. And when Ramón said,
>
> RAMÓN (*simply*): Thanks . . . sisters . . . and brothers.

The people smile softly. A few of them lift their hands in a wave of acknowledgment. They begin to leave.

CLOSE UP SHOT: THE QUINTERO FAMILY ON PORCH.

Ramón holds the baby in the crook of his arm. He hands the portrait of Juárez to Luís. The boy gazes at it with respect, wipes the dust off it, and readjusts the torn frame. Ramón heaves a long sigh. Unsmiling, he looks off at the receding convoy. Esperanza watches him.

There is a pause. Still not looking at her, Ramón says haltingly:

> RAMÓN: Esperanza . . . thank you . . . for your dignity.

Esperanza's eyes fill with tears.

> RAMÓN: You were right. Together we can push everything up with us as we go.
>
> ESPERANZA'S VOICE: Then I knew we had won something they could never take away — something I could leave to our children — and they, the salt of the earth, would inherit it.

Esperanza places her hand in Ramón's. With the children they walk into the house.

FADE OUT

Chapter 9
The United States
and the Cold
War: Salt of the
Earth *(1954)*

REVIEWS AND
NEWS STORIES

Excerpted from a review by Otis L. Guernsey, Jr., New York Tribune, *March 15,
1954, p. 13.*

Without Savor

The much-discussed "Salt of the Earth," which opened last night at the Grande
Theater at 160 E. 86th St., aims a blow at American society's most vulnerable
spot: abuse of minorities. It is a hard blow, but a glancing blow, a slanted
blow. . . .

At the same time it cannot be dignified with the word "controversial" — it
seems to be aimed not so much at examining an honest controversy, or starting
one, but at creating resentment and confusion. Its conflict is so loaded in favor
of the workers that its picture of conspiracy among bosses, police and law is absurd as a sample of modern American injustice. Obviously it is supposed to be a
dramatic object lesson and if an object lesson has a responsibility to tell all of the
relevant truth, then "Salt of the Earth" is a lie by omission — all the more un-
healthy because it is very cleverly told in terms of the movies.

A movie review is not the proper place to take up labor ethics or the alleged
political connections of those who make films. But there are occasions of misrepresentation so glaring that they involve the essential purpose of the cinema
as a form of the press, and "Salt of the Earth" is one of these occasions.

The technique is realistic, but the social villainy is not. Everyone concerned
with the mining company from the foreman up is an oily dilettante, caring little
whether the miners get killed on the job. The president of the company is sym-
bolized in a slick "Man of Distinction" magazine layout indicating that he goes
lion-hunting in Africa every year while the workers starve. The police don't
care whom they brutalize — they try to plow through a women's picket line in
an automobile.

There is a union organizer attached to the local outfit, but evidently, he does
not know that there are laws to protect labor, or free press channels for public
protest. These workers are defenseless, and yet this story is no antique from the
bad old days — there is a reference to the Taft-Hartley Act in it. No, it is simply and purely a game played with loaded dice by producer Paul Jarrico, director Herbert J. Biberman and writer Michael Wilson at the expense of the whole
truth.

The movie craftsmanship is excellent. There is a severe beauty in the location photography of a desperately poor community, and enormous affection and sympathy for these olive-skinned Americans, most of them played by actual members of the International Union of Mine, Mill and Smelter Workers, who co-sponsor the movie. . . .

In this bleak community of gray wooden shacks inhabited by people who carry their shoulders straight under work-stained clothing, there are many acute vignettes of character, including Will Geer's performance of the sheriff who is an errand-boy for the company. The work is capable throughout, and those who challenge the right of "Salt of the Earth" to be shown publicly are lending credence to its specious protest against a straw man of public evil. Let it be shown by all means, but let it be recognized for what it is: a corruption of screen journalism.

Excerpted from a review by Bosley Crowther, New York Times, *March 15, 1954, p. 20.*

Salt of the Earth Opens at the Grande — Filming Marked by Violence

Against the hard and gritty background of a mine workers' strike in a New Mexican town — a background bristling with resentment against the working and living conditions imposed by the operators of the mine — a rugged and starkly poignant story of a Mexican-American miner and his wife is told in "Salt of the Earth," a union-sponsored film drama, which opened last night at the Grande Theatre on East Eighty-sixth Street.

It is the story of a husband's firm objection to women — and, especially, his wife — mixing in the grim affairs of the strikers, and of the strong determination of the wife to participate, along with other women, in the carrying on of the strike. . . .

[*Crowther then discussed the difficulties the film company encountered in making and distributing the film.*]

In the light of this agitated history, it is somewhat surprising to find that "Salt of the Earth" is, in substance, simply a strong pro-labor film with a particularly sympathetic interest in the Mexican-Americans with whom it deals. True, it frankly implies that the mine operators have taken advantage of the

Chapter 9
The United States
and the Cold
War: Salt of the
Earth *(1954)*

Mexican-born or descended laborers, have forced a "speed up" in their mining techniques and given them less respectable homes than provided the so-called "Anglo" laborers. It slaps at brutal police tactics in dealing with strikers and it gets in some rough, sarcastic digs at the attitude of "the bosses" and the working of the Taft-Hartley Law.

But the real dramatic crux of the picture is the stern and bitter conflict within the membership of the union. It is the issue of whether the women shall have equality of expression and of strike participation with the men. And it is along this line of contention that Michael Wilson's tautly muscled script develops considerable personal drama, raw emotion and power.

CONFLICT OF PERSONALITIES

For this conflict of human personalities, torn by egos and traditions, is shown in terms of sharp clashes at union meetings, melees on dusty picket lines, tussles with "scabs" and deputy sheriffs and face-to-face encounters between the husband and wife in their meager home. It is a conflict that broadly embraces the love of struggling parents for their young, the dignity of some of these poor people and their longings to see their children's lot improved.

Under Mr. Biberman's direction, an unusual company made up largely of actual miners and their families plays the drama exceedingly well. Miss Revueltas, one of the few professional players, is lean and dynamic in the key role of the wife who compels her miner-husband to accept the fact of equality, and Juan Chacon, a non-professional, plays the husband forcefully. Will Geer as a shrewd, hard-bitten sheriff, Clinton Jencks as a union organizer and a youngster named Frank Talevera as the son of the principals are excellent, too.

The hard-focus, realistic quality of the picture's photography and style completes its characterization as a calculated social document. It is a clearly intended special interest film.

Excerpted from Variety, *March 17, 1954, pp. 1, 15.*

Fear Reds May Season "Salt of Earth" with Paprika in Foreign Showings

Fear is widely expressed by film executives and film critics in New York lest a recent independent feature, "Salt of the Earth," fall into the hands of Russian or satellite Communists and they use it as a new "Grapes of Wrath" picturing life in capitalistic America as a tooth-and-fang struggle of oppressed poor people against monsters who own everything but hearts. An even greater concern is the potential of negative world reaction in countries this side of the Iron Curtain in the event — and not unlikely — of a distorted or specially angled presentation.

Even today, after 15 years, "Grapes of Wrath" is still a yumium item with the Red.

With one or two notable exceptions, the reaction of those who have seen the controversial union film stand on the principle that, whatever the production's faults, there should be no interference with its showings anywhere. But at the same time there is concern over the kind of impression "Salt" will create abroad. Its first showing outside the U.S.A. will be in Mexico City.

As Otis L. Guernsey, Jr., the N.Y. Herald Tribune reviewer, put it, "I believe the same export rules should apply to this film as to any other. However, I would be as sorry to see anyone here or abroad get their ideas about the U.S. from this picture as from a film like "My Son John." . . .

[Variety *then summarized Guernsey's* Tribune *review.*]

In striking contrast, a spokesman for Independent Productions Corp., which is releasing "Salt," said this week that ["]the picture was a worthy ambassador for the American film industry abroad. Certainly it's a lot better than some of the bad pictures now being shipped to the foreign market." "Salt" doesn't as yet have a foreign release, although the Mexican opening is virtually arranged.

"Salt," made in cooperation with the International Union of Mine, Mill & Smelter Workers, which has been accused of Red leanings, tells of a strike by Mexican workers at a mine in New Mexico. Its theme, apart from a plea for equality for women within the union, is the company's brutal attempt to break the strike. Discrimination against Mexicans also figures prominently.

Opinion that "Salt" shouldn't be exported since it paints an untrue picture of conditions in this country and does not represent a typical labor situation was voiced by Arthur Mayer, Independent Motion Picture Distributors Assn. prexy, in N.Y. "This matter goes beyond freedom of expression," he held. "I have fought censorship long and hard, but somewhere one must draw the line. And it seems to me 'Salt of the Earth' is it."

ALIENS LACK A FRAME

Distress expressed by most of those who have seen the film is that it will be widely misinterpreted abroad. "In this country we have a necessary perspective

Chapter 9
The United States
and the Cold
War: Salt of the
Earth *(1954)*

and frame of reference, we know that this kind of thing doesn't go on as a permanent condition," was one comment. "Send this kind of thing abroad and it's bound to become a weapon in the hands of the Communists. Chances are they'd make out that these are the conditions whereas the balancing picture provided by Hollywood is just propaganda."

Problem of controlling exports without entering into the realm of censorship has plagued the industry for decades. The major distribs exercise a certain selectivity in their choice of pix going abroad. For instance, 20th-Fox recently had in mind reissuing "Grapes of Wrath" but changed its mind when it was realized that this would feed ammunition to hostile elements abroad.

The government occasionally takes an indirect hand. There were some talks between the U.S. Information Agency and Columbia re the foreign release of "From Here to Eternity." Theodore C. Streibert, the agency's director, said Monday that he was heartily in favor of voluntary action on the part of the industry in exercising export selectivity. But he added:

"I would be very cautious and hesitant to suggest government action. We don't want government controls in these matters. This kind of thing always works two ways, and never satisfactorily. You shouldn't tamper with films any more than with news dispatches."

According to the "Salt" producers, their picture will be shown abroad in exactly the same version being exhibited in the U.S. They have no intention of affixing a foreword that would indicate that the situation depicted in the film represents the exception rather than the rule.

With the exception of the two papers that didn't bother reviewing "Salt" — the Mirror and the Journal-American — all of the N.Y. critics agreed that any attempt to stop the film's export would constitute censorship.

Kate Cameron of the N.Y. Daily News, who thought in her review that the picture "has its strong points," commented that some scenes should be deleted from the film before it is sent abroad. "I don't think it's an honest picture," she said.

Bosley Crowther of the N.Y. Times, in his review, tagged the picture "a calculated social document . . . a clearly intended special interest film," and, on tracing the pic's "agitated history," expressed surprise in finding it "simply a strong pro-labor film." Crowther was the only one to detail the political record of those connected with the production.

Alton Cook in the N.Y. World-Telegram & Sun noted that "Salt" "loads its dice so heavily, all chance for sympathy is lost." He expressed apprehension over the film being used for anti-American propaganda in Latin American countries.

Following "Salt" lensing at Silver City, New Mexico, there were queries from Rep. D. Jackson (R., Cal.) to both the State and Commerce Depts. on what could be done to flash the red light on the export of "Salt." He was told that it was largely up to the conscience of the individual producer.

From Newsweek, *March 29, 1954, p. 87.*

'Salt' — One Brand

Last spring there was a civic uproar in the area of Silver City, N.M., while an independent film company was making a picture called "Salt of the Earth" (*Newsweek,* March 2, 1953). An anti-Red parade confronted the film makers with such slogans as: "We don't want Communism; respect the law; no violence, but let's show them we don't like it." In Washington, D.C., Republican Rep. Donald L. Jackson of California declared that the film was being produced under "Communist auspices." Many film people involved had lost their Hollywood jobs for suspected Communism, and the picture was sponsored by the International Union of Mine, Mill, and Smelter Workers, which was ousted from the CIO on charges of Communist domination.

Last week "Salt of the Earth" opened in New York City. The story by Michael Wilson ("A Place in the Sun," "Five Fingers") was inspired by the strike of 1951 and 1952 at the Silver City plant of the Empire Zinc Co.

The keynote of the plot is an uprising of the miners' wives when their husbands are enjoined from forming a picket line. And when the company obtains a dispossess order against one of the strike leaders, the community at large takes his furniture back into his house as fast as the sheriff's men can remove it. Under Herbert Biberman's direction, the film has a good deal of pictorial force. Against the harsh New Mexican landscape there are many effective figures, especially Rosaura Revueltas, as the strike leader's wife, and an impressive nonprofessional actor, Juan Chacon, as the leader himself. But the company men are represented, simply, as so many sleek vipers.

Summing Up. The film's final effect is wholly propagandistic — Red-tinged.

Chapter 9
The United States
and the Cold
War: Salt of the
Earth *(1954)*

Excerpted from a review in Time, *March 29, 1954, p. 92.*

Salt & Pepper

Salt of the Earth was asking for trouble. Written, produced and directed by three of Hollywood's blacklisted fellow travelers — Michael Wilson, Paul Jarrico and Herbert Biberman — the picture was sponsored by the International Union of Mine, Mill and Smelter Workers (expelled from the C.I.O. in 1950 for being Communist-dominated).

When production started near Silver City, N. Mex. (pop. 7,000), the townspeople rioted and warned the moviemakers to get out of town before they were shipped out "in black boxes" (*Time,* March 16, 1953). Under police protection, Jarrico & Co. kept shooting until the leading lady, Mexican Actress Rosaura Revueltas, was deported as an illegal alien.

Salt of the Earth had its world première last week in a tiny third-run-and-revival house in Manhattan's Yorkville district. The critics had a variety of reactions. The *Herald Tribune*'s Otis Guernsey denounced *Salt* as "a game played with loaded dice . . . at the expense of the whole truth." The *Time*'s Bosley Crowther called it simply "a strong pro-labor film." A more inspired appraisal came from the *Daily Worker*'s Joseph North: "This movie stands with the best ever made, here or anywhere across the waters . . ."

[*The reviewer then summarized the plot of the film.*]

. . . In the story of Ramon Quintero (Juan Chacon) and his wife Esperanza (Rosaura Revueltas), the moral of the strike is lived out in sweat and painful growing.

All the issues, private and public, find reconciliation in the climax as the company gives up and the workers win. The dice, without doubt, are loaded. Every boss who crosses the screen is either a sleek deceiver or a leering flunky, and the police are slavish doers of the corporate will. Nevertheless, the film, within the propagandistic limits it sets, is a work of vigorous art. It is crowded with grindingly effective scenes, through which the passion of social anger hisses in a hot wind; and truth and lies are driven before it like sand.

The passion carries the actors along too in its gale. The workers, actual miners of the New Mexico local, carry conviction in their savage setting as trained actors could never do. The best of the worker-players is Juan Chacon, real-life president of the union local. Ugly and cold as an Aztec amulet, his

[282]

heavy face comes slowly to life and warmth as the picture advances, and in the end seems almost radiant.

Three days after *Salt of the Earth's* première, the tradesheet *Variety* posed an interesting problem: Will *Salt,* if shown in theaters overseas, give the Communists ready-ground propaganda with which to pepper the U.S.? Since Jarrico & Co. are independent of the powerful Motion Picture Association, they are free to show the film wherever bookings can be had (*i.e.,* with non-M.P.A. foreign distributors). First scheduled foreign showing of *Salt of the Earth:* in Mexico City, this month.

Questions to Consider

1. What is Representative Jackson's major concern? What does he want to be done to address this concern?

2. What does Roy M. Brewer of the Hollywood AFL promise to do? Why does he mention the Taft-Hartley Act?

3. What does Howard Hughes believe that the government should do? What does he say that the motion picture industry should do?

4. How does the Secretary of Commerce think that the government might help? What problems does he foresee?

5. What additional suggestions does the Assistant Secretary of State make?

6. What kinds of people do you think read national magazines such as *Time* and *Newsweek*?

7. What impressions would readers obtain from the three *Newsweek* items, all written before the film was shown?

8. *Salt of the Earth* opens with Esperanza talking about the town as it used to be. What is the purpose of this scene? How does the argument between Barton and Ramón reinforce this point?

9. What is the nature of the conflict between Esperanza and Ramón early in the film? What does the viewer learn from the scene at the Saint's Day party? Is Esperanza and Ramón's behavior toward each other different in public and in private? Why?

10. The workers at the union meeting emphasize the "solidarity of working men." How do the men treat the women at this meeting?

11. Frank, the union organizer, and Ramón have a serious argument. What is the nature of this conflict?

Chapter 9
*The United States
and the Cold
War:* Salt of the
Earth *(1954)*

How is Frank portrayed in his subsequent argument with Ruth, his wife?

12. How do the men react to their wives' offer to picket in their places? Why do they finally give their approval?

13. When violence breaks out on the picket line, how do the women react? How do the men react? What is the result?

14. What is the significance of the conversation between Ramón and Antonio? How have the circumstances affected Ramón's opinion, if at all?

15. Why is the attempted eviction of the Quintero family a turning point in the film? How have both Esperanza and Ramón changed by the end of the film?

16. On what points do all the film reviewers agree? On what points do they disagree?

17. Do any reviewers find the film objectionable? Why?

18. Do any reviewers believe that the film's distribution should be restricted? Why?

Once you have answered these specific questions based on the evidence from the *Congressional Record, Newsweek,* the screenplay, and the film reviews, you will be ready to evaluate the collective mood of Americans during the time period. What three major issues were raised by *Salt of the Earth?* Which of these issues do *you* think was central to the film? What do you believe Americans of the 1950s saw as the central issue? Why were certain people especially concerned about the film being shown abroad? In what ways did government officials, the motion picture industry, film reviewers, and private citizens try to obstruct the production and distribution of the film? Why?

Epilogue

The national hysteria known as the second Red Scare had begun to wane by the 1960s. Senator Joseph McCarthy had been discredited in the 1954 Army hearings, was censured by the United States Senate in that same year, and died in 1957. Gradually Americans came to believe that it was better to try to negotiate with Communists in the Soviet Union, China, and elsewhere than to try to eradicate them. And although crises continued to occur, the uneasy detente for the most part seemed to be holding.

Those that had been unable to find work in the Hollywood studios for years gradually drifted back into the industry, a few even recapturing their former prominence. Dalton Trumbo and Ring Lardner, Jr., both members of the Hollywood Ten, actually increased in prestige, Trumbo as the screenwriter for *Spartacus* (1960) and Lardner for his work on *The Cincinnati Kid* (1965) and *M*A*S*H* (1970). Carl Foreman, who wrote the script for *High Noon,* remained in England where he wrote or co-wrote the screenplays for *The Bridge on the River Kwai, The Mouse That Roared, The Guns of Navaronne,* and *The Victors.* In some cases, however, his work was uncredited, for some major studios still feared repercussions if they openly reemployed blacklisted artists.

Those connected with *Salt of the Earth* for the most part did not fare so well. Actress Rosaura Revueltas was deported from the United States in 1954 and never had the Hollywood career that some felt she so richly deserved. Actor Will Geer was able to work only sporadically in films and television until he finally achieved celebrity status as Grandpa on the television series "The Waltons." Screenwriter Michael Wilson wrote a number of scripts in the 1950s and 1960s for which he received no credit: *Friendly Persuasion* (1956); *The Bridge on the River Kwai,* with Carl Foreman (1957); and *Lawrence of Arabia* (1962). Finally emerging from the blacklist, Wilson was credited for his work on *The Sandpiper* (1965), *Planet of the Apes* (1968), and *Che!* (1969). He died in 1978.

Herbert Biberman, the director of *Salt of the Earth,* filed suit against distributors and various unions, claiming that a conspiracy had been formed to prohibit the distribution and showing of the film. The case dragged on for a decade, and Biberman finally lost. His last film, *Slaves* (1969), inspired by Harriet Beecher Stowe's *Uncle Tom's Cabin,* was received without enthusiasm by most American film critics. Biberman died in 1971.

While *Salt of the Earth* was not distributed in the United States until 1965, the film enjoyed considerable success in Europe, so much so that some United States Information Agency (USIA) officials wanted to block its distribution, claiming that it portrayed life in the United States unfavorably.[13] Yet the film was voted the best picture of 1954 by the French Motion Picture Academy, won the top prize at the Czechoslovakian Karlovy Vary Film Festival in 1954, and was very popular in European nations on both sides of the iron curtain. While prints of *Salt of the Earth* were lying in their cans in 1954, the Academy Award for best picture that year went to *On the Waterfront,* ironically another film about a labor union but with a much different theme.

Few film critics today would call *Salt of the Earth* an excellent movie. Yet a study of the controversy sur-

---

13. The USIA was able to make it difficult for *Salt of the Earth* to be shown overseas, largely by hindering the process of currency exchange. Other films that encountered difficulties in the 1950s included *All the King's Men, All Quiet on the Western Front,* and *Blackboard Jungle.* See *New York Times,* May 24, 1959.

Chapter 9
*The United States
and the Cold
War:* Salt of the
Earth *(1954)*

rounding its making and distribution can tell students of American history a great deal about the collective mentality of Americans and their leaders in the 1950s. In that sense *Salt of the Earth* is an important piece of historical evidence. Moreover, the issues raised by the film itself (labor unions, racial discrimination, feminism) and by the controversy surrounding it are as timely and important today as during the second Red Scare.

Chapter 10

A Generation in War and Turmoil: The Agony of Vietnam

On May 4, 1970, a group of students at Kent State University in Ohio were protesting against the United States' military activities in Vietnam. Such protests had been spreading across college campuses since President Nixon had announced an "incursion"[1] into Cambodia in a television speech four days earlier. In response to the protests, the Ohio National Guard was called out to keep order. While a large crowd gathered, some protesting students gave flowers to the guardsmen, many of whom were about the same age as the students, and urged them to "make love, not war." But others threw stones at the guardsmen and taunted them. Tensions rose until shots rang out — the guardsmen had fired into a crowd of protesting students. Four students were killed, and eleven were wounded.

Shock spread across the nation. Many college students went on strike, disrupting or shutting down more than 250 college campuses. Increasing numbers of antiwar protesters went to Washington, D.C., to demonstrate against the widening war in Southeast Asia.

Not all Americans, however, were outraged by the National Guard's actions at Kent State. On May 8 in New York City, a group of angry construction workers clashed violently with a group of equally angry antiwar demonstrators. The issue was the American flag at City Hall, which had been lowered to half staff as a sign of

---

1. This word was used as a euphemism for air strikes and a land invasion.

mourning for the dead Kent State students. The construction workers wanted to raise the flag to full staff. The construction workers won the battle — city officials raised the flag.

What caused the deep divisions that exploded among Americans in the wake of Kent State? A partial answer to this question involves understanding two long-term trends: the United States' involvement in Southeast Asia, and the socioeconomic changes in American life that simultaneously were taking place.

The United States emerged from World War II as a superpower confronting another superpower, its former wartime ally, the Soviet Union. Both nations and their allies struggled to influence neutral countries in Europe, Latin America, Africa, and Asia. As we know, the resulting tensions and confrontations were characterized as the cold war. The basic bipartisan[2] foreign policy of the United States during this period was containment: a commitment to stop the spread of communism (and the influence of the Soviet Union) by all means short of total war. Regional defense alliances like NATO and SEATO, massive economic aid and programs like the Marshall Plan, technological and advisory military aid envisioned in the Truman and Eisenhower Doctrines, and bilateral defense treaties like that between the United

States and South Korea were all part of containment.[3]

The Japanese defeat of Western colonial powers, particularly Britain and France, in the early days of World War II had encouraged nationalist movements[4] in both Africa and Asia. The final surrender of Japan in 1945 left an almost total power vacuum in Southeast Asia. While Britain struggled with postwar economic dislocation and, within India, the independence movement, both the United States and the Soviet Union moved into this vacuum, hoping to influence the course of events in Asia.

Vietnam had long been a part of the French colonial empire in Southeast Asia and was known in the West as French Indochina. At the beginning of World War II, the Japanese had driven the French from the area. Under the leadership of Vietnamese nationalist Ho Chi Minh, the Vietnamese cooperated with American intelligence agents and fought in guerrilla-style warfare against the Japanese. When the Japanese were finally driven from Vietnam in 1945, Ho Chi Minh declared Vietnam independent.

3. NATO stands for North Atlantic Treaty Organization; SEATO stands for Southeast Asia Treaty Organization. The Marshall Plan called for massive economic aid to western Europe. The Truman and Eisenhower Doctrines offered military and technical aid to countries resisting communism.

4. Those in nationalist movements seek independence for their countries.

2. Bipartisan means supported by both political parties.

This declaration, however, was not recognized by the Western nations. At the end of World War II, France wanted to reestablish Vietnam as a French colony, but seriously weakened by war, France could not reestablish itself in Vietnam without assistance. At this point the United States, eager to gain France as a postwar ally and viewing European problems as being more immediate than problems in Asia, chose to help the French reenter Vietnam as colonial masters. From 1945 to 1954 the United States gave over \$2 billion in financial aid to France so that it could regain its former colony.

Ho Chi Minh and other Vietnamese felt that they had been betrayed. They believed that in return for fighting against the Japanese in World War II, they would earn their independence. The reentry of France, with the United States' assistance, was viewed by many Vietnamese as a broken promise. Almost immediately, war broke out between the forces of the French and their westernized Vietnamese allies and the forces of Ho Chi Minh, who by now had embraced communism. In the cold war atmosphere of the late 1940s and early 1950s the United States gave massive aid to the French who, it was maintained, were fighting against monolithic communism.

The fall of Dien Bien Phu in 1954 spelled the end of French power in Vietnam. Rather than let the area fall to the Communists, however, President Eisenhower and his secretary of state John Foster Dulles sought to stabilize the situation by dividing Vietnam temporarily into two countries — South Vietnam, ruled by westernized Vietnamese formerly loyal to the French, and North Vietnam, governed by the Communist Ho Chi Minh.

Free and open elections to unify the country were to be held in 1956. However, the elections were never held because American policymakers feared that Ho Chi Minh would easily defeat the unpopular but pro–United States Ngo Dinh Diem, the United States' choice to lead South Vietnam. From 1955 to 1960 the United States supported Diem with more than \$1 billion of aid, while civil war between the South Vietnamese and the Northern Viet Minh (later called the Viet Cong) raged across the countryside and in the villages.

President Kennedy did little to improve the situation. Facing his own cold war problems with the building of the Berlin Wall and the Bay of Pigs invasion,[5] Kennedy simply poured more money and more "military advisers" (close to seventeen thousand by 1963) into the troubled country. Finally, in the face of tremendous Vietnamese pressure, the United

5. The Berlin Wall is a barricade created to separate East Berlin (Communist) from West Berlin. The Bay of Pigs invasion was a U.S.-sponsored invasion of Cuba in April 1961 that failed. The American role was widely criticized.

States turned against Diem, and in 1963 South Vietnamese generals, encouraged by the American Central Intelligence Agency, overthrew the corrupt and repressive Diem regime. Diem was assassinated in the fall of 1963, shortly before Kennedy's assassination.

Lyndon Johnson, the Texas Democrat who succeeded Kennedy in 1963 and won election as president in 1964, was an old New Dealer[6] who wished to extend social and economic programs to needy Americans. The "tragedy" of Lyndon Johnson, as one sympathetic historian saw it, was that the president was increasingly drawn into the Vietnam War. Actually, President Johnson and millions of other Americans still perceived Vietnam as a major test of the United States' willingness to resist the spread of communism.

Under Johnson, the war escalated rapidly, and in 1964 the Viet Cong controlled almost half of South Vietnam. Thus, when two American ships were attacked by the North Vietnamese that year, Johnson used the occasion to obtain sweeping powers from Congress[7] to conduct the war as he wished. Bombing of North Vietnam

6. Johnson had served in Congress during the 1930s and was a strong supporter of New Deal programs.

7. The Tonkin Gulf Resolution gave Johnson the power to "take all necessary measures to repel any armed attack against the forces of the United States and to prevent further aggression."

and Laos was increased, refugees were moved to "pacification" camps, entire villages believed to be unfriendly were destroyed, chemical defoliants were sprayed on forests to eliminate Viet Cong hiding places, and troops increased until by 1968 about 500,000 American men and women were serving in Vietnam.

As the war effort increased, so did the doubts. In the mid-1960s, the chair of the Senate Foreign Relations Committee, J. William Fulbright, raised important questions about whether the Vietnam War was serving our national interest. Several policymakers and members of the administration (including George Kennan, author of the original containment policy) maintained that escalation of the war could not be justified. Television news coverage of the destruction and carnage along with reports of atrocities such as the My Lai massacre[8] disillusioned more and more Americans. Yet Johnson continued the bombing, called for more ground troops, and offered peace terms that were completely unacceptable to the North Vietnamese. Not until the Tet offensive — a coordinated North Vietnamese strike across all of South Vietnam in January 1968, in which the Communists captured every provincial capital and even entered Saigon (the capital of

8. This incident occurred in March 1968 when American soldiers destroyed a Vietnamese village and killed many of the inhabitants, including women and children.

South Vietnam) — did President Johnson change his mind. Two months later, Johnson appeared on national television and announced to a surprised nation that he had ordered most of the bombing to stop, had asked North Vietnam to start real peace negotiations, and had withdrawn his name from the 1968 presidential race. While we now know that the Tet offensive was a setback for Ho Chi Minh, it was seen in the United States as a major setback for the West, evidence that the optimistic press releases about our imminent victory simply were not true.

And yet America's "longest war" and the growing disillusionment that accompanied it went on. The new president, Richard M. Nixon, announced that he was committed to "peace with honor" — a double-edged policy that encompassed the gradual withdrawal of American forces and their replacement by South Vietnamese troops (Vietnamization), and the escalation of bombing of North Vietnam and neighboring areas. As you'll recall, it was Nixon's announcement of the secret incursion into Cambodia that sparked the Kent State antiwar demonstrations in May 1970.

At the same time that the United States was becoming increasingly entangled in Vietnam (1945–1970), significant changes were taking place in American society. Veterans came home from World War II eager to reestablish "normal" lives — to

marry, complete their educations, obtain steady jobs, have children, and buy homes, automobiles, and other material goods. One result was massive suburbanization, as inexpensive tract housing developments sprang up like mushrooms outside major and medium-sized cities across the nation. The birth rate almost doubled for white middle-class Americans, reversing the demographic trend toward smaller families that had begun during the late colonial era. Married women left (or were removed from) their wartime jobs by the millions, some returning to full-time jobs and others to part-time typical "female" jobs. Traditional sex roles were reinforced by popular literature and the media, and a smaller proportion of women completed college degrees or sought professional education than in previous generations. Pent-up consumer demand burst forth after wartime scarcity and rationing, only to be satisfied by more and more purchases of television sets, refrigerators and other household appliances, camping equipment, clothing, furniture, and new automobiles. According to one observer, America's "affluent society" was in full bloom by the late 1950s.

There was, however, an underside to the so-called affluent society. Indeed, many Americans did not share in its benefits at all. As middle-class whites fled to the suburbs, cities declined. Increasingly populated by the poor — blacks, Latin American immigrants, the elderly, and unskilled

[291]

white in-migrants — urban areas struggled to finance essential city services such as police and fire protection. Moreover, poverty and its victims could also be found in rural areas, as Michael Harrington pointed out in his classic study, *The Other America,* first published in 1962. Small farmers, tenants, sharecroppers, and migrant workers were not only poor, but they often lacked any access to even basic educational opportunities and health-care facilities.

The "baby boom" generation of the postwar era came of age in the late 1960s, just as the Vietnam War was escalating. The shining idealism surrounding the election of John Kennedy in 1960 had been tarnished by a series of assassinations, riots in the cities, and increasing violence in reaction to the black civil-rights movement.[9] At the same time, college enrollments increased dramatically as millions of upper- and middle-class (as well as those who aspired to be middle-class) students flocked to campuses to earn undergraduate, graduate, and professional degrees. Many of these students began to question their parents' values, especially those connected with materialism, sexual mores and traditional sex roles, corporate structure and power, and the kind

of patriotism that supported the Vietnam War. Increasingly alienated by impersonal university policies and by the actions of authority figures like police, administrators, and politicians, many students turned to new forms of religion, music, and dress as well as to the use of drugs to set themselves apart from the older generation.

Other young people who lacked the money or who were not brought up with the expectation of earning college degrees tended to continue in more traditional life patterns. They completed their educations with high school or before, although others attended a year or two at a local vocationally oriented community college or trade school. They often married younger than their college counterparts, sought stable jobs, and aspired to own their own homes. In other words, they rarely rejected the values of their parents' generation.

The issue of the draft, however, touched the lives of both groups of this younger generation. The draft, or conscription, in time of war was not new to America, nor were deferments or exemptions for various reasons. Both the Union and the Confederacy had exempted men who were well-off financially — those who could "buy" a substitute or those who owned at least twenty slaves. In World War I there were physical, mental, and financial hardship exemptions, and when ten million men were drafted for World War II, those who held jobs essential to the war effort (as well

9. Assassinations included those of John Kennedy, Robert Kennedy, and Martin Luther King. City riots, beginning with the Watts riot in Los Angeles in 1964, spread across major cities for the next several years.

as students preparing for essential professions such as engineering and medicine) were added to the list of those exempted or deferred. The post–World War II "peacetime" draft expanded the exemption and deferment categories to include all college students up to age twenty-six, and married men with children. Further, those whose religious beliefs rejected military service (such as Quakers) have, historically, been offered alternative service or exempted.

As long as military needs, and thus draft quotas, were low (1954–1964), the draft was not of great concern to young men. As late as 1966 only 7 percent of high school sophomores reported that they were concerned about the draft. But by 1969 that figure had risen to 75 percent. Although women were not included in the draft, wives, mothers, sisters, friends, and lovers were deeply concerned too.

As the need for troops increased, deferments and exemptions became somewhat more difficult to obtain. College students had to maintain good grades, graduate-student deferments were ended, and draft boards were frequently unsympathetic to pleas for conscientious-objector status.[10] But the Selective Service, headed by General Lewis Hershey since 1948, was extremely decentralized and antiquated in its procedures and record-keeping. As two observers noted, there were

four thousand local draft boards with four thousand different policies. Avoiding the draft became a desperate game for many, while draft counselors and lawyers aided young men in evasions based on physical or mental impairments, legal technicalities, conscientious-objector status, or "safe" enlistments and reserve duty.[11] Of the approximately 27 million young men who reached draft age between 1964 and 1973, almost 25 million did not serve. Although some fled to Canada, Sweden, or other countries and a few remained in the United States, resisted the draft, and were prosecuted, most of these 25 million men simply avoided the draft through loopholes in the system. According to a Harris poll in 1971, most Americans believed that those who did go to Vietnam were "suckers" who could have avoided it.

In fact those who did serve in the military and/or went to Vietnam were the less affluent, less well-educated whites and blacks. Of those who served in the military, 45 percent were high-school graduates whereas 23 percent were college graduates. Of the high-school graduates, 21 percent went to Vietnam, but only 12 percent of the college graduates served there. Figures based on family income are equally revealing: 40 percent of men from low-income families served in

10. Conscientious objectors are those whose religious beliefs are opposed to military service.

11. Safe enlistments are assignments to desk jobs or areas in which no actual fighting is taking place (such as Europe or the U.S. during the Vietnam War).

the military (19 percent of them in Vietnam), while 24 percent of men from high-income families served in the military (9 percent in Vietnam). Casualty figures show yet another side of the story. In the early part of the war, blacks (who made up about 11 percent of the American population) constituted 23 percent of the Vietnam War fatalities. Later this percentage fell to 14 percent, still disproportionately high.

As the arbitrary and unfair nature of the draft became increasingly evident, President Nixon finally replaced General Hershey and instituted a new draft system, the lottery. In this system, draft-age men drew numbers and were drafted in order from lowest to highest number until the draft quota was filled. With this action the very real threat of the draft spread to those who had previously felt relatively safe. Already divided, an entire generation had to come face to face with the Vietnam War.

In this chapter your task is to analyze the experiences of two members of the baby-boom generation in order to understand how and why public opinion became so deeply divided about the Vietnam War.

The Method

You already have some experience with oral history. In the chapter on the Great Depression you not only in-terviewed someone but you also analyzed that interview. In that exercise you compared an individual's history with the aggregate experiences of Americans during the 1930s as portrayed by your readings. In this chapter the focus is somewhat different. Two concepts will be helpful to you here.

The first is that of *birth cohort* — those people born within a few years of one another who form a historical generation. Members of a birth cohort experience the same events — wars, depressions, assassinations, as well as such personal experiences as marriage and childbearing — at approximately the same age and often have similar reactions to them. Sociologist Glen Elder showed that a group of people who were relatively deprived as young children during the Great Depression grew up and later made remarkably similar decisions about marriage, children, and jobs. Others have used this kind of analysis to provide insights into British writers of the post–World War I era and to explain why the Nazi party appealed to a great many young Germans.

Yet even within a birth cohort, people may respond quite differently to the same event(s). *Frame of reference* refers to the *personal background* of an individual, which may influence his or her beliefs, responses, and actions. For example, in the Great Depression chapter you may have found that men and women coped differently with unemployment, or that blacks and whites differed in their perceptions of how hard the times were. In this chapter, both interviewees are white males of the generation that came of age during the Vietnam War. In analyzing their frames of reference, then, neither age, race, nor gender will provide you with clues. However, other factors such as socioeconomic class, family background, values, region, and experiences may be quite important in determining the interviewees' frames of reference and in understanding their responses to the Vietnam War. When a group of people share the same general frame of reference, they are a generational subset who tend to respond similarly to events. In other words, it may be possible to form tentative generalizations from the interviewees about how others with the same general frames of reference thought about and responded to the Vietnam War.

In addition to the interviews, there are two other kinds of evidence included in this chapter: photographs and popular music lyrics. Many historians are now using such nontraditional sources to give us a fuller and richer view of the past, particularly the past of people who were not well known or famous. Both posed pictures and unposed snapshots can be revealing when studied carefully. For example, the pioneer families who settled the Great Plains often dressed in their best clothes and lined up in front of their houses to have their pictures taken to send back East to their relatives. Consider what these photographs must have revealed. The size and composition of the families, the relative modesty of their finest clothes, the limited comfort of their sod houses — in fact, the very isolation and backbreaking work of settling the plains — would be evident. Similarly, snapshots of backyard barbecues and new family cars can tell us a great deal about suburban life in the 1950s.

The final piece of evidence is "For What It's Worth," a very popular Stephen Stills song of the late 1960s. Almost every piece of music contains some sort of message. Some messages are shallow (love between a boy and a girl is a wonderful thing), while others are more profound (Tschaikovsky's *1812 Overture,* which celebrates the strength and fortitude of a people and a nation). Some messages cause songs to become classics and transcend time, while other messages are time-bound and do not mean much to listeners years later. Yet, whether it is sophomoric or sophisticated, universal or temporally limited, there is a message in almost every song.

In the mid-1950s popular music known as rock 'n' roll literally burst upon the scene. While adults either greeted this music with disgust or waited patiently for the "fad" to pass, young people almost universally embraced it. The rock music industry eventually became a $3 billion per year phenomenon, with 70 percent of that money spent by people between the ages of fourteen and twenty-five. On college campuses folk music became another popular musical form in the late 1950s. Folk music lyrics often possessed a quality that early rock 'n' roll lyrics lacked, for they dealt with social issues like poverty, racism, and war. By the mid-1960s rock too was becoming more conscious of the world around it, and some artists merged the two musical forms into hybrid folk-rock, with lyrics laden with social comment. In analyzing the lyrics of "For What It's Worth," answer the following questions carefully:

1. What is the message of the song?

2. How is that message conveyed?

3. What is the tone of the lyrics (for example, sad, angry, strident)?

4. What events were taking place in the year in which this song was released (1967)?

The Evidence

FIGURE 1   **John and His Family. Left to Right: John's Father, John, John's Mother, and John's Brother**

John

[John was born in 1951. His father was a well-to-do and prominent physician, and John grew up in a midwestern town that had a major university. He graduated from high school in 1969 and enrolled in a four-year private college. John dropped out of college in 1971 and returned home to live with his parents. He found work in the community and associated with students at the nearby university.]

My earliest memory of Vietnam must have been when I was in the seventh grade [1962–1963] and I saw things in print and in *Life* magazine. But I really don't remember much about Vietnam until my senior year in high school [1968–1969].

I came from a repressive private school to college. College was a fun place to hang out, a place where you went after high school. It was just expected of you to go.

At college there was a good deal of apprehension and fear about Vietnam — people were scared of the draft. To keep your college deferments, you had to keep your grades up. But coming from an admittedly well-to-do family, I somehow assumed I didn't have to worry about it too much. I suppose I was outraged to find out that it *could* happen to me.

No, I was outraged that it could happen to *anyone*. I knew who was going to get deferments and who weren't going to get them. And even today my feelings are still ambiguous. On one hand I felt, "You guys were so dumb to get caught in that machine." On the other, and more importantly, it was wrong that *anyone* had to go.

Why? Because Vietnam was a bad war. To me, we were protecting business interests. We were fighting on George III's side, on the wrong side of an anti-colonial rebellion. The domino theory didn't impress me at all.[12]

I had decided that I would not go to Vietnam. But I wasn't really worried for myself until Nixon instituted the lottery. I was contemplating going to Canada when my older brother got a CO.[13] I tried the same thing, the old Methodist altar boy gambit, but I was turned down. I was really ticked when I was refused CO status. I thought, "Who are you to tell me who is a pacifist?"

My father was conservative and my mother liberal. Neither one intervened or tried to pressure me. I suppose they thought, "We've done the best we could." By this time I had long hair and a beard. My dad had a hard time.

12. The domino theory, embraced by presidents Eisenhower, Kennedy, and Johnson, held that if one nation fell to the Communists the result would be a toppling of other nations, like dominos.

13. CO stands for conscientious objector.

The antiwar movement was an intellectual awakening of American youth. Young people were concentrated on college campuses, where their maturing intellects had sympathetic sounding boards. Vietnam was part of that awakening. So was drugs. It was part of the protest. You had to be a part of it. Young people were waking up as they got away from home and saw the world around them and were forced to think for themselves.

I remember an argument I had with my father. I told him Ho Chi Minh was a nationalist before he was a Communist, and that this war wasn't really against communism at all. It's true that the Russians were also the bad guys in Vietnam, what with their aid and support of the North Vietnamese, but they had no business there either. When people tried to compare Vietnam to World War II, I just said that no Vietnamese had ever bombed Pearl Harbor.

The draft lottery certainly put me potentially at risk. But I drew a high number, so I knew that it was unlikely that I'd ever be drafted. And yet, I wasn't concerned just for myself. For example, I was aware, at least intellectually, that blacks and poor people were the cannon fodder in Vietnam. But I insisted that *no one,* rich or poor, had to go to fight this war.

Actually I didn't think much about the Vietnamese people themselves. The image was of a kid who could take candy from you one day and hand you a grenade the next. What in hell were we doing in that kind of situation?

Nor did I ever actually know anyone who went to Vietnam. I suppose that, to some extent, I bought the "damn baby napalmers" image. But I never had a confrontation with a veteran of Vietnam. What would I think of him? I don't know. What would he think of me?

Kent State was a real shock to me. I was in college at the time, and I thought, "They were students, just like me." It seemed as if fascism was growing in America.

I was part of the protest movement. After Kent State, we shut down the campus, then marched to a downtown park where we held a rally. In another demonstration, later, I got a good whiff of tear gas. I was dating a girl who collapsed because of the gas. I recall a state policeman coming at us with a club. I yelled at him, telling him what had happened. Suddenly he said, "Here, hold this!" and gave me his club while he helped my date to her feet.

But there were other cops who weren't so nice. I went to the counter-inaugural in Washington in June 1973. You could see the rage on the cops' faces when we were yelling, "One, two, three, four, we don't want your f---ing war!" It was an awakening for me to see that much emotion on the subject coming from the other side. I know that I wasn't very open to other opinions. But the other side *really* was closed.

By '72 their whole machine was falling apart. A guy who gave us a ride to the counter-inaugural was a Vietnam vet. He was going there too, to protest against the war. In fact, he was hiding a friend of his who was AWOL,[14] who simply hid rather than go to Vietnam.

Then Watergate made it all worthwhile — we really had those f---ers scared. I think Watergate showed the rest of the country exactly what kind of "Law and Order" Nixon and his cronies were after!

I have no regrets about what I did. I condemn them all — Kennedy, Johnson, Nixon — for Vietnam. They all had a hand in it. And the war was wrong, in every way imaginable. While I feel some guilt that others went and were killed and I didn't, in retrospect I feel much guiltier that I wasn't a helluva lot more active. Other than that, I wouldn't change a thing. I can still get angry about it.

How will I explain all that to my son? I have no guilt in terms of "duty towards country." The *real* duty was to fight *against* the whole thing. I'll tell my son that, and tell him that I did what I did so that no one has to go.

[*John chose not to return to college. He learned a craft, which he practices today. He married a woman who shares his views ("I wouldn't have known anyone on the other side, the way the country was divided"). They have one son. Both John and his wife work outside the home, and they share the responsibilities of child care.*]

"For What It's Worth," Words and Music by Stephen Stills

There's something happenin' in here,
What it is ain't exactly clear,
There's a man with a gun over there
A'tellin' we got to beware.

Chorus
I think it's time we stop children,
What's that sound?
Everybody look what's goin' down.

14. This is an acronym for "absent without leave."

There's battle lines being drawn,
But nobody's right if everybody's wrong,
Young people speakin' their minds
A'gettin' so much resistance from behin'
Time we
(repeat chorus)

What a field day for the heat,
A thousand people in the street,
Singin' songs and a'carryin' signs
Mostly say "Hooray for our side."
It's time we
(repeat chorus)

Paranoia strikes deep,
Into your life it will creep,
It starts when you're always afraid — Step out of line,
    the man will come and take you away;
You better
(repeat chorus twice)

FIGURE 2   Photo of Mike in Vietnam

Mike

[Mike was born in 1948. His family owned a farm in West Tennessee, and Mike grew up in a rural environment. He graduated from high school in 1966 and enrolled in a community college not far from his home. After two quarters of poor grades, Mike left the community college and joined the United States Marine Corps in April 1967. He served two tours in Vietnam, the first in 1967–1969, and the second in 1970–1971.]

I flunked out of college my first year. I was away from home and found out a lot about wine, women and song but not about much else. In 1967 the old system of the draft was still in effect, so I knew that eventually I'd be rotated up and drafted — it was only a matter of time before they got me.

My father served with Stilwell in Burma and my uncle was career military. I grew up on a diet of John Wayne flics. I thought serving in the military was what was expected of me. The Marines had some good options — you could go in for two years and take your chances on the *possibility* of not going to Vietnam. I chose the two-year option. I thought what we were doing in Vietnam was a noble cause. My mother was against the war and we argued a lot about it. I told her that if the French hadn't helped us in the American Revolution, then we wouldn't have won. I sincerely believed that.

I took my six weeks of basic training at Parris Island [South Carolina]. It was sheer hell — I've never been treated like that in my life. Our bus arrived at Parris Island around midnight, and we were processed and sent to our barracks. We had just gotten to sleep when a drill instructor threw a thirty-two-gallon garbage can down the center of the barracks and started overturning the metal bunks. We were all over the floor and he was screaming at us. It was that way for six weeks — no one ever talked to us, they shouted. And all our drill instructors geared our basic training to Vietnam. They were always screaming at us, "You're going to go to Vietnam and you're gonna f--- up and you're gonna die."

Most of the people in basic training with me were draftees. My recruiter apologized to me for having to go through boot camp with draftees. But most of the guys I was with were pretty much like me. Oh, there were a few s--- birds, but not many. We never talked about Vietnam — there was no opportunity.

There were a lot of blacks in the Corps and I went through basic training with some. But I don't remember any racial tension until later. There were only two colors in the Marine Corps: light green and dark green. My parents drove down to Parris Island to watch me graduate from basic training, and they brought a black woman with them. She was from Memphis and was the wife of one of the men who graduated with me.

After basic training I spent thirteen weeks in basic infantry training at Camp Lejeune [North Carolina]. Lejeune is the armpit of the world. And the harassment didn't let up — we were still called "scumbag" and "hairbag" and "whale---." I made PFC [private first class] at Lejeune. I was an 03-11 [infantry rifleman].

From Lejeune [after twenty days home leave] I went to Camp Pendleton [California] for four-week staging. It was at Pendleton where we adjusted our training at Parris Island and Lejeune to the situation in Vietnam. I got to Vietnam right after Christmas 1967.

It was about this time that I became aware of antiwar protests. But as far as I was concerned they were a small minority of malcontents. They were the *protected*, were deferred or had a daddy on the draft board. I thought, "These people are disloyal — they're selling us down the drain."

We were not prepared to deal with the Vietnamese people at all. The only two things we were told was don't give kids cigarettes and don't pat 'em on the heads. We had no cultural training, knew nothing of the social structure or anything. For instance, we were never told that the Catholic minority controlled Vietnam and they got out of the whole thing — we did their fighting for them, while they stayed out or went to Paris or something. We had a Catholic chaplain who told us that it was our *duty* to go out and kill the Cong, that they stood against Christianity. Then he probably went and drank sherry with the top cats in Vietnam. As for the majority of Vietnamese, they were as different from us as night and day. To be honest, I still hate the Vietnamese SOBs.

The South Vietnamese Army was a mixed bag. There were some good units and some bad ones. Most of them were bad. If we were fighting alongside South Vietnam units, we had orders that if we were overrun by Charley[15] that we should shoot the South Vietnamese first — otherwise we were told they'd turn on us.

I can't tell you when I began to change my mind about the war. Maybe it was a kind of maturation process — you can only see so much death and suffering until you begin to wonder what in hell is going on. You can only live like a nonhuman so long.

I came out of country[16] in January of 1969 and was discharged not too long

---

15. "Charley" was a euphemism for the Viet Cong.

16. "Country" was Vietnam.

after that. I came home and found the country split over the war. I thought, "Maybe there *was* something to this antiwar business after all." Maybe these guys protesting in the streets weren't wrong.

But when I got back home, I was a stranger to my friends. They didn't want to get close to me. I could feel it. It was strange, like the only friends I had were in the Marine Corps. So I re-upped[17] in the Marines and went back to Vietnam with a helicopter squadron.

Kent State happened when I was back in Vietnam. They covered it in *Stars and Stripes*.[18] I guess that was a big turning point for me. Some of the other Marines said, "Hooray! Maybe we should kill more of them!" That was it for me. Those people at Kent State were killed for exercising the same rights we were fighting for for the Vietnamese. But I was in the minority — most of the Marines I knew approved of the shootings at Kent State.

Meanwhile I was flying helicopters into Cambodia every day. I used pot to keep all that stuff out of my mind. Pot grew wild in Vietnam, as wild as the hair on your ass. The Army units would pick it and send it back. The first time I was in Vietnam nobody I knew was using. The second time there was lots of pot. It had a red tinge, so it was easy to spot.

But I couldn't keep the doubts out of my mind. I guess I was terribly angry. I felt betrayed. I would have voted for Lyndon Johnson — when he said we should be there, I believed him. That man could walk on water as far as I was concerned. I would've voted for Nixon in '68, the only time I ever voted Republican in my life. I believed him when he said we'd come home with honor. So I'd been betrayed twice, and Kent State and all that was rattling around in my head.

I couldn't work it out. I was an E5 [sergeant], but got busted for fighting and then again for telling off an officer. I was really angry.

It was worse when I got home. I came back into the Los Angeles airport and was spit on and called a baby killer and a mother raper. I really felt like I was torn between two worlds. I guess I was. I was smoking pot.

I went back to school. I hung around mostly with veterans. We spoke the same language, and there was no danger of being insulted or ridiculed. We'd been damn good, but nobody knew it. I voted for McGovern in '72 — he said we'd get out no matter what. Some of us refused to stand up one time when the national anthem was played.

17. "Re-upped" means reenlisted.
18. *Stars and Stripes* is a newspaper written and published by the armed forces for service personnel.

What should we have done? Either not gotten involved at all or go in with the whole machine. With a different attitude and tactics, we could have *won*. But really we were fighting for just a minority of the Vietnamese, the westernized Catholics who controlled the cities but never owned the backcountry. No, I take that back. There was no way in hell we could have won that damned war and won anything worth winning.

I went to Washington for the dedication of the Vietnam veterans' memorial. We never got much of a welcome home or parades. The dedication was a homecoming for me. It was the first time I got the whole thing out of my system. I cried, and I'm not ashamed. And I wasn't alone.

I looked for the names of my friends. I couldn't look at a name without myself reflected back in it [the wall].

One of the reasons I went back to school was to understand that war and myself. I've read a lot about it and watched a lot of TV devoted to it. I was at Khe Sanh and nobody could tell about that who wasn't there. There were six thousand of us. Walter Cronkite said we were there for seventy-two days. I kept a diary — it was longer than that. I'm still reading and studying Vietnam, trying to figure it all out.

[*Mike returned to college, repeated the courses he had failed, and transferred to a four-year institution. By all accounts he was a fine student. Mike is now employed as a park ranger. He is married, and he and his wife have a preschool child. He is considered a valuable, respected, and popular member of his community. He rarely speaks of his time in the service.*]

Questions to Consider

As you read through both interviews, try to get a sense of the tone and general meaning of each. Then try to establish the respective frames of reference for John and Mike by comparing and contrasting their backgrounds. From what socioeconomic class does each come? From what region of the country? What influences did their fathers have on them? Their mothers? What did they think was expected of them? What was college like for each?

After the brief time each spent in college, John's and Mike's experiences diverged greatly. Why did Mike join (and rejoin) the Marines? What was his experience like? Why did John become involved in the antiwar protest movement? What was it like? What do you think each man learned from his experiences?

Next, consider the views expressed by each interviewee. What did each young man actually know about Vietnam and the Vietnamese? How did each use his understanding of the American Revolution to justify his position on the Vietnam War? What meaning did Kent State have for each of them? What role did drugs play in their lives? What did each think about the draft? About the protesters? About the returning veterans? How did they react to national political leaders? What is each man's final analysis of our involvement in Vietnam — its meaning and the personal roles each man played?

Now look at both photographs carefully. Are they posed or unposed? For whom might they have been intended? What "image" of each man is projected? How does each man help to create that image?

Both men also mentioned the song "For What It's Worth" when they were being interviewed. Using the guidelines presented in the Method section of this chapter, analyze the message and tone of these lyrics, as well as their historical context. What do you suppose this message meant to John? To Mike?

Finally, try to link each man's views and image with his background and experiences. Can you find any reasons why each man might have thought and acted the way he did?

Can you understand each position? These two men have never met. Do you think they could meet and talk about the war today? If so, why? If not, why not?

Epilogue

In the spring of 1971 fifteen thousand antiwar demonstrators disrupted daily activities in the nation's capital by blocking the streets with trash, automobiles, and their own bodies. Twelve thousand were arrested, but the protest movement across the country continued. In June the Pentagon Papers, a secret 1967 government study of the Vietnam War, was published in installments by the *New York Times*. The Pentagon Papers revealed that government spokespersons had lied to the American public about several important events, particularly about the Gulf of Tonkin incident.

As part of his reelection campaign in 1972, President Nixon traveled first to China, then to the Soviet Union, and finally began to pull American troops out of Vietnam. "Peace," his advisor Henry Kissinger announced, "is at hand." Withdrawal was slow and painful, and created a new group of refugees — those Vietnamese who had supported the Americans in South Vietnam. Nixon became mired in the Watergate scandal and resigned from office in 1974 under the threat of impeachment. The North Vietnamese entered Saigon in the spring of 1975 and began a "pacification" campaign of their own in neighboring Cambodia. Nixon's successors, Gerald Ford and Jimmy Carter, offered "amnesty" plans that were utilized by a relatively small number of draft violators. Many who were reported Missing in Action in Vietnam (MIAs) were never found, either dead or alive. The draft was replaced by a new concept, the all-volunteer army.

The Vietnam veterans who never had their homecoming parades and who had been alternately ignored or maligned finally got their memorial. A stark, simple, shiny black granite wall engraved with the names of the 57,000 war dead, the monument is located on the mall near the Lincoln Memorial in Washington, D.C. The idea came from Jan Scruggs (the son of a milkman), a Vietnam veteran who

was wounded and decorated for bravery when he was nineteen years old. The winning design was submitted by twenty-year-old Maya Lin, an undergraduate architecture student at Yale University. A representational statue designed by thirty-eight-year-old Frederick Hart, a former antiwar protester, stands beside the wall of names. All one hundred United States senators cosponsored the gift of public land, while the money to build the memorial was raised entirely through 650,000 individual public contributions. Not everyone was pleased by the memorial, and some old emotional wounds were reopened. Yet more than 150,000 people attended the dedication ceremonies on Veterans' Day, 1982, while the Vietnam veterans paraded down Constitution Avenue. Millions of Americans have already gone to see the monument, now one of Washington's most visited memorials.

Chapter 11

Searching for the Good Life in an Evil World: Cartoonists Analyze Contemporary America

The Problem

Although few could have foreseen it, in many ways the 1968 Democratic National Convention and its eruptive aftermath probably marked the high point of protest in mid–twentieth-century America. To be sure, much of the agony of Vietnam still lay ahead, and the shock of Kent State (May 1970) was still to be felt throughout almost the entire nation. Moreover, serious dissent still raged over questions such as civil rights, the environment, and equal rights for women. But the 1972 landslide reelection of President Richard Nixon against Democratic candidate George Mc-Govern (who was portrayed by Republicans as "too radical") seemed to connote a kind of popular drawing back from reform, change, and even from controversy. Watergate could still fill people with outrage, but it was more outrage against a man than against a "system," an "Establishment," or a "military-industrial complex," all key words in the 1960s. More than anything else, Americans appeared to want to return to "things as normal" and not to be disturbed by the often harsh and strident tones of protest. Indeed, Americans seemed to have embraced a new collective mentality or mood far different from that of the controversy-filled 1960s.

Two of the most prevalent characteristics of this mood of the 1970s and early 1980s were self-centeredness and cynicism, leading social observer

Chapter 11
Searching for the
Good Life in an
Evil World:
Cartoonists
Analyze
Contemporary
America

Tom Wolfe to characterize the 1970s as the "Me Decade" and political scientist Andrew Hacker to speak of a society of "200 million egos." On college campuses that but a few years before had been havens of idealistic causes and scenes of bitter protest, hair styles for men became shorter, beards and mustaches more trimmed. Dormitory stereos blared out more music from the Beach Boys than from Bob Dylan, and collegiate "bull sessions" tended to be more about "majors" and jobs than about the immorality of war or the necessity of equal rights for all people. There was a revival of interest in social fraternities and sororities, and homecoming-queen ceremonies once again became respectable. Many white males talked bitterly about what they called "reverse discrimination," complaining about the practice of giving preference for jobs or admission to professional schools to blacks and women who in the past had often been excluded. By the late 1970s "preppies" had even reappeared, complete with their own clothes, vocabulary, and values. And while many college students mocked and ridiculed preppies, it was clear that even the critics were considerably different from college students of but a few years before.

The self-centeredness and cynicism were reminiscent of collegians of the 1920s or even the 1950s. The world, many of the students believed, was an evil place in which the winners were those who possessed discipline, luck,

and commitment to their individual goals. Most felt that the world could not be changed for the better by selfless devotion to causes, by dissent, or by protest. The solution was to be "laid back" (loose translation: unflappable, unconcerned) and to "go with the flow." Campus political clubs and issued-oriented groups dwindled in membership, while premedical, prelaw, prebusiness and pre-engineering societies swelled. Once again college faculty members and administrators became concerned with student cheating, as it appeared that many students felt that any way to "get ahead" was acceptable. In all, the message seemed to be clear: the world outside the college classroom was badly flawed and contained unfairness, injustice, and wrong. But, many were convinced, earlier protests to correct those ills had accomplished little, had damaged the lives and careers of many of the participants, and, while morally correct, had been in the end ineffective.

This mood was not confined to America's college campuses. Self-centeredness and cynicism seemed to be dominant features throughout American society. These characteristics could be seen nearly everywhere: in the sharp decline of people's loyalty to the company they worked for (previous generations, in the 1920s through the 1950s, had been fiercely loyal to their companies), in the increased interest in individual improvement and physical fitness, in the growing materialism of the age (as home computers, cable television, and video cassette player-recorders became badges of self-worth). Even anti-Establishment figures of the 1960s seemed to join in, with Jerry Rubin becoming a stockbroker and Gary Hart a United States senator from Colorado and presidential aspirant. To their consternation, Vietnam veterans were not so much praised or condemned as ignored, living reminders of a war most Americans appeared all too willing to forget. The ultracynical and nasty J. R. Ewing of the television show "Dallas" and the cool, laid-back "Fonz" of "Happy Days" became heroes to replace those of the recent past.

Some people were puzzled by this kind of mass schizophrenia that saw the world as evil but unchangeable, society as flawed but holding the keys to personal fulfillment, materialism as a false god but at the same time a mark of success. Was American society simply going through a phase, or had the pain of its recent past driven it to madness? How would such a society confront the problems and challenges that still faced it, problems such as racism, sexism, the environment, economic recession and inflation, crime, and others?

There were people in the 1970s and early 1980s who wrote about and spoke to those issues either directly or indirectly, people like the Reverend Jesse Jackson, Gloria Steinem, John Updike, Christopher Lasch, Tom Wolfe, and Joyce Carol Oates. But perhaps the best known of the social observers and critics of the 1970s and early 1980s were the new wave of cartoonists, people who used humor to point out to society its own shortcomings and foibles. Since the comic pages were the most widely read part of American newspapers, this new wave of newspaper cartoonists attracted almost immediate attention, with reactions ranging from mass popularity to almost apoplectic outrage.

Two of the best known of this new wave were Garry Trudeau, the creator of the *Doonesbury* comic strip, and Berke Breathed, the originator of *Bloom County*. Born in New York City in 1948, Trudeau began doing a comic strip entitled *Bull Tales* for the student newspaper while an undergraduate at Yale University. The central character of that comic strip was Mike Doonesbury ("doone" was a Yale slang term for a "good-natured fool"), an innocent who was equally ineffective with women and with making sense out of his world. In 1970 Trudeau was "discovered" by two scouts for Universal Press Syndicate who were looking for cartoon strips that would attract young adults. Trudeau's work seemed promising, and *Doonesbury* made its first appearance beyond Yale in October 1970. Many readers were shocked by Trudeau's lampooning of President Nixon, soon-to-be Secretary of State Henry Kissinger, and liberal and conservative heroes alike. Some newspapers even dropped

Chapter 11
Searching for the
Good Life in an
Evil World:
Cartoonists
Analyze
Contemporary
America

the strip. But *Doonesbury*'s attacks coupled with its sensitivity toward difficult issues such as women's rights, black equality, and Vietnam veterans attracted and held a host of followers and devotees. In 1974 Trudeau won the Pulitzer Prize for cartooning, the first time the award had been given to an artist whose work usually appears on the comics page, and by 1981 *Doonesbury* was carried in approximately six hundred newspapers and recirculated in twenty-one books. Controversy continued to surround the comic strip, two recent examples being a 1980 series on "the mysterious world of Ronald Reagan's brain" and a series on Senator John Warner and his then-wife Elizabeth Taylor, the latter drawing a censure from the Republican caucus of the Virginia General Assembly. In the fall of 1982 Trudeau announced that he was taking an extended leave-of-absence from *Doonesbury* to "recharge his batteries" and bring the strip's characters more up-to-date.

Those who mourned the temporary absence of *Doonesbury* from their daily comics pages were delighted to discover the work of another new-wave cartoonist. Berke Breathed had attended the University of Texas, where he had developed the comic strip *Academia Waltz* for the student newspaper. That effort became the genesis of *Bloom County,* an imaginary area in "America's heartland" populated by precocious children, a Vietnam veteran in a wheelchair, a feminist, the local leader of the Moral Majority, a macho but bumbling preppie, a talking but befuddled penguin, and other assorted characters. Just as audacious as Trudeau, Breathed was in and out of trouble for his portrayals of the nation's leaders, institutions, and values. When Trudeau took his leave of absence, many newspapers replaced *Doonesbury* with *Bloom County,* and numerous nearly fanatical followers of Trudeau became equally devoted to the work of Breathed.

When the new wave of American cartoonists appeared in the 1970s, many readers attacked the cartoonists for editorializing on the "funny pages." Yet those pages of America's newspapers had been expressing points of view and criticizing society almost from the very beginning (cartoon strips became regular features of American newspapers in the 1890s). In 1913 George McManus created *Bringing Up Father* (known to some readers as *Jiggs and Maggie*), a humorous satire of the "new rich" and their pretensions. Harold Gray's *Little Orphan Annie* (1924), Chester Gould's *Dick Tracy* (1931), and Al Capp's *Li'l Abner* (1934) were frankly editorial in tone, as was Walt Kelly's magnificent *Pogo* (1949), and others. Even the so-called noneditorial comic strips, like *Peanuts* (1950), *B.C.* (1958), and *The Wizard of Id* (1964), made comments on the human condition and societal values. Hence, in 1971, when Trudeau defended his work before a convention of newspaper editors by "invoking the precedent of great cartoonists through the centuries," he was historically accurate. That is not to say, however, that all agreed that the new wave of cartoon-strip creators belonged on the comic pages (roughly one-seventh of the newspapers that carried *Doonesbury* put it on their editorial pages) or that the cartoonists' observations were always right. But the cartoonists were, like many of us, seeking to understand the society in which we live. Our society is filled with both bright light and frightening shadows, with economic, technological, and social problems that we have just begun to address, and with uncomfortable memories of the recent past and timorous hopes for the future.

Your task in this chapter is threefold: (1) to identify the principal issues and problems addressed in the evidence, (2) to identify the cartoonist's point of view about each issue, and (3) to determine how the cartoons collectively can be used to gain insight into the time in which they were created (the 1970s and early 1980s).

The Method

At first it may appear that analyzing our own times and our own society will be considerably easier than analyzing past times and societies, those in which we did not live. After all, we can recall most of the important events and significant trends from our own memories or from newspapers, magazines, and books we have read or television news programs or documentaries we have watched. We are comparatively familiar with most of the central characters and major events, having discussed them over meals or in informal conversations. Moreover, the evidence provided here is cartoon strips that many of us have read since childhood. In sum, then, the task of identifying the key issues these cartoon strips raise, understanding the cartoonist's point of view concerning these issues, and analyzing how those cartoon strips characterize their times may seem, on the surface, to be an easy one.

But none of this is as simple as it first appears. For one thing, we may be too close to the people, events, and trends of our own time to understand their true meaning. Some of us actually may have been caught up in or participated in some of the issues the following cartoon strips address. At the same time, we may not be able to recognize ourselves in these strips. Are we there? And if so, how do we appear? In sum, we need to gain some perspective on ourselves before we can understand how the following cartoon strips reflect the times in which they were created.

One way to do this is to imagine that you are a person one hundred years from now who is trying to learn about and understand the 1970s and

Chapter 11
Searching for the
Good Life in an
Evil World:
Cartoonists
Analyze
Contemporary
America

early 1980s. In other words, it is like *you*, living in the 1980s, trying to understand America of the 1860s and 1870s by using the work of cartoonist Thomas Nast. How would you go about doing that?

Begin by looking at each cartoon strip individually. What issue, problem, or situation is being dealt with? How does the cartoonist feel about that issue, problem, or situation? Who or what is being satirized or made to look silly, ridiculous, or wrong? As you analyze each cartoon, it might be helpful to jot down a few notes, and again a brief chart such as Table 1 may prove helpful.

After you have examined all the cartoons in the evidence, look through the notes you took on the main points addressed in each cartoon. If you were looking at these cartoons from a one-hundred-year perspective, what conclusions would you reach about American society in the 1970s and early

1980s? How did that society react to the principal problems, trends, and events of the preceding decade, the 1960s? What were the problems of the 1970s and early 1980s, and how were they addressed? Now begin to think of some adjectives (probably just one adjective will not do) that will accurately complete the following sentence:

The 1970s and early 1980s can be characterized as a period of _____

_____.

Once you have completed the above sentence, think about whether it is an accurate description of the age in which you live. If it is not, what is wrong with it? Has something been left out? If so, go back and see whether the cartoonists have dealt with it. (In other words, have you missed something?)

TABLE 1

Cartoon	Subject	Cartoonist's Point of View	Additional Observations
College Reunion	The public image of the oil industry	Thinks they're "greedheads"	Makes oil people look defensive & shallow, but not enough to change their ways. Also waiter may *think* they're "greedheads" but won't *do* anything about it.

Figures 1–4 from Garry Trudeau, Speaking of Inalienable Rights, Amy (New York: Holt, Rinehart and Winston, © 1976). Figure 5 from Garry Trudeau, An Especially Tricky People (New York: Holt, Rinehart and Winston, © 1977). Figures 6–8 from Garry Trudeau, He's Never Heard of You Either (New York: Holt, Rinehart and Winston, © 1981).

Doonesbury, by Garry Trudeau

FIGURE 1   Nixon and Kissinger

FIGURE 2   Student Protesters of the 1960s

FIGURE 3   Liberal Education

[314]

FIGURE 4 **The Quest**

FIGURE 5 **College Reunion**

FIGURE 6 Watergate Reunion

FIGURE 7 The National Mood

FIGURE 8   George Bush on Campus

From *Berke Breathed, Bloom County (Boston: Little, Brown and Company, ©*
1983).

Bloom County,
  by Berke Breathed

FIGURE 9 Politics — The Senator's Visit

FIGURE 10 Politics — Left Wingers

FIGURE 11 · Politics — Hunting Liberals

FIGURE 12   Campus Life — Disarmament Rally

FIGURE 13   Campus Life — The Wheelchair

FIGURE 14 Vietnam Vet

FIGURE 15 Technology — Mr. Rogers and Politics

FIGURE 16 Technology — Class Material

FIGURE 17 Technology — Instant Banking

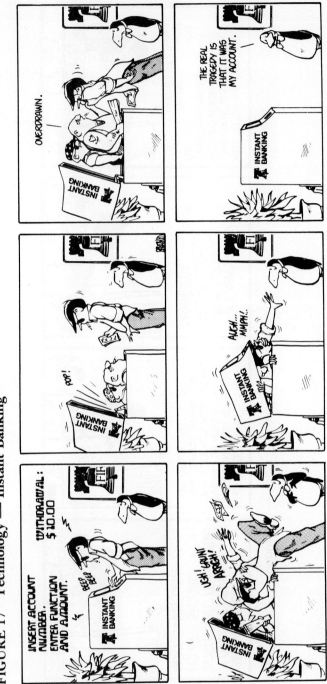

You may find it helpful to read about the 1960s and 1970s before you begin to analyze the cartoons. List the important issues and problems that existed during those decades. Add to your list some of the important shifts in public mood and behavior noted. If your list becomes too long and cumbersome, you might consider dividing the points by topic (political, economic, foreign policy, social life, life in college, and so forth).

Once you have done this, you will be ready to analyze the cartoon strips. Start by linking each cartoon strip to one (or more) of the topics you have identified. For example, look at Figure 5 (Trudeau's *College Reunion*). What topic is addressed? Clearly, the strip has to do with the oil business and the general public's image of the oil industry. Look at each cartoon strip in the same way.

Your second task is to identify how the cartoonist feels about the topic. For example, in Berke Breathed's cartoon *Politics — The Senator's Visit* (Figure 9) clearly Senator Bedfellow is meant to symbolize both politicians and the political system. How does Breathed portray Senator Bedfellow? What does the precocious Milo think of Bedfellow and, by implication, of the American political system? Therefore, what does Breathed think of the American political system of the 1970s? Why?

Because cartoon strips are meant for audiences generally familiar with the trends and events being mentioned, sometimes the characterizations are more subtle and at other times the cartoon strips are satirical (see, for example, Trudeau's *Watergate Reunion*). You may have to go back to your readings occasionally to pick up some of these subtleties.

A number of the cartoon strips deal with college life (see Figures 2, 3, 4, and 12). What changes had taken place in American colleges from the 1960s to the late 1970s? How do Trudeau and Breathed feel about those changes?

After you have identified the topic of each cartoon strip and what the cartoonist thinks about that topic, you will be ready to analyze how these comic strips reflect the times in which they were created. In one sense, this involves combining your answers to the first two questions. However, something more is required. What was going on in America that would cause each cartoon strip to be drawn? For example, look at Figure 16 (*Technology — Class Material*). Ostensibly this strip is about the paucity of good programs on television (what former FCC Commissioner Newton Minow called a "vast wasteland"). However, according to the strip, who is responsible for the poor programs on television? Is it the television networks? Are they solely responsible? What about the television viewer? How does *Technology — Class Material* reflect the

Chapter 11
Searching for the
Good Life in an
Evil World:
Cartoonists
Analyze
Contemporary
America

1970s? What does the strip say about American society during that period? Ask the same types of questions for each of the comic strips.

Finally, if you gather all of the cartoon strips together, what do they collectively tell us about the 1970s? What kind of an era was it? What adjectives best describe it? This is a difficult question, but close analysis of your readings and the evidence should allow you to find the answer.

Epilogue

It is impossible to predict with any degree of accuracy what the future holds for ourselves and for our society. We have some clues, but little more. For instance, we know that technology (especially computer and telecommunications technology) will bring great changes in our education, working lives, home and family lives, recreation, health, safety, and countless other areas we can barely imagine. Moreover, we know that energy concerns and environmental problems will command an increasing amount of our attention and the attention of our political, economic, and social institutions. Fields such as medicine, engineering, architecture, and business are changing so rapidly that they may be barely recognizable a few decades

from now. But beyond these points and a few other sureties, about the only thing we are certain of is change itself, and the possibility that change will occur with more and more rapidity.

For this reason, the ability to analyze and understand the times in which we live will be especially crucial as we attempt to absorb the changes, control them, and ascertain where they are leading us. And yet the evidence that is needed to understand the riddle of our own times is all around us, in cartoon strips and movies, in advertisements and statistics, in architecture and speeches, in novels and popular music, in art and court decisions. Indeed, the evidence continues to bombard us daily.

The ability to absorb that evidence, sort it, analyze it for clues and meaning, and fit it into an overall explanation will be indispensable to people who hope to lead satisfying, fulfilling, and productive lives. This book has attempted to show you how you can use selected pieces of evidence to understand the American past. More important, *you* have analyzed the past; the analysis was not something told to you by someone else. You have already used the greatest of human properties, the human mind, to understand your past. As you come to analyze the times in which you live, the skills you have learned will prove essential.